Alex Boese is a graduate student at the University of California at San Diego, where he is completing his doctoral dissertation. He is the creator and curator of www.museumofhoaxes.com, which began in 1997 as research notes for his dissertation. His website has received acclaim from *Yahoo!* as well as *USA Today, Parade,* and other newspapers around the world. He lives in San Diego, California.

THE
MUSEUM
OF
HOAXES

*A History of Outrageous
Pranks and Deceptions*

ALEX BOESE

A PLUME BOOK

PLUME
Published by the Penguin Group
Penguin Group (USA) Inc., 375 Hudson Street, New York, New York 10014, U.S.A.
Penguin Books Ltd, 80 Strand, London WC2R 0RL, England
Penguin Books Australia Ltd, 250 Camberwell Road,
Camberwell, Victoria 3124, Australia
Penguin Books Canada Ltd, 10 Alcorn Avenue, Toronto, Ontario, Canada M4V 3B2
Penguin Books India (P) Ltd, 11 Community Centre, Panchsheel Park,
New Delhi – 110 017, India
Penguin Books (N.Z.) Ltd, Cnr Rosedale and Airborne Roads,
Albany, Auckland 1310, New Zealand
Penguin Books (South Africa) (Pty) Ltd, 24 Sturdee Avenue,
Rosebank, Johannesburg 2196, South Africa

Penguin Books Ltd, Registered Offices: 80 Strand, London WC2R 0RL, England

Published by Plume, a member of Penguin Group (USA) Inc.
Previously published in a Dutton edition.

First Plume Printing, November 2003

10 9 8 7 6 5 4 3 2 1

Ⓟ REGISTERED TRADEMARK—MARCA REGISTRADA

The Library of Congress has catalogued the Dutton edition as follows:
Boese, Alex.
The museum of hoaxes / Alex Boese.
p. cm.
Includes bibliographical references and index.
ISBN 0-525-94678-0 (hc.)
ISBN 0-452-28465-1 (pbk.)
1. Imposters and imposture—Museums. 2. Fraud—Museums. I. Title.

HV6751 .B64 2002
001.9'5—dc21   2002026780

Printed in the United States of America
Original hardcover design by Eve L. Kirch

BOOKS ARE AVAILABLE AT QUANTITY DISCOUNTS WHEN USED TO PROMOTE PRODUCTS OR SER-
VICES. FOR INFORMATION PLEASE WRITE TO PREMIUM MARKETING DIVISION, PENGUIN GROUP (USA)
INC., 375 HUDSON STREET, NEW YORK, NEW YORK 10014.

To Beverley Walton and
Charlie Curzon, my new family

Contents

THE GULLIBILITY TEST (QUESTIONS)   ix

INTRODUCTION   1

CHAPTER ONE • BEFORE 1700
Female Popes and Vegetable Lambs   7

CHAPTER TWO • THE EIGHTEENTH CENTURY
Rabbit Babies and Lying Stones   29

CHAPTER THREE • 1800–1868
Lunar Bison and Solar Armor   51

CHAPTER FOUR • 1869–1913
Stone Giants and Antlered Rabbits   77

CHAPTER FIVE • 1914–1949
New Jersey Martians and Van Gogh's Ear   104

CHAPTER SIX • 1950–1976
Naked Animals and Swiss Spaghetti Trees   133

CHAPTER SEVEN • 1977–1989
Australian Icebergs and Cockroach Pills   157

CHAPTER EIGHT • 1990–1999
Crop Circles and Cross-Dressing Ken   182

CHAPTER NINE • AFTER 2000
Bonsai Kittens and Monster Cats   207

AFTERWORD   235

THE GULLIBILITY TEST (ANSWERS)   239

ENDNOTE   245

SUGGESTIONS FOR FURTHER READING   247

HOAXES BY CATEGORY   257

INDEX OF STORY TITLES   263

ACKNOWLEDGMENTS   267

ABOUT THE AUTHOR   269

THE GULLIBILITY TEST

(QUESTIONS)

☛ Imagine that you're an editor at a newspaper. A reporter has just handed you a story that contains the following statements. Unfortunately, this reporter has a reputation for embellishing stories with wild claims that are completely untrue. Using common sense and what you know about history and the natural world, you've got to decide which statements are true and which are false before the paper goes to print. Saying "I don't know" isn't an option. Could your readers depend on you to weed out the hoax information for them?

★ History and Culture ★

1) Sir Thomas Crapper invented the toilet.
___True   ___False

2) The Eskimo language has over a hundred words for snow.
___True   ___False

3) Early Dutch traders acquired the entire island of Manhattan from a Native American tribe for a few goods worth around $700 in today's currency.
___True   ___False

4) When the English Pilgrims landed in the New World they were surprised to discover that one of the first Native Americans they met had lived in England for many years.
___True   ___False

5) Mud throwing was an official event at the 1904 Olympics.
___*True*   ___*False*

6) There is a lake in Massachusetts called Lake Chargoggaggoggman-chaugagoggchaubunagungamaug. The name is a Native American word that means "You fish on your side, I'll fish on my side, nobody fish in the middle."
___*True*   ___*False*

7) When Columbus sailed to America in 1492, most Europeans believed that the earth was flat.
___*True*   ___*False*

8) The ancient Sumerians worshiped Ninkasi, a goddess of beer.
___*True*   ___*False*

9) Thomas Jefferson and John Adams, two of America's founding fathers, both died on July 4, 1826, fifty years to the day after the signing of the Declaration of Independence.
___*True*   ___*False*

10) Marco Polo introduced ice cream to Europe after watching it being made in China.
___*True*   ___*False*

★ *Science and Nature* ★

11) Cockroaches can survive for up to a month with their heads cut off.
___*True*   ___*False*

12) Sharks do not get cancer.
___*True*   ___*False*

13) Long-tailed South American monkeys have an unusual way of crossing rivers. Clinging to each other, they form their bodies into a living bridge that stretches between the trees on either side of a river. Other members of the pack then climb across this "monkey chain" to reach the other side.
___*True*   ___*False*

14) The laws of physics change over time.
___*True*   ___*False*

15) Turtles never die of old age.
___*True*   ___*False*

16) Lemmings commit suicide by hurling themselves, en masse, off cliffs.
___*True*   ___*False*

17) There is a small village in Ecuador, called Vilacabamba, whose inhabitants have an average life-span of over a hundred years.
___*True*   ___*False*

18) Lightning has been known to imprint photographic images of surrounding scenery onto the skin of those it has struck.
___*True*   ___*False*

19) Physicists recently announced that they were able to slow down light waves until the waves were almost frozen in place.
___*True*   ___*False*

20) Gravity has a stronger pull at the Earth's poles than it does at the equator. As a result a person who weighs 150 pounds at the equator would weigh almost a pound more if they stood at the North Pole.
___*True*   ___*False*

THE
MUSEUM
OF
HOAXES

Hoax *v.* To deceive or take in by inducing to believe an amusing or mischievous fabrication or fiction; to play upon the credulity of.

—*Oxford English Dictionary,* 1985

Contriving wonderful stories for the publick. . . . This waggery has recently received the elegant term of hoaxing.

—James P. Malcolm,
*Anecdotes of the Manners
and Customs of London,* 1808

INTRODUCTION

Hoax *n.* dodge, fake, flimflam, forgery, fraud, humbug, imposture, jeu d'esprit, practical joke, prank, put-on, quiz, ruse, scheme, sell, stunt, sham, tall tale. —**hoax** *tr.v.* bamboozle, cheat, con, deceive, diddle, dupe, hornswoggle, hoodwink, lie, swindle, trick.

Today it's become commonplace to declare that we live in the Age of Information. But more often it seems like the Age of Misinformation.

Deception surrounds us everywhere: on TV, on the radio, in newspapers, and on the Internet. Especially on the Internet. In its brief existence the Internet has become the great incubator of every lie, rumor, and half-baked idea imaginable. Internet message boards brim over with slanders and false allegations. And it's a matter of jest that the nineteen-year-old college student from San Diego you think you're sharing a chatroom with is probably a fifty-year-old weirdo from Wichita.

How did this happen? Why has our society, with all the advanced tools at its disposal for finding the truth, become such a haven for untruth? That is the question this book sets out to answer by telling the history of one particular variety of untruth: the hoax.

What Is a Hoax?

Our culture describes many different activities as hoaxes. When a newspaper knowingly prints a fake story, we call it a hoax. We also describe misleading publicity stunts, false bomb threats, scientific frauds, business scams, and bogus political claims as hoaxes. What is the common thread that runs through all of these?

First of all, they are all deceptive acts, or lies. But not just any deceptive act qualifies as a hoax. A small white lie, such as when an employee falsely calls in sick to take a day off work, doesn't qualify as a hoax. Nor do most forms of criminal deception, such as identity theft, counterfeiting, perjury, or plagiarism. To become a hoax a lie must have something extra. It must be somehow outrageous, ingenious, dramatic, or sensational. Most of all, it must command the attention of the public. A hoax, then, is a deliberately deceptive act that has succeeded in capturing the attention (and, ideally, the imagination) of the public.

The key word in this definition is "public." In my opinion there is no such thing as a private hoax. A deception rises to the level of a hoax by achieving public notoriety. The broader the public impact a hoax achieves, the higher it ranks in the hoax honor roll of infamy. This characteristic can be used to mark out the similarities and differences between hoaxes and four other forms of deception: frauds, pranks, urban legends, and tall tales.

Frauds are a criminal form of deception. Often people draw a sharp distinction between hoaxes and frauds. Frauds, they say, are perpetrated simply to make money, whereas hoaxes touch on something deeper.

But a fraud can become a hoax when the method of acquiring financial return generates a broad enough public impact, or is unusual enough to capture the public's imagination. In this sense the only element differentiating frauds and hoaxes is the reaction of the public. For this reason a variety of notorious stock-market frauds whose motive was solely financial gain have achieved the status of hoax, such as the Great Stock Exchange Hoax of 1814 (Chapter Three) and the Emulex Hoax of 2000 (Chapter Nine).

It is the same with pranks. A prank is a mischievous trick, such as putting a whoopee cushion beneath a chair, or short-sheeting a bed. However, if a prank attracts the attention of a wide public audience it can rise to the level of a hoax. For instance, making a prank phone call to a friend might generate a few laughs, but it will never be reported on the front page of the paper. It will always remain just a prank. But making a prank phone call to the queen of England, and broadcasting that call over the radio to millions of people, certainly would raise that prank to the level of a hoax (see Chapter Eight, "A Call to Queen Elizabeth"). It is all just a question of the degree of public interest in the act.

Urban legends are false stories that circulate throughout the culture, often spread via e-mail or word of mouth. Like hoaxes, they are examples of falsehoods that people swallow, and, like them, often achieve broad public notoriety. The difference is that urban legends are unintentionally deceptive, whereas hoaxes are intentionally so. Urban legends do not have single authors. Instead, they seem to spring from the society itself. Often they are old stories that have been subtly recycled to match new circumstances. People tell these stories to their friends and acquaintances not out of a deliberate desire to fool, but because they think the stories might be true. Hoaxes, by contrast, are purposeful acts. There is always a hoaxer who deliberately perpetrates them, intending to fool other people. If it were discovered that an urban legend had a single author who created the story with an intent to deceive, then it would cease to be a legend and become a hoax. Since they are not purposefully deceptive, there are no urban legends here in the museum.

Finally, there are tall tales. Tall tales are a specialized type of hoax, a subgenre of the larger category of hoaxing. Whereas the standard hoax is an act of deception perpetrated by a single person (or sometimes a group of people), tall tales are acts of deception in which entire communities winkingly participate.

For instance, Santa Claus, the Easter bunny, jackalopes, and fur-bearing trout (see Chapter Four) may not exist in a literal sense (though don't tell anyone I said that), but almost our entire culture collaborates in maintaining the fiction that they do. When individuals invent tall tales, the larger community will usually recognize what they are up to and play along with the jest. Standard hoaxes, by contrast, will eventually be debunked. Of course, most tall tales, like most pranks and frauds, never achieve wide circulation, but those that do earn a proud place in this collection.

Why Are There So Many Hoaxes?

So why have hoaxes become so ubiquitous? One possibility is that people have grown more gullible and therefore offer easier prey to deceivers. But even a quick glance at the record of human history assures us that credulity has been a constant theme throughout the ages. When compared to our ancestors we are certainly not more gullible, though we probably are *just as* gullible. Of course, the lies that we are willing to believe today are quite different from the ones that passed muster three hundred years ago. The Native of Formosa (see Chapter Two) probably would not find many believers today. This is because what people believe to be possible has changed as their understanding of the world has changed. But humanity's inherent propensity toward belief, its preference for trust over skepticism, has remained constant.

Instead the answer may lie with the changing context in which hoaxers operate. Modern society has given people both more opportunity to hoax, and more incentive to do so. It has also given people more incentive to expose hoaxes. The driving force behind all this hoaxing and hoax busting is, paradoxically, the rise of democracy.

Beginning around the early eighteenth century, the rise of democracy in the West made the public far more important than it had ever been before. It gave people a strong incentive both to shape public opinion and to attract the public's attention. Hoaxing, as it turned out, was an excellent method of doing both. If you desperately wanted to attract the public's eye (to promote your business, for instance, or to make a political statement, or simply to make yourself feel important), yet you lacked a legitimate way of doing so, telling an outrageous lie was an attractive option for achieving your goal. It was certainly an option that many people throughout the past three centuries chose. Nineteenth-century hoaxers such as P. T. Barnum (see Chapter Three) soon discovered that the public didn't even mind being lied to, as long as the lies were more sensational and entertaining than the dull, everyday truth. By the same token, the public loved the spectacle of frauds unmasked and deceivers brought to justice. Hoaxes, to put it bluntly, made sensational news. And the public loved sensation. This fortuitous alignment provided a rich soil in which hoaxes multiplied and grew.

Modern democracy has had an uneasy relationship with sensationalism and hoaxing. Communication innovations, such as the mass circulation of newspapers in the 1830s and the Internet in the 1990s, were each hailed as advances for democracy upon their introduction because they promoted the free exchange of ideas and information. But to the chagrin of many, they also promoted mindless entertainment and deception. This was because these technologies made it easier for individuals to connect with mass audiences. They removed barriers between the public and those (such as hoaxers, showmen, and con artists) who wanted to address it.

This is a paradox at the heart of democracy. The freer people are to communicate with each other, the freer they are to deceive and manipulate each other. This places the burden on those who participate in democracies to learn about the ways of misinformation in order to defend and benefit from the freedoms they enjoy. This also allows us safely to predict that any future technology that makes it easier for people to share information will usher in a new and even greater era for hoaxing, repeating the pattern established by newspapers and the Internet. Given the pace of technological development, such a time is probably not far away. The Museum of Hoaxes will dutifully add a new wing when it arrives.

Visit the museum online at www.museumofhoaxes.com

CHAPTER ONE

BEFORE 1700

Female Popes and Vegetable Lambs

In the modern world we make a sharp distinction between fact and fantasy. We are quite certain that there is a difference between the "real" and the "not real." As a result we treat statements as either being true or not true. In the medieval world, by contrast, these lines were not as sharply drawn.

The medieval world treated the concept of truth allegorically and spiritually, while we treat it scientifically. Claims that we would regard as obviously false were regarded by the medieval mind as true if they revealed a deeper underlying metaphysical meaning about the world. Belief in things that we would regard as curious half-truths, superstitious fantasies, and outright lies persisted for centuries throughout the medieval era, completely unchallenged, even when contradictory evidence was clearly available. People whom we would label as hoaxers, they labeled as heroic tellers of the truth.

The medieval world view was shaped by two events: the division of the Roman empire during the fourth century A.D. and the publication of Saint Augustine's *City of God* in the fifth century. The division of the empire resulted in the gradual decline and isolation of the western empire (Europe) as it withered beneath the onslaught of barbarian invasions. Europe became a

rural, poverty-stricken, inward-looking society lacking centralized institutions. Public life was highly localized and fragmented.
Sharing of information between communities was sporadic and
unreliable. As a result secrecy, not openness, became the foun-
dation of medieval knowledge. Augustine's *City of God* set the
philosophical tone for this era. It taught that there were two
kingdoms, the earthly and the heavenly. The more people of
the medieval era sought after the truth of the heavenly kingdom, the less they seemed to be concerned when truths of the
earthly kingdom were bent or misrepresented.

The modern world view, with its more literal scientific concept of truth, began to emerge around the fourteenth and fifteenth centuries during the Renaissance. Classical learning was
rediscovered, and along with it ancient methods of critical in-
quiry. Scholars began to take a more skeptical look at texts and
became more concerned about the authenticity of manuscripts.
The sixteenth-century Protestant Reformation sharpened this
mood of skepticism even further by giving scholars strong ideo-
logical reasons to prove that their Protestant or Catholic opponents were either wrong or lying. Accusations flew back and
forth, and out of this heated cultural environment, in which
sensitivity to deception was greatly heightened, the modern
concept and awareness of hoaxing emerged. The word itself
dates from this era. It is said that Protestant jesters and con-
jurors began ridiculing the Latin phrase intoned by Catholic
priests during the Mass, *Hoc est corpus meum,* by corrupting it
into the nonsense phrase *hocus-pocus.* They shouted this phrase
whenever they performed a trick. From *hocus-pocus* it was a
simple contraction to arrive at the word *hoax.*

Forgeries of the Medieval Church

Taken as a whole, medieval monks and clerics were probably the most prolific forgers of all time. For centuries they con-

trolled access to official documents, placing them in a perfect position to alter or forge those documents, should they so desire. Their superiors could be counted on to overlook, or even approve, any textual inventions that benefited the Church.

Papal bulls were a frequent object of forgery. In one notorious case a count of Armagnac bribed a papal official to produce a fake papal bull allowing him to marry his sister. Letters, church histories, lives of saints, and deeds to land were other common creations of clerical forgers.

Almost all of these forgeries went undetected for centuries, until the revival of historical scholarship that began during the Renaissance. As the vast scope of the deception gradually became evident, some scholars began to wonder whether there were any medieval church documents whose authenticity could be trusted. In 1675 the Jesuit scholar Daniel van Papenbroeck published his conclusion that all ancient deeds were falsifications created by eleventh-century monks. His announcement brought the wrath of the Church down upon him, and a few years later he humbly begged forgiveness for his doubt. Another seventeenth-century scholar, Jean Hardouin, became convinced that the majority of classical Greek and Roman literature, as well as all extant Greek and Roman coins, had actually been forged by medieval Benedictine monks. Hardouin declared that when he died he would he would leave behind a scrap of paper on which was written the reason why the monks had committed this forgery. Unfortunately, Hardouin's mysterious scrap of paper was never found.

The Donation of Constantine

The Donation of Constantine was a document supposedly written by Emperor Constantine (285–337 A.D.) granting the Catholic Church ownership of vast territories within the western Roman empire. The document stated that he made this generous gift out of gratitude to Pope Sylvester I, who had converted him to Christianity and had cured him of leprosy. For centuries the Donation legitimated the Church's possession of the papal lands in Italy. Unfortunately, the Donation was entirely fake, as even the Church eventually acknowledged.

The truth is that the Church only officially acquired the papal lands in 756 A.D., when King Pepin of the Frankish empire gave them to the Church as a gift. The same year, 756 A.D., also appears to be the time when the text of the Donation first appeared. It was probably created by a cleric either in Rome or the Frankish court. Its purpose may have been to allow the king to claim that he was *returning*, not giving, the papal lands to the Church. In this way the fiction of the Donation added legitimacy to a convenient political marriage between the Catholic Church and the Frankish state.

The Donation was not revealed to be a forgery until 1440. In that year Lorenzo Valla published his *Discourse on the Forgery of the Alleged Donation of Constantine*, in which he enumerated the large number of historical anachronisms that pervaded the work. For instance, it referred to Byzantia as a province when in the fourth century it was only a city, it referred to temples in Rome that did not yet exist, and it referred to "Judea," which also did not yet exist. Valla could have added that Emperor Constantine never had leprosy, making it impossible for Pope Sylvester to have cured him of this disease. The Catholic Church suppressed Valla's work for years. Centuries later it publicly conceded that the Donation was a fake.

The History of Crowland

Crowland Abbey is located in the south Lincolnshire fens of England. Its history dates back to the early ninth century, when Saint Guthlac moved out into the fens to find solitude. The abbey was established some time after his death, in his honor.

For centuries the monks of the abbey lived a quiet, solitary existence. But they were not immune to the intrusions of the outside world. In particular they had to guard against a steady stream of threats to the abbey property. These threats peaked during the early fifteenth century, when the neighboring abbey of Spalding claimed a portion of Crowland's lands as their own. The case was brought to court in 1413. To bolster their own position the monks of Crowland produced a volume known as the *Historia Crowlandensis* (or History of Crowland), which was a string of historical land charters woven together into a general history of the abbey. The *History* and charters were accepted as legitimate, Crowland Abbey won its case, and details of the *History* passed into wider circulation. During the seventeenth and eighteenth centuries it was widely quoted by historians.

It was not until the nineteenth century that the *History of Crowland* was fully realized to be a fraud, at which time scholars identified many details that should have been giveaways. For instance, the *History* referred to numerous place names and historical figures anachronistically, using fourteenth-century terms in passages that were supposedly written in the tenth century. It described monks of the abbey as having studied at Oxford University in years before the university existed. It made mention of the construction of a triangular bridge during the tenth century, even though such bridges were not built until the fourteenth century. Finally, and perhaps most tellingly, it credited the monks of the abbey with remarkable health, for according to the *History* the inhabitants of the abbey had regularly attained such ripe old ages as 148, 142, and 115.

Pope Joan: The Female Pope

John Anglicus left England in the early ninth century and traveled to Athens, where he gained a reputation for his knowledge of the sciences. Eventually he moved to Rome and lectured at the Trivium, boosting his fame and reputation even higher. He became a cardinal, and when Pope Leo IV died in 853 A.D., John Anglicus was unanimously elected pope. As Pope John VIII, John Anglicus ruled for two years, until 855 A.D. But one day he took ill while riding from St. Peter's to the Lateran. He had to stop by the side of the road and, to the astonishment of everyone present, proceeded to give birth to a child. It turned out that Pope John VIII had been concealing the fact that he was a woman. In other words, Pope John was really Pope Joan.

According to legend, upon discovering the pope's true gender, the people of Rome tied her feet together and dragged her behind a horse while stoning her until she died. Another legend has it that she was sent to a faraway convent to repent her sins and that the child she bore grew up to become the bishop of Ostia.

It is uncertain whether the story of Pope Joan is true. The first known reference to her comes from the thirteenth century, 350 years after her supposed reign. The Catholic Church at first seemed to accept her reality but backed away from this position during the sixteenth-century Reformation. At the same time Protestant writers insisted she was real. After all, the existence of a female pope was a scandalous piece of anti-Catholic propaganda. Modern scholars have been unable to settle the question, but if it is true that she existed, then it qualifies as one of the most startling cases of gender concealment ever perpetrated.

The Medieval Relic Trade: True Crosses and Fake Shrouds

Medieval Europe hosted a thriving trade in holy relics, many of them fake. The sixteenth-century Protestant reformer John Calvin, who believed the veneration of relics to be a form of false worship, commented that if all the relics were brought together in one place it would be obvious that most of them were fake because "it would be made manifest that every apostle has more than four bodies, and every saint two or three."

The relics collected and worshiped by medieval Europeans ranged from the mundane to the truly bizarre. Bones or body parts of saints and martyrs were always in high demand. One church proudly displayed the brain of Saint Peter, until the relic was accidentally moved and revealed to be a piece of pumice stone. Relics of Christ or the Virgin Mary were also extremely valuable and included items such as the milk of the Virgin Mary, the teeth, hair, and blood of Christ, pieces of the Cross, and samples of the linen Christ was wrapped in as an infant. The monks of Charrox even claimed to possess Christ's foreskin, cut off during his circumcision. But this claim faced a challenge from a rival foreskin displayed in the Church of Joannes Lateranensis in Rome.

The true value of relics lay in their ability to perform miracles. A relic that was an acknowledged fake could become "real" if it performed a miracle. The European faithful regularly made pilgrimages over hundreds of miles to visit the most powerful relics. This pilgrimage traffic had an enormous impact on local economies, leading towns to go to extreme lengths to obtain the relics that would draw the most pilgrims.

Some of the lengths to which towns would go in their quest to obtain the most popular relics have been documented by Patrick Geary in his book *Furta Sacra: Thefts of Relics in the Central Middle Ages*. He notes that towns were usually reluctant to simply buy or trade relics. After all, why would anyone willingly sell or part with a miracle-performing relic? Presumably they would only do so it if it no longer possessed its powers, meaning that the relic was worthless. Instead, towns often stole the relics they desired, or surreptitiously bought them while publicly claiming to have stolen them. Relic thefts were highly organized affairs, and the successful thieves were treated as local heroes. Geary tells the story of the Italian town of Bari, which in 1087 commissioned a team of thieves to obtain the remains of Saint Nicolas from the Turkish town of Myra. The expedition was a success, and for decades Bari basked in the glory of being the town that owned the stolen bones of Saint Nick, known more popularly today as Santa Claus.

The Shroud of Turin

The relic that has generated the most controversy over the years continues to be the Shroud of Turin. It is a fourteen-foot piece of cloth that bears the image of a naked man. Its supporters claim that it is the cloth in which Christ was wrapped after his crucifixion.

The Shroud first came to the attention of the European public around 1355, when it was exhibited at the Church of St. Mary in Lirey, France. It had been given to the church by a French knight, Geoffroy de Charny, who probably acquired it in Constantinople.

The shroud soon became the subject of controversy. A 1389 report to Pope Clement written by Bishop Pierre d'Acis argued that the shroud was merely a painting, and that it was being falsely displayed as a true relic in order to solicit donations to the church. As a consequence Pope Clement declared the relic a fraud. In 1443 the shroud was acquired by de Charny's granddaughter, who eventually sold it to the duke of Savoy. The Savoys exhibited it for many decades, until in 1532 it was almost destroyed in a fire. The shroud still displays burn marks from this incident. The Savoy family eventually donated the shroud to the Catholic Church in 1983.

Throughout the twentieth century researchers dueled back and forth over the shroud's authenticity. In 1982 a group calling itself the Shroud of Turin Research Project declared it to be genuine after studying samples lifted from the cloth using tape. But radiocarbon tests performed later during the 1980s dated the shroud to approximately the fourteenth century, indicating that the relic was a fake. Nevertheless, shroud supporters found many reasons to dispute the radiocarbon testing, and so the debate raged on and likely will for the foreseeable future.

Medieval Travel Lies

As the western Roman empire declined during the fourth and fifth centuries A.D., Europe lost contact with the rest of the world. Classical knowledge of the outside world receded, and what emerged in its place was a peculiar mixture of fact and fiction. European scholars populated the lands to their east with unicorns, cyclopses, and other fantastic creatures. One persistent rumor spoke of the barbarian tribes of Gog and Magog, whom Alexander the Great had supposedly imprisoned behind giant brass gates somewhere in the East. It was said that the escape of Gog and Magog would signal the imminent end of the world. With the gradual revival of commerce during the thirteenth and fourteenth centuries, Europeans once more began to venture beyond their borders and returned to tell of what they had seen. But these travelers seldom gave what we would consider to be factual accounts. Instead, they told bizarre stories that confirmed the existence of the imaginary kingdoms and creatures that Europeans had so long dreamed about and feared. We can only assume that the popularity of these travel lies was another manifestation of the medieval preference for allegorical truths over literal ones.

The Letter of Prester John

In 1144 the Muslim armies won a stunning victory against the Christian crusaders at Edessa. It was soon after this that a rumor began to circulate around Europe about a Christian king of great wealth named Prester John who ruled in the East and was willing to come to the aid of the defeated crusaders. Naturally the European rulers who heard this rumor were intrigued. If such a king actually existed, he could help shift the tide of the wars back in their favor.

Twenty years later the rumor received apparent validation when a letter turned up written by Prester John himself and addressed to the Byzantine emperor Manuel Comnenus. In this letter Prester John described his immense kingdom, which he said stretched from India to the land where the sun rises. He wrote that fantastic creatures inhabited his land—seven-horned bulls, birds so large that they could lift and kill an armored man, and horned men with three eyes in the back of their heads. Finally, he claimed that there was a fountain in his kingdom whose waters allowed men to stay young forever.

After reading this letter European rulers could scarcely believe their luck. They began to dream about enlisting the aid of this faraway king to help bring about the worldwide triumph of Christianity. It is said that the pope, compelled by this vision of a global Christian kingdom, instructed his personal envoy to travel east, search for Prester John, and deliver a reply to his letter. But what was unclear to medieval readers of the Prester John letter is quite obvious to its readers today: The letter was nothing more than a skillful hoax. Its author remains unknown, though he was probably a European cleric who constructed its fantasies out of old legends, such as the tales of Alexander the Great's adventures in the East. The letter was probably intended to offer hope to the Christian armies fighting the Crusades, and in this respect it certainly succeeded, even though the hope was a false one. In fact, it succeeded so well that the legend of Prester John lay like a heavy, unavoidable shadow over the next four centuries of European exploration. The quest for his mythical kingdom became an obsession for European explorers. Wherever they went in the world, they searched for it. Many explorers, including the famous Marco Polo, even claimed that they had found it. Since it is quite certain that his kingdom never existed, these claims must be taken as prime examples of the medieval travel lie.

Marco Polo's Description of the World

Marco Polo wrote his *Description of the World* around 1298 (or rather, he told his story to a man named Rustichello, who did the actual writing). His account, which was a description of his travels throughout China, offered Europeans unique information about what was to them the mysterious land of the East.

Even as late as 1492 Polo's book was still considered to be the best source of information about the Far East, as shown by Columbus's decision to take a copy of it with him on his transatlantic voyage. But a number of modern scholars now suspect that Polo never went to China. This suspicion has been laid out most forcefully by Frances Wood of the British Library in her book *Did Marco Polo Go to China?*

Wood's argument focuses on a set of curious omissions. She questions how Polo could have spent so many years in China, and yet have failed to include in his account the following aspects of its culture: the custom of drinking tea, the use of chopsticks, the peculiarities of Chinese script, the art of woodblock printing, the practice of foot-binding (which fascinated all other European travelers), and, most significantly, the imposing presence of the Great Wall. She concludes that he omitted these details because he actually never set foot in China and so was ignorant of them.

Defenders of Polo, who are in the majority, argue that these omissions could have resulted from Polo's reluctance to tell all he knew, for fear of being branded a liar. As it was, many of his contemporaries found his tales so fantastic that they called him a liar anyway. His defenders also point out that Mongol control in China at the time of Polo's visits would have lessened the prevalence of traditional Chinese customs. Finally, they note that Polo did describe many important Chinese innovations, such as porcelain, paper money, and the use of coal, all of which were unknown to Europeans in the thirteenth century.

Wood notes these arguments, but suggests that Polo could have gathered a great deal of information about China without ever having traveled farther than his family's trading posts on the Black Sea. Here he would have had access to Persian and Arabic guidebooks about China, from which he could have pieced together his account without ever having set foot there himself.

The Travels of Sir John Mandeville

The seventeenth-century writer Sir Thomas Browne declared that the explorer Sir John Mandeville was "the greatest liar of all time." The travel book attributed to Mandeville, which first appeared around 1371, was certainly one of the most popular books of the late Middle Ages (hundreds of medieval manuscript copies of it have survived to the present day), and it was definitely filled with bizarre fabrications. But Browne's assessment of Mandeville's character is undermined by the fact that Mandeville probably never existed.

The Travels of Sir John Mandeville described the adventures of an English knight who left home around 1322 and journeyed throughout Egypt, Ethiopia, India, Persia, and Turkey. The stories that Mandeville returned with were fantastic, by any measure. He told of islands whose inhabitants had the bodies of humans but the heads of dogs, of a tribe whose only source of nourishment was the smell of apples, of a people the size of pygmies whose mouths were so small that they had to suck all their food through reeds, and of a race of one-eyed giants who ate only raw fish and raw meat. All of this fantasy was interwoven with other, geographical, descriptions that were perfectly accurate.

The authorship of Mandeville's *Travels* remains unknown. Historians cannot decide whether the author was French or English, though they agree that the book was originally composed in French. The character of Mandeville, as already indicated, was almost certainly fictitious. The name might have been adapted from an earlier French romance titled *Mandevie* that also involved a hero who embarked on an imaginary journey.

It is not clear how seriously medieval readers took Mandeville's stories. It is tempting, as a modern reader, to think that they must have recognized the tales as works of fiction, but this is not necessarily the case. Again we return to the puzzle of the medieval concept of truth. Medieval culture made sense of the world by viewing it through the lens of religious imagery and fantastic legends. In this respect the book did offer an alle-

Illustration from the earliest printed edition of *The Travels of Sir John Mandeville*. Shown are a sample of the various races and species that Mandeville claimed to have encountered, including: 1) the dog-headed folk; 2) the flat-faced people; 3) the wild men with horns and hoofs; 4) the people with eyes in their shoulders; 5) the vegetable lamb; and 6) the folk that have but one foot.

gorical truth of a kind, though not one that modern readers are
likely to grasp.

Waiting for the Apocalypse

The medieval mind fixated on the end of the world. Predictions of imminent, world-encompassing disaster turned up with
almost clockwork regularity. This atmosphere of constant dread
had its ridiculous elements. For instance, we read about medieval survivalists frantically storing up grain or heading to high
ground in anticipation of the final days. But it also had serious
consequences for the course of European history. Many of the
crusaders of the twelfth and thirteenth centuries viewed themselves as taking part in battles that would anticipate Judgment
Day. Even Christopher Columbus seems to have been driven by
a belief that he needed to help bring about universal conversion before the end of the world.

Predictions of disaster and catastrophe were usually made
with no intention to deceive. They were motivated by genuine
beliefs inherited from the cultural tradition of early Christianity
and ancient Judaism. Such beliefs helped to provide a framework of meaning within which to understand catastrophic events
such as wars and plagues. They could also serve as rallying
points for efforts to reform or change society. Nevertheless, the
predictions often lent themselves to fraud and manipulation.

For instance, in 1184 a document called the Toledo Letter
appeared and rapidly spread throughout Europe. An ominous
conjunction of the planets, it claimed, foretold the imminent end
of the world in September 1186. When the letter reached the
archbishop of Canterbury in England, it prompted him to order
a three-day fast to prepare for the final days. September 1186
came and went, and the world didn't end. But this didn't deter
the letter's true believers. They simply changed the doomsday
date and kept circulating the letter for several more centuries.

One of the most famous prophets of doom of all time was Michel de Notredame, better known as Nostradamus (1503–1566). Supported by the patronage of the French queen Catherine de Médicis, he wrote numerous verses predicting the downfall of her great rival, Elizabeth I of England. Obviously these predictions did not pan out. But Nostradamus's great genius was in writing his prophecies in an ancient form of French worded so ambiguously that it could be interpreted to mean almost anything a reader desired. As a result, ever since his death his followers have continued to reinterpret his writings, reading into them predictions of calamitous events: the great London fire of 1666, the rise of Adolf Hitler, the Iranian revolution of 1979, the events of September 11, 2001. Some of his more zealous fans have even gone to the effort of penning new, more specific verses, after such events have already occurred, and attributing the "predictions" to him (see Chapter Nine).

After the sixteenth century, apocalypticism waned in southern Europe. But in northern Europe it remained influential, in the sixteenth century among German Protestant reformers, and in the seventeenth among English Puritans. The Puritans exported their apocalypticism to America, where predictions of imminent doom have found willing audiences ever since.

Pranks and Truth Spells

A number of texts have preserved the efforts of everyday medieval tricksters. The notebook of Thomas Betson, a fifteenth-century monk at Syon Abbey in Middlesex, records his joke of hiding a beetle inside a hollowed-out apple. When the apple began to mysteriously rock back and forth, people believed it to be possessed. Other manuscripts include instructions for more mischievous tricks, such as how to make beds itchy and meat appear wormy. The *Secretum Philosophorum,* which was a kind of fourteenth-century guide to trickery, offered a recipe for magically transforming water into wine. The trick was to secretly drop pieces of bread into the water, after first soaking the bread pieces in dark wine and then drying them in the sun.

Of course, with all this trickery and deception afoot it was also useful to know how to make people tell the truth. One magic spell suggested this method: Place the heart and left foot of a toad over a sleeping person's mouth. When the sleeper awoke, they would respond truthfully to whatever question they were asked. Unfortunately, user feedback for this spell was not recorded.

Renaissance Forgeries

The Renaissance stirred a new interest in the classical world. Wealthy merchants and princes scrambled to build magnificent collections of classical artifacts. Scholars pored over manuscripts that had been lost to Europeans for centuries. Much of this activity represented genuine excitement at the rediscovery of lost knowledge and art. But some was driven by the fact that the acquisition of classical artifacts had become a new way to display status. Instead of collecting the bones and body parts of saints, towns and wealthy rulers now collected fragments of the ancient world. And just as with the relic trade, demand far outstripped supply. Therefore, the forgers once again stepped in to fill the gap.

Curiously, some of the greatest scholars and artists turned out to be the most notorious forgers. A highly respected fifteenth-century scholar named Giovanni Nanni (aka Annius) forged elaborate ancient texts and inscriptions in order to invent a glorious past for his native town of Viterbo. In 1583 Carlo Sigonio, one of the most renowned scholars of his day, faked a new complete work by Cicero titled *De Consolatione*, perhaps motivated by a desire to display his mastery of Ciceronian scholarship. But the most famous case of Renaissance fraud involved the young Michelangelo. In 1496 he sculpted a sleeping cupid, which he buried in acidic earth to give it an appearance of great age. He then sold it through a dealer to Cardinal Riario of San Giorgio. The cardinal eventually learned of the forgery and demanded his money back from the dealer. Michelangelo, however, was able to keep his percentage of the sale. In fact, everyone was so impressed by Michelangelo's obvious talent that they all simply overlooked his youthful indiscretion. Unfortunately, Michelangelo's cupid was lost in the ensuing years and was never found again. It would undoubtedly command an imposing price today as a genuine Michelangelo fake.

Lusus Naturae and Museums of Hoaxes

Medieval natural history contained a strong appreciation for hoaxing. This appreciation was displayed through the taxonomical category known as *Lusus naturae,* or joke of nature.

The term *Lusus naturae* described any creature or specimen that defied efforts at classification. One famous example was the Scythian lamb, also known as the vegetable lamb (see *The Travels of Sir John Mandeville*). This bizarre creature, whose existence was long rumored but never confirmed, was part plant and part animal. It consisted of a lamb from whose belly grew a thick stem that was firmly rooted in the ground. Thus rendered immobile, the creature survived by eating the grass that grew around it. Medieval naturalists labeled the creature a *Lusus naturae* because it defied classification, being neither plant nor animal.

The category of *Lusus naturae* was not simply a way for medieval naturalists to avoid classifying puzzling creatures. It actually symbolized a belief that nature was an active, sentient force that enjoyed playing jokes on man, that enjoyed confounding his expectations and subverting his classification schemes. In other words, medieval naturalists believed that nature was the greatest hoaxer of all.

Lusus naturae could also include inanimate objects. The naturalist Athanasius Kircher kept a collection of objects in which he had discovered the shapes of crosses. He believed that nature had purposefully placed the crosses in the objects as a kind of game, intending for him to find them. The seventeenth-century Veronese collector Lodovico Moscardo greatly prized a stone in which he discerned the shapes of trees, houses, and countrysides. He thought it was an example of nature parodying human art by creating an image in a stone similar to something a man might draw.

During the sixteenth and seventeenth centuries the growing interest in the study of nature prompted the establishment of the first museums in Europe. They appeared initially in Italy but soon spread to the rest of the continent. These early museums were, to use the phrase of the historian Paula Findlen, like "repositories of wonders," full of bizarre natural specimens: fossils, birds, bones, monstrosities, and *Lusus naturae*. Remains of legendary creatures such as the unicorn rested alongside examples of more mundane creatures. The curators of these museums also created elaborate jokes of their own, designed to mimic nature's capacity for joking: optical-illusion shows involving magic lanterns and distorting mirrors, or levitation tricks that used magnets and string. Because these museums gathered together the jokes of nature and the jokes of man, they can be considered the original Museums of Hoaxes.

By the end of the seventeenth century the concept of *Lusus naturae* was disappearing. In its place emerged the modern scientific view that nature does not joke, but instead follows strict rules and laws that men can learn and manipulate. *Lusus naturae* exhibits were eventually relocated from museums to circus sideshows, but wherever they were displayed, they continued to fascinate audiences with their category-defying mystery.

The Museum of Marchese Ferdinando Cospi. Museums of this kind served as "repositories of wonder" in early modern Europe.   From Lorenzo Legati, *Museo Cospiano annesso a quello del famoso Ulisse Aldrovandi . . .* (Bologna, 1677).

THE ORIGIN OF APRIL FOOLS' DAY

The question of when April Fools' Day began is shrouded in mystery, but the most widespread theory about its source involves the Gregorian calendar reform of the late sixteenth century. According to this theory observance of the day began in 1582, when France became the first country to switch from the Julian to the Gregorian calendar, following the directive of the pope. This switch meant that the beginning of the year was moved from the end of March to January 1. During the confusion of the change, those who persisted in celebrating the new year in April had various jokes played on them. For instance, pranksters would surreptitiously stick paper fish to their backs and taunt them with the name *"Poisson d'Avril,"* or "April Fish." Thus, April Fools' Day was born.

The calendar-change hypothesis might provide a reason why April 1 specifically became the date of the modern holiday, but it is clear that the idea of a springtime festival honoring pranks and mayhem had far more ancient roots. For instance, a rival French legend links spring prank-playing and the origin of the term *"poisson d'avril"* to the abundance of fish found in streams and rivers during early April. These young, newly hatched fish were easy to fool with a hook and lure. Therefore, the French called them *"poissons d'avril"* and celebrated this season of easy fishing by playing pranks on each other. It is still the custom in France to celebrate April Fools' Day by eating chocolate fish. But even as far back as Roman times celebrations such as Hilaria honored spring mischief, while farther afield in India revelers observed Holi, the festival of color, and in northern Europe the festival of Lud, a Celtic god of humor, provided an excuse for merrymaking.

Anthropologists explain that the tradition of spring foolery relates to the transition from winter to spring. During such moments of seasonal transition, in that moment when winter passes away and spring begins, society is momentarily in a state of flux. It is as if the world holds its breath, waiting to see if the cycle of seasons will continue unbroken. In that moment of suspense, social rules are suspended and normal behavior does not govern. Raucous partying and trickery are briefly allowed. Other festivals marking moments of transition, such as New Year's Eve, Halloween, and May Day, similarly involve partying and pranks.

For more theories, myths, and legends about
the origin of April Fools' Day go to
www.museumofhoaxes.com/aprilframe.html

The Cerne Abbas Giant

The Cerne Abbas giant is a gigantic naked chalk figure carved into the side of a hill near Dorchester, England. It is one of a number of presumably ancient hill figures that dot the English countryside, such as the Long Man of Wilmington and the White Horse of Uffington. But the Cerne Abbas giant is unique for the large club that it holds and the erect phallus that it sports. Despite its "impudent anatomy" (or really because of it), the giant occupies a treasured place in British culture. As the historian Glyn Daniel notes, postcards of it are the only images of a naked man cheerfully accepted by the British post office. But in recent years controversy has swirled around the giant. A growing number of historians have begun to suggest that the figure is not as ancient as most people assume. Instead, they argue that the giant may be nothing more than an enormous seventeenth-century hoax.

On May 23, 1996, a mock trial was held in the town of Cerne Abbas to settle once and for all the question of the giant's age. A jury listened to the arguments both of those who defended the giant's antiquity and of those who suggested the figure was of far more recent origin.

The case for a modern giant focused on the puzzling lack of references to the figure before 1694. The historian Ronald Hutton argued that, given the many surveys and descriptions of the Cerne Abbas region that survive from before the seventeenth century, surely some reference to the giant should be found, if he had existed at that time. Joseph Betty then presented an even more specific case for a modern giant. He argued that a local landowner named Denzil Holles created the giant in the seventeenth century during the English Civil War. Holles was known for harboring a passionate hatred of the Puritan commander, Oliver Cromwell. Cromwell's followers often portrayed their leader as a modern-day, club-wielding Hercules. Therefore, what better way for Holles to satirize the commander, Betty suggested, than to plaster a 180-foot crude caricature of the image of Hercules on a hilltop in the middle of England? Of course, Holles would have concealed his authorship of the giant in order to avoid unpleasant forms of retaliation.

The defenders of the giant's antiquity countered these arguments by noting that an absence of evidence (the lack of references to the figure before 1694) is not evidence of absence.

Their argument also focused on the undeniable antiquity of the hill-carving tradition and the blatant pagan symbolism of the giant itself. They insisted that the themes expressed by the the giant ("violence, nakedness, sexual arousal") were simply not the kind of themes memorialized by Christian societies through large public works of art.

When the jury cast its votes, fifty percent of them supported the ancient-origin theory. But thirty-five percent of them sided with Hutton and Betty. Fifteen percent remained ambivalent. Although the trial was supposed to end the debate over the giant's age, it almost certainly inflamed the issue by bringing it before an even wider audience. This means that scholars will probably be arguing for years over what the giant really is: prehistoric art, or an enormous seventeenth-century hill hoax.

The Cerne Abbas Giant. Modern hill hoax or prehistoric art?
Source: Yann Arthus-Bertrand/CORBIS

CHAPTER TWO

THE EIGHTEENTH CENTURY

Rabbit Babies and Lying Stones

If any era can be said to have raised hoaxing to a noble art, it was the eighteenth century. In the hands of Enlightenment artists and philosophers hoaxing became more than just a tool to cheat, scam, fool, and deceive others. It became a means of educating and enlightening the people, and of improving the human condition itself.

International commerce had dramatically increased the wealth of Europe and America by the eighteenth century. As a result a prosperous middle class had emerged that was committed to the forward-looking ideals of education and progress. But as the members of this middle class looked around themselves, they saw a popular culture still mired in medieval superstitions and bedeviled by vice and credulity. It was this lingering medievalism that the educated classes felt had to be swept away in order for society to progress. To this purpose they launched into a project of improving themselves and the surrounding society. They read more and wrote more than any previous culture. They developed new ways of sharing information, such as dictionaries, encyclopedias, scientific surveys, newspapers, and periodicals. They also met frequently to discuss and share their knowledge in new social spaces such as coffeehouses and salons. Above all they believed that the secrecy which had shrouded the creation of knowledge during medieval times had to be done away with. They believed that openness and free public debate were the only paths toward true knowledge. Charlatanry, credulity, and vice had to be forcibly dragged out of the shadows in which they lurked and exposed to the light of public reason. Hoaxing, and its cousin satire, proved to be powerful means to this end.

The idea of luring people into false belief in order to expose their credulity was not a new one. But the Enlightenment honed it to a high art. Writers and thinkers such as Benjamin Franklin, Jonathan Swift, and Daniel Defoe crafted skillful deceptions that they then let loose upon the public. Sometimes their goal would be achieved by the spread of the deception itself, as a subversive idea disseminated throughout the culture. Other times the hoax would only achieve its purpose at the moment of exposure, the "gotcha" moment, when the victim's vice or pomposity would be exposed to public view. But always education and enlightenment were the final purposes of the hoax.

Of course, not every hoax perpetrated during the Enlightenment was motivated by such lofty ideals. The larger popular culture that surrounded the educated elite gave birth to a broad variety of charlatanry and deceit, and the spread of education, and the proliferation of new ways of sharing information, ironically created many new opportunities for forgers and fakes to practice their arts. But educational and satirical hoaxes were among the most visible and celebrated deceptions of the century. Following the eighteenth century, entrepreneurs would realize that the publicity generated by a skillful hoax could more profitably be used for public entertainment or advertisement than for education, but for the moment idealism and public-spiritedness still prevailed.

The Native of Formosa

Those who journeyed on European roads at the start of the eighteenth century must have met many unusual characters during their travels, but one character wandering the byways in those years proved more unusual than the rest. This man was in his early twenties. His skin was white; his hair was blond; he spoke fluent Latin with a hint of a Dutch accent; and he claimed to be a native of Formosa (now known as Taiwan). His eccentric behavior provided proof of his claim. For instance, he worshiped the sun and the moon; he slept upright in a chair with a lamp burning; and he ate heavily spiced raw meat. What better evidence of foreignness could anyone possibly want?

In 1702 the man who claimed to be from Formosa (he had no other name, at that time) arrived in Holland, where he met a Scottish clergyman named William Innes. Innes converted him to Anglicanism, baptized him with the Christian name George Psalmanazar, and brought him to England. There the Formosan, now known as Psalmanazar, became an instant celebrity. After all, the English had never met anyone from Formosa before. Psalmanazar was introduced to the bishop of London and was then ushered around to all the high-society events, where the elite gentlemen and ladies treated him as an exotic curiosity. Even the members of the Royal Society took an interest in him.

Soon Psalmanazar capitalized on his fame by writing a book titled *An Historical and Geographical Description of Formosa*, in which he offered British readers an intriguing and sensational glimpse at Formosan culture. He claimed that in Formosa convicted murderers were hung upside down and shot full of arrows, that polygamy was allowed, and that every year twenty thousand young boys were sacrificed to appease the gods (this latter claim was accompanied by a gruesome illustration of "The Gridiron upon which the hearts of the young Children are burnt"). Psalmanazar also obtained an appointment at Oxford College to translate religious literature into Formosan.

But not everyone was quite so ready to believe that Psalmanazar was who he claimed to be. The Jesuit Father Fontaney, who had traveled extensively throughout Asia, challenged Psalmanazar to explain why his skin was not darker in color like that of other people from Asia. Psalmanazar coolly replied that in Formosa the nobility, of which he was a member, lived indoors and therefore had lighter skin than the laborers who worked outside. Since Fontaney had never been to Formosa, he was powerless to deny the truth of this assertion.

But doubts continued to circulate about Psalmanazar's true identity. His critics became more and more insistent until finally, in 1706, ostensibly motivated by a religous revelation, he confessed to his imposture. He spent the rest of his life working as an editor and a writer on Grub Street. Many years later he wrote a long confession titled *Memoirs of ****, Commonly Known by the Name of George Psalmanazar*. This work was published posthumously in 1765, a year after his death.

Who was Psalmanazar really, and why did he perpetrate this deception? Surprisingly little is known about his true identity. In his memoir he claimed to be of French Catholic heritage. He wrote that he adopted the life of a vagabond after growing bored with his studies as a young man. While on the road he discovered that posing as a foreigner was a convenient way to con funds from sympathetic strangers. But he claimed that the deception only rose to a greater level because of the ambition of the clergyman Innes, who had immediately seen through the imposture but desired to advance his career by presenting the church with an exotic convert. Given Psalmanazar's record of dishonesty, it is not clear whether this explanation is the truth, or yet another of his fabrications.

The Hoaxes of Jonathan Swift

The relationship between satire and hoaxing is complex. Satire is defined as the use of wit to expose stupidity or vice, whereas a hoax is a sensational act of deception. But frequently hoaxes can have a satirical effect. Jonathan Swift (1667–1745) was one of the pioneers of satirical hoaxing. For instance, his most famous work, *Gulliver's Travels,* ostensibly told the true story of a man's journey to a series of incredible lands, but was actually more of a comment on English society. Likewise, in "A Modest Proposal for Preventing the Children of Poor People in Ireland from Being a Burden to Their Parents or Country," he pretended to make a serious case for the benefits to be had by feeding poor children to the rich, although he clearly was making a dark comment on the inhumanity of the rich toward the poor. In both these instances the deception was fairly obvious. This was also the case in most of his other satirical hoaxes. His Bickerstaff hoax, described below, was probably his most successful deception, as well as being one of the earliest recorded examples of an elaborately planned April Fools' Day prank.

The Predictions of Isaac Bickerstaff

Sometime in February 1708 an almanac went on sale in London titled *Predictions for the Year 1708,* written by a previously unknown astrologer, Isaac Bickerstaff. One of the events predicted by Mr. Bickerstaff was the death "by a raging fever" of the famous rival astrologer John Partridge. Bickerstaff predicted that Partridge would die at exactly 11:00 P.M. on March 29 of that year.

Londoners were shocked and amused by this bold claim. Almost immediately Partridge issued an angry reply, claiming that Bickerstaff was nothing but a fraud. "His whole Design was nothing but Deceit,/ The End of March will plainly show the Cheat," Partridge declared. The gauntlet having been thrown down, everyone waited to see who would be proven right, Partridge or Bickerstaff.

On the night of March 29 Bickerstaff declared that he was proven right because Partridge had died. He released an elegantly printed, black-framed *Elegy* to commemorate the man's death. This was followed up the next day by an anonymously penned pamphlet titled "The Accomplishment of the First of

Mr. Bickerstaff's Predictions," which explained that Bickerstaff's prediction had come true, but noted that its timing had been off by four hours, since Partridge had died at 7:05 P.M., not 11:00 P.M. Given the slow speed at which news traveled, the word of Partridge's death only became generally known throughout London on April 1, April Fools' Day .

But Partridge was actually still alive. On April 1 he was woken by the sexton outside his window, who wanted to know if there were any orders for his funeral sermon. Then, as he walked down the street, people he knew stared after him or stopped him to inform him that he looked exactly like a deceased acquaintance. Enraged, Partridge published a pamphlet insisting that he was still alive and that Bickerstaff was a fraud. Bickerstaff coolly responded that Partridge was obviously dead since no living man could have written the rubbish that had appeared in his last almanac.

Bickerstaff, of course, was a pseudonym for Jonathan Swift. Swift's intention had been to embarrass and discredit Partridge, apparently because he was annoyed by the astrologer's attacks upon the church. In this sense the hoax was a complete success. It humbled and humiliated the astrologer, who eventually had to stop publishing his almanacs because he could never shake the ridicule of having been declared dead.

The Lying Stones of Dr. Beringer

Dr. Johann Bartholomew Adam Beringer (1667–1740) was dean of the Faculty of Medicine at the University of Würzburg in Germany. He was known to be an arrogant, overbearing man with many enemies, but he was also a passionate naturalist always in search of new curiosities of nature. In May 1725 he paid some local boys to explore nearby Mount Eivelstadt and bring him any interesting objects they might find. Soon they returned with a boxful of spectacular finds: stone fossils that displayed in sharp, three-dimensional relief the shapes of various plants, animals, astronomical objects, and even Hebrew letters.

Dr. Beringer was genuinely puzzled by the stones. He considered many different theories about what they might be. Were they ancient pieces of sculpture carved hundreds of years ago by pagans? Were they relics of the Great Flood? Were they the product of "the marvelous force of petrifying moisture"? He rejected all these possibilities but could arrive at no satisfactory answer of his own, save that they were a wonderful example of the creativity of nature. He was convinced that he had come across the greatest natural-history discovery of the century.

Almost a year passed, and still the boys were bringing Beringer more of the mysterious stones. In the meantime he had written an entire book about them, complete with carefully drawn illustrations. According to legend, just as the first copies of the book were rolling off the printing press, the boys presented Beringer with a final stone, one that had his own name carved in it. Finally he realized that he had been the victim of an elaborate, extended hoax.

In a state of panic Beringer frantically tried to buy up all the existing copies of his book (all extant copies of it are now rare collector's items). He also brought criminal charges against two junior faculty members at the university whom he believed to be the masterminds of the hoax, J. Ignatz Roderick and Georg von Eckhart. These fellow professors, irritated at Beringer's overbearing manner and wanting to bring him down a notch, had paid the boys to bring him the miraculous stones. The case came to court on April 13, 1726, and Beringer eventually won a conviction against the men. But he was not able to save his historical reputation. Today Beringer is principally remembered because of the hoax, not for his work as a scholar.

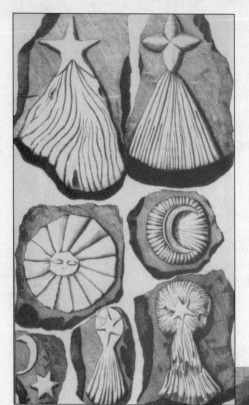

The Mount Eivelstadt stones bore many unusual marks, such as the astronomical symbols shown here. Beringer insisted the marks were the work of nature, not of man. From Beringer's *Lithographie Wirceburgensis (1726).*

Photograph of an extant "lying stone."

The Hoaxes of Benjamin Franklin

Benjamin Franklin (1706–1790) was born the son of a candle- and soapmaker, but by his own efforts and intellect he rose to become arguably the most admired man of the eighteenth century. Throughout his long and illustrious career he was many different things: a printer, a philosopher, a man of science, a man of letters, and a statesman. He was also a hoaxer. Like other eighteenth-century literary figures such as Jonathan Swift and Daniel Defoe, he used hoaxes for satirical ends, to expose foolishness and vice to the light of public censure. The efforts of Franklin and other Enlightenment hoaxers to address the public through hoaxes reveals the increasing importance placed upon public opinion throughout this period. Franklin was a master of the art of public relations before that concept had even been dreamed up. The very image of himself that he presented to the world, as a simple but wise American rustically dressed in a raccoon-skin hat, was actually a carefully crafted public persona that belied the reality that he was one of the most sophisticated, cosmopolitan men of his era.

Silence Dogood

In 1722 a series of letters appeared in the *New-England Courant* written by a middle-aged widow named Silence Dogood. The letters poked fun at various aspects of life in colonial America, such as the drunkenness of locals and the fashion of hoop petticoats. Silence was particularly fond of ridiculing Harvard, complaining that it had been ruined by corruption and elitism, and that most of its students learned nothing there except how to be conceited. The readers of the paper thought she was a charming woman. So charming, in fact, that a few of the male readers wrote in offering to marry her. She coyly hinted that she might be willing to entertain such offers. But unfortunately, Silence Dogood didn't really exist. She was the invention of sixteen-year-old Benjamin Franklin, whose older brother,

James, was a Boston printer. It is not known whether James was privy to the true identity of Silence Dogood, or whether, like the rest of Boston, he was fooled by his younger brother. This was the first of Franklin's many hoaxes.

The Death of Titan Leeds

Poor Richard's Almanac was a yearly publication supposedly written by a henpecked, poverty-stricken scholar named Richard Saunders. It first appeared in 1733, offering a collection of wit, poetry, and prophecies. In its first year it included the prediction that the rival almanac-writer Titan Leeds would die on "Oct. 17, 1733, 3:29 P.M., at the very instant of the conjunction of the Sun and Mercury." Titan Leeds failed to die. In fact, he lived to chastise Saunders for his falsehood and stubbornly continued to publish his almanac. Saunders responded to Leeds's impertinent refusal to die by theorizing that Leeds actually had died, but that someone had usurped his name and was using it to falsely publish the almanac. For the next five years Saunders continued to insist that Leeds was dead until finally, in 1738, Leeds actually did die. This prompted Saunders to congratulate the men who had usurped Leeds's name on their decision to end the pretense. Saunders was, of course, the pseudonym of Franklin. The hoax (adapted from Jonathan Swift's similar Bickerstaff hoax of 1708) represented his method of mocking the popular art of prophecy.

Polly Baker

Eighteenth-century laws made it illegal for women to have sexual relations with men out of wedlock. In 1747 the text of a speech delivered in a court by a woman accused of this crime began to circulate around Europe. The evidence that she had committed the crime was fairly compelling: she had just given birth and was unmarried. Therefore, she didn't contest her guilt. Instead, she contested the justice of the law itself. She pointed out that she had already been fined four times for the same crime, while her accomplices (the men who had fathered her children) had never been fined at all. In fact, she argued, she would have been willing to marry any one of these men, but all of them had abandoned her. For this reason, she maintained, she was really being punished for their crime. After hearing this speech the judges supposedly not only declared her innocent, but one of them married her the next day. The text of Polly Baker's speech was reprinted in many papers throughout Europe and America and caused a great sensation. Everyone accepted it as a true account of an actual event. But thirty years later Franklin confessed that he had written the speech himself and that there was no Polly Baker. His intention had been to draw attention to the unfairness of the law that punished mothers, but not fathers, for having children out of wedlock.

A Supplement to the Boston Independent Chronicle

In 1782 a shocking letter was printed in the *Supplement to the Boston Independent Chronicle* and soon began to circulate throughout Europe. It alleged that Indian warriors were sending hundreds of American scalps as war trophies across the Atlantic to British royalty and members of Parliament. The scalps included those of women, as well as young girls and boys. The allegation shocked European public opinion. But in fact, the British had not received scalps from any Indians. The *Supplement to the Boston Independent Chronicle* was a fake newspaper that Franklin himself had printed up and distributed to his friends. Franklin saw his hoax as aiding the American war effort by turning European opinion against the British.

For more hoaxes by Benjamin Franklin go to
www.museumofhoaxes.com/hoaxes18.html.

APRIL FOOLS' DAY HOAXES

 During the eighteenth century April Fools' Day (or All Fools' Day, as it was usually called at that time) became increasingly popular throughout Europe and America. But few accounts of large-scale, elaborate pranks survive from this period (Jonathan Swift's 1708 hoax described previously is a significant exception). Instead the day seems to have been a holiday embraced by the common people for the simple pleasure of tormenting each other with numerous small, mischievous tricks. One strict custom that prevailed was that the foolery could begin at midnight of April 1 but had to end by noon. Pranksters who failed to observe this rule themselves became the April fools.

Sleeveless Errands

The most common prank was to send a victim on a "sleeveless errand." This meant sending some poor soul on a fruitless quest in search of an item that did not exist. Young apprentices working in the shops of tradesmen were frequent victims of this trick. They might be sent to the market to search for a variety of goods, including hen's teeth, pigeon's milk, striped paint, a soft-pointed chisel, a box of straight hooks, sweet vinegar, a stick with one end, or a penny's worth of elbow grease. Alternatively, they might be sent to a saddler's shop to ask for some "strong strapping," at which point, if they were not careful, they would receive a strong strapping across their shoulders. Or they might be sent to ask for a "long stand," whereupon they would be told that they could stand for as long as they wished. The Scottish developed a special variety of this prank, which they referred to as "hunting the gowk" (*gowk* being a term for a cuckoo bird). When sent on a "gowk hunt," a victim would be asked to deliver a note that, unbeknownst to him, read, *Never laugh, never smile,/Hunt the gowk another mile*. Recipients of this note would duly redirect its bearer elsewhere until the victim had been run all over town.

Street Pranks

The English were particularly fond of playing pranks on unsuspecting strangers in the streets. The most popular gag (still in use today) was to pin a sign reading KICK ME onto a victim's back. Other tricks included gluing a penny to the pavement and watching as someone tried to pick it up, putting a brick beneath a hat and waiting for someone to kick it out of the way, or tying a string to a purse and yanking it out of the grasp of whoever bent down to lift it up. Street urchins were also famous for pulling the coattails of gentlemen and then running rapidly away as they surreptitiously dropped a handkerchief. The gentlemen, seeing the handkerchief and believing they had been pickpocketed, would run fruitlessly after the boys for blocks before giving up the chase.

Mary Toft and the Rabbit Babies

England during the reign of King George I (1660–1727) was full of oddities, shams, and charlatans. But for sheer strangeness nothing surpassed the infamous case of Mary Toft of Godalming and her rabbit babies.

In September 1726 Mary Toft began to give birth to rabbits. The local surgeon, John Howard, responding to her family's summons, hurried to their house, where, to his amazement, he soon helped her deliver nine more of the animals. They were all born dead, and they were actually rabbit parts rather than whole rabbits. Nevertheless, this didn't lessen the amazing fact that she was giving birth to them.

John Howard excitedly wrote to other men of science around the country, urging them to help him sort out this bizarre phenomenon. Soon two prominent men, sent by the king himself, arrived to investigate: Nathanael St. Andre, surgeon-anatomist to the king, and Samuel Molyneux, secretary to the Prince of Wales. Mary explained to these men that she had recently miscarried, but that during the pregnancy she had intensely craved rabbit meat. After unsuccessfully attempting to chase down several rabbits she had dreamt that there were rabbits in her lap. The next thing she knew, she was giving birth to rabbits.

In the presence of the doctors Mary continued to give birth to even more rabbits. The men performed tests to verify the reality of the phenomenon. For instance, they placed a piece of the lung of one of the rabbits in water and noted that it floated. This meant that the rabbit must have breathed air before its death, which could not have happened inside a womb. Amazingly, the doctors ignored this evidence and decided that there was no deception involved—that Mary really was giving birth to rabbits.

On November 29 Mary was brought to London. By now her case had become a national sensation, and huge crowds surrounded the house where she was lodged. But when kept under constant supervision Mary stopped giving birth to rabbits, and her case quickly began to unravel. Witnesses came forward who claimed that they had supplied Mary's husband with rabbits. Then, when a famous London physician, Sir Richard Manningham, threatened that he might have to surgically examine Mary's uterus in the name of science, she wisely decided to confess. She explained that she had simply inserted the dead rabbits inside her womb when no one was looking, motivated by a desire for fame and the hope of receiving a pension from the king. She was briefly imprisoned for fraud but was released without trial. It is said that she managed to give birth to a normal human child less than a year later. John Howard and Nathanael St. Andre, the two surgeons who had most passionately believed and defended her, fared less well. Their medical careers were both ruined.

The Patagonian Giants

When Commodore John Byron (grandfather of the poet Lord Byron) returned to London in 1766 after circumnavigating the globe, an intriguing rumor accompanied him. His crew mem-

Credulity, Superstition, and Fanaticism by William Hogarth, 1762. The figure of Mary Toft is shown in the bottom left-hand corner. Rabbits are running out from beneath her dress. Other symbols of eighteenth-century popular credulity fill the remainder of the scene. The nail-vomiting Boy of Bilston crouches to the right of Mary Toft, and in the pulpit above, a preacher denounces witchcraft. A credulous, leering audience looks on behind.   Source: Heritage-Images/Corporation of London

bers whispered that they had encountered a tribe of twelve-foot giants in Patagonia, South America. The rumor first appeared in print on May 9, 1766, in the *Gentleman's Magazine,* but other newspapers and journals soon picked up the story.

Explorers had been spreading stories about Patagonian giants for over two hundred years, so there was a good deal of history to give the tale credibility. There was also the matter of scientific rivalry. Georges Louis Leclerc de Buffon, a French natural philosopher, had famously argued that the animals and plants of the New World were small and degenerate in comparison to their European counterparts. If giants were found in the Americas, this would prove Buffon wrong. Therefore his rivals seized on the rumor and gleefully promoted it.

Naturally, not everyone believed the rumor. The Frenchman Charles Marie de La Condamine argued that the report was just a hoax spread by the English in order to camouflage the real reason that they were sending a boat back to Argentina (which was to explore a mine newly discovered there, according to him). Horace Walpole joked that some of the Patagonian women should be brought back to England and used to improve the English race. Despite these notes of skepticism widespread belief in the rumor persisted.

It was only seven years later, when the official account of Byron's voyage appeared in print, that the rumor was laid to rest. The account revealed that Byron had indeed encountered a tribe of Patagonians, but that the tallest among them measured only six feet six inches. In other words, they were tall, but not twelve-foot giants. The tribe that Byron met was probably the Tehuelches, who were wiped out by the Rocca expedition in 1880.

Eighteenth-Century Literary Hoaxes

The eighteenth century is known as the great age of literary forgery. Fakes poured forth from the pens of writers. A number of factors contributed: First, this was the period during which print culture became ascendant over oral culture. Literacy rates rose dramatically. Therefore, it was natural that more people would turn their hands to print-based hoaxes. Second, the keen popular interest in antiquities and history that developed during this period gave forgers a ready market for any "ancient" manuscripts that they could produce. The sheer volume of forgery ironically promoted the advance of scholarship because it forced scholars to improve their analytical skills in order to separate authentic from inauthentic texts. The forgers, in turn, responded by becoming better at faking manuscripts. This "arms race" between scholars and forgers continues to this day. Any improvement in skills or techniques on one side immediately prompts a corresponding improvement from the other side.

James Macpherson and the Ossianic Controversy

In 1760 a young Edinburgh schoolmaster named James Macpherson (1736–1796) published a translation of ancient Scottish verse titled *Fragments of Ancient Poetry Collected in the Highlands of Scotland.* Prompted by the enthusiastic response this work received, Macpherson next translated two longer epic poems, *Fingal* and *Temora,* both supposedly composed by a third-century bard named Ossian. The poems were instant international successes and propelled Macpherson to fame and riches. Eighteenth-century readers found that the simple, melancholy virtues of Ossian's heroic characters provided an appealing contrast to the complexity and deceit of the modern world. In addition, the discovery of an ancient literature older than any England could boast gave a boost to Scottish cultural nationalism. But not all were impressed. While touring Scotland in 1773 Samuel Johnson searched for the original Gaelic manuscripts that Macpherson had translated. He could not find them, and he returned home to denounce Macpherson as a fraud, suggesting that Macpherson had actually written the poetry himself. What followed was an almost fifty-year controversy about the authenticity of the Ossianic poetry. Macpherson kept promising to produce the originals, but it was not until his death that scholars really got a chance to examine his sources. Then it became clear that while there were some legitimate manuscript sources, Macpherson had greatly expanded and altered them. Although Macpherson is now principally remembered as a fraud, he did help to draw attention to the ancient and disappearing oral tradition of Scottish balladry, which was real.

Thomas Chatterton and the Rowley Poems

As a young boy growing up in Bristol, Thomas Chatterton (1752–1770) spent a great deal of time with his uncle, who was sexton of the St. Mary Redcliffe Church. A sensitive, artistic child, Chatterton began to imagine what the life of the monks who had lived in the church during the fifteenth century must have been like. He even invented in his mind the character of a fifteenth-century priest named Thomas Rowley. Most children manage to maintain a line between their imaginary life and reality, but Chatterton drew no such line. His medieval fantasy world became real when he claimed to have found poetry tucked away in a back room of the church that had been written by his imaginary priest. He showed it to the law partner of his employer, a Bristol attorney, who believed it to be authentic fifteenth-century material and bought it from him. Emboldened by this success, Chatterton began "finding" more of Rowley's poetry. He also produced poems using his own name, but these were ignored, whereas work by Rowley was eagerly sought after. In April 1770 Chatterton left for London, determined to make it on his own merits as a writer, without any help from Rowley. But a mere four months later, unable to find any work, without money, and near starvation, he penned a farewell poem and poisoned himself with arsenic. He was only seventeen years old. Paradoxically, upon his death Chatterton found the appreciation for his own work that had eluded him during his brief life. His poetry was discovered and published, and ended up exerting an enormous influence upon the rising generation of Romantic poets. Wordsworth referred to him as "the marvelous boy" and Keats dedicated *Endymion* to him. Some argue that Chatterton, the boy forger, was, in fact, the very first Romantic poet.

William Henry Ireland's Shakespeare Forgeries

As literacy rates rose during the eighteenth century, a cultlike reverence for the great literary master William Shakespeare emerged. Theaters staged his plays repeatedly, and collectors eagerly sought out any relics related to his life. The book-seller Samuel Ireland was one of the most passionate of these Shakespeare-worshiping relic hunters. He devoted his life to the pursuit of Shakespeariana, in the process neglecting his talented young son, William Henry Ireland (1777–1835). That is, until 1794, when eighteen-year-old William Henry brought home from the law office where he worked a mortgage docu-ment supposedly signed by Shakespeare himself. The boy claimed that he had found the document among the estate papers of a client who desired to remain anonymous. Samuel Ireland was ecstatic, and grew even more so as his son continued to bring home other spectacular finds, including a love letter written by Shakespeare to Anne Hathaway and a previously unknown his-torical drama by the Bard titled *Vortigern*. Arrangements were made for this play to be performed at the Drury Lane Theater on April 2, 1796. The theater's owner, though half suspecting a fraud, decided that there was enough public interest in even a fake Shakespeare play to warrant a performance. But the actors were not so willing to play along. To indicate their displeasure they hammed their way through the performance, and when the lead actor, J. P. Kemble, arrived at some lines that read, "And when this solemn mockery is ended," he delivered them with such emphasis that everyone in the audience knew he was re-ferring to the play itself. This prompted a riotous outburst of laughter and applause. After that infamous opening night the play was never performed again. A few weeks later William Henry confessed that the play and other documents were all his own work. His father, however, refused to believe his son's con-fession. He went to his grave insisting that the treasured finds were really the work of his idol, William Shakespeare.

The Great Chess Automaton

Enlightenment virtuosi thrilled audiences by constructing ingenious mechanical contraptions called automata. For instance, Jacques de Vaucanson (1709–1782) built a famous mechanical duck that quacked, ate food, and defecated just like the real thing (he claimed that it was actually digesting the food, but this was a hoax). These automata were widely praised and admired, but none more so than the Great Chess Automaton of Baron Wolfgang von Kempelen (1734–1804).

The device consisted of a wooden figure dressed in Turkish clothes (and usually referred to as the "Turk"), whose trunk emerged out of a large wooden box filled with gears and wires. When wound up the Turk played chess against human opponents. This involved the machine lifting up chess pieces and moving them around a board by its own volition. Unlike mere mechanical contraptions such as the duck, the chess automaton was billed as being an actual "thinking machine."

Kempelen, who was a Hungarian nobleman, built the chess automaton in 1769 and then toured throughout Europe with it, exhibiting it before audiences filled with royalty and aristocrats. He invited audience members to challenge the machine to a match. These challengers, who included such luminaries as Benjamin Franklin, usually lost to it. Before each show Kempelen made a point of opening sliding doors on the side of the box to prove that it was occupied only by clockwork gears, and each time the automaton moved the noise of grinding machinery could be heard, emphasizing that this was indeed only a machine.

The secret of the automaton's operation was a source of constant speculation. The leading theory was that a dwarf was somehow hidden inside the box and was controlling its movements, but many were convinced that the automaton actually was a chess-playing machine. In 1790 Kempelen finally dismantled the device and stored it away. But this was not the end of its career, because in 1805 Kempelen's family, following his death, sold the machine to Johann Nepomuk Maelzel (1772–1838), a German university student.

Maelzel reconstructed the automaton and toured with it throughout Europe before bringing it to America in 1826. Again it entertained and fascinated audiences, while regularly beating challengers, and again people tried to guess the trick that made it work. Edgar Allan Poe famously surmised that someone was hidden inside the wooden figure of the Turk. But this was incorrect.

The real secret was that a full-grown man (and not a dwarf) was ingeniously concealed inside the gearbox. A series of sliding panels and a rolling chair allowed this man to remain hidden while the interior of the machine was displayed. He then controlled the Turk by means of a "pantograph" device that synchronized his arm movements with those of the wooden figure. Magnetic chess pieces allowed him to know what pieces were being moved on the board above his head. The hidden operator was usually a chess master. Johann Allgaier and Aaron Alexandre are among those known to have served in this capacity.

An article that ran in the *Philadelphia National Gazette Literary Register* in 1837 partially revealed the method of the automaton's operation. But when the machine was accidentally destroyed by a fire in 1854, its secrets were still a mystery to most. A complete exposé appeared three years later in 1857. The historian Tom Standage has recently reassembled the entire illustrious career of the automaton in *The Turk: The Life and Times of the Famous Eighteenth-Century Chess-Playing Machine*.

The Duckbilled Platypus

In 1799 the naturalist George Shaw, who was keeper of the Department of Natural History at the British Museum, received a truly bizarre animal specimen from Captain John Hunter in Australia. It appeared to be the bill of a duck attached to the skin of a mole. Shaw dutifully examined the specimen and wrote up a description of it in a scientific journal known as the *Naturalist's Miscellany,* but he couldn't help confessing that it was "impossible not to entertain some doubts as to the genuine nature of the animal, and to surmise that there might have been practised some arts of deception in its structure."

Despite Shaw's doubts about the reality of the animal, he gave it a name: *Platypus anatinus,* or flatfoot duck. The scientific name was later changed to *Ornithorhynchus anatinus,* but it popularly remained known as the duckbilled platypus.

Other naturalists were equally suspicious that the creature was just a hoax. The surgeon Robert Knox later explained that because the specimens arrived in England via the Indian Ocean, naturalists suspected that Chinese sailors, who were well known for their skill at stitching together hybrid creatures, might have been playing some kind of joke upon them. "Aware of the monstrous impostures which the artful Chinese had so frequently practised on European adventurers . . . ," Knox noted, "the scientific felt inclined to class this rare production of nature with eastern mermaids and other works of art."

It was only when more platypus specimens arrived in England that naturalists finally, grudgingly, granted that the creature was real. This made the platypus one of the more famous instances of a hoax that proved not to be a hoax after all.

CHAPTER THREE

1800–1868

Lunar Bison and Solar Armor

The first half of the nineteenth century witnessed wrenching social change. Thousands of people left their small farm communities to find work in the fast-growing cities and factory towns spawned by the industrial revolution. Canals and railways connected these crowded metropolises together, while cheap newspapers mass produced on new steam-powered printing presses fed information to the city inhabitants. The modern age had arrived, together with all its stresses and tensions.

With the rise of the modern age, hoaxes acquired two new forms of significance. First, they became the rhetorical weapon of choice of the new newspapers that began appearing during the 1830s, the "penny papers." These penny papers were low priced and proudly lowbrow. They catered to the democratic masses and not to the elite businessmen, who read the more established, more socially conservative "six-cent" papers. Again and again the penny papers hoaxed the "six-cent" newspapers, thereby implying that the six-cent papers represented an older, more gullible generation, whereas the penny papers were the voice of a quick-witted younger generation. The strategy worked. The six-cent papers were soon run out of business, while the penny papers evolved to become the newspapers we read today. This initial success with hoaxing proved to be the start of the media's love affair with sensationalism.

Second, just as eighteenth-century philosophers had used hoaxes to help publicize and promote the values of the Enlightenment, nineteenth-century entrepreneurs and showmen now used hoaxes to publicize and promote the market-oriented values of the urban world. The great showman P. T. Barnum was one of the masters of this art. He always dressed up his hoaxes in the language of the Enlightenment, claiming that they served an educational purpose by helping people to learn how to recognize fraud and deception. They might have done this, but his sensational pranks and cons also brought publicity to his businesses and put a surprisingly charming spin on the deceptive practices that prevailed in the urban marketplace, making such practices seem more mischievous than malicious. Hoaxers like Barnum helped to convince people that although the new urban world could be dangerous, threatening, and full of deceit, these same qualities also made it exciting and entertaining in a way that life back in the small towns and farm communities never had been. In fact, with Barnum we find the roots of the advertising industry's ambivalent relationship with truth, because he pioneered the acceptance of the idea that it's forgivable to be misleading, as long as you succeed in being entertaining.

The Berners Street Hoax

In 1810 London was the largest, wealthiest city in the world, linked by trade with every continent and fed by the manufacturing might of northern British cities such as Liverpool and Manchester. Almost anything could be obtained in its shops, and on November 10 all of this mercantile abundance was focused for one brief day upon a single residential address located in a sleepy middle-class neighborhood: 54 Berners Street.

It began at nine o'clock in the morning when Mrs. Tottenham, the unsuspecting occupant of that address, answered her door and was greeted by a coal man delivering an order of coal. Mrs. Tottenham hadn't ordered any coal, but she thought nothing of it. After all, such mix-ups occur all the time. Then more delivery men began to arrive, bearing everything imaginable from the city's huge markets: furniture, musical instruments, flowers, bread, fish, fresh vegetables, a wedding cake, and even tanks of lager piled high on a brewer's dray. Just when it seemed that there was nothing left in the city to deliver to her front door, tradesmen began to show up claiming that their services had been requested: chimney sweeps, physicians, dentists, wigmakers, gardeners, housemaids, undertakers. The list went on and on. Finally, dignitaries began to arrive. The governor of the Bank of England showed up, searching for the widow who had written him of her intent to settle a sizable endowment on the bank. The archbishop of Canterbury was close behind, followed by prominent businessmen, cabinet ministers, dukes, and finally the lord mayor of London.

By this time so many were people were crowded into the narrow street that it was hard even to move. Somehow a cart was knocked over, fights broke out, and a near riot ensued. It was well past dark by the time the crowd began to thin out.

When the dust had all settled, two men emerged from a neighboring house, shook hands, and exchanged a guinea. The two men were Theodore Hook, a writer of popular comic operas, and his friend Samuel Beazley. Hook had bet Beazley a guinea that he could transform any house in London into the most talked-about address in the city within a week. Hundreds of letters later Hook won his bet. Although he eventually confessed to being the mastermind behind the hoax, he never faced any punishment for it.

Charles Redheffer's
Perpetual Motion Machine

On January 21, 1813, eight commissioners from the city of Philadelphia arrived to inspect a mysterious machine that Charles Redheffer had constructed in his house. He had been proclaiming to anyone who would listen that it was the world's first working perpetual-motion machine. In other words, it could run indefinitely without any source of energy. If the commisioners determined that it worked as he claimed, they were prepared to give him city funds to build an even larger version of the machine.

Under Redheffer's watchful eye the eight men carefully inspected the machine. But whenever they approached too closely he motioned them away, claiming that he was concerned they might damage it. They were almost ready to announce the contraption a success, when one of the commissioners spied the trick that made it work. Power was being secretly routed to it from elsewhere through a carefully disguised system of belts and gears. The commissioner could have exposed Redheffer on the spot, but instead he decided to lay a trap for him. The next time Redheffer ventured downtown he discovered, to his astonishment, that a duplicate version of his machine was humming away in city hall. Realizing his secret had been found out, Redheffer hurriedly packed his bags and skipped town. But his career as a con man wasn't over. He simply relocated his scam to New York City.

Back then, news traveled slowly between cities, so Redheffer was able to work the same scheme again without fear of being recognized. Once again he spread the word around town about his miraculous invention, and soon people were coming from all over to admire it. One of these visitors was the well-known mechanical engineer Robert Fulton. Fulton noticed that the machine was wobbling slightly and deduced from this that someone operating a hidden hand-crank was actually powering the machine. So Fulton offered Redheffer a challenge. He claimed that he could prove that the machine was a fraud, and that if he failed to do so he would pay for any damages he might cause in trying. Eyeing the crowd that had gathered around Fulton, Redheffer reluctantly agreed to this, whereupon Fulton pried loose a board from a wall neighboring the machine and revealed a long cord made of catgut hidden inside the wall. Fulton saw that the cord disappeared through the ceiling, so he ran upstairs where he discovered an old bearded man sitting alone in a room, eating a crust of bread with one hand, while he turned a hand crank with the other. The crowd that had followed Fulton realized the scam, grew angry, and demolished the "perpetual motion machine." Redheffer fled and was never heard from again.

The Great Stock Exchange Hoax of 1814

The Napoleonic wars were a long and trying experience for the British. Therefore, when a man wearing the uniform of a British military officer showed up at an inn on the coast of the English Channel announcing that the war was over, that a party of Cossacks had killed Napoleon, and that the Bourbon government was restored, everyone who heard the news was ecstatic.

Swift horses were dispatched to speed the news to London. In the capital people rejoiced, and jubilant investors bid up the stocks on the London exchange. Then the bad news arrived. Napoleon was still alive. The report of his death had just been a hoax.

The investigation that followed uncovered a scheme to manipulate prices on the London stock exchange. Some circumstantial evidence indicated that a popular military and political hero, Lord Thomas Cochrane, had masterminded the plan. He was arrested, tried, and imprisoned.

But as time passed many began to question whether Cochrane was really guilty, or whether he had been framed by his political enemies. After all, there was no evidence that Cochrane had profited from the stock market's rise. Cochrane escaped from prison and was thrown back inside again before finally being released due to the popular support that he enjoyed. In 1831 the king pardoned him of any involvement in the stock market hoax. Historians now agree that Cochrane was probably not behind the scheme to defraud investors, but the real perpetrator of this notorious financial hoax remains unknown.

Princess Caraboo

On April 3, 1817, a strange woman appeared in Almondsbury, a small town near Bristol in England. She was five foot two, extremely attractive, and wore a black shawl twisted turban-style around her head. She spoke no known language and had to communicate with the people of the town through gestures. She appeared to be a foreigner. For the people of Almondsbury she was a complete riddle. They had no idea who she was or where she had come from.

Wandering vagrants were normally sent to the poorhouse in Bristol, but in this instance Mrs. Worrall, the wife of the local magistrate of the county, took a personal interest in the woman's case. She put the woman up at Knole Park, the nearby manor house where she lived with her husband, and set out to solve the puzzle of who this woman was.

Mrs. Worrall soon learned that the woman's name was Caraboo. Or, at least, the woman would frequently say the word *caraboo* while pointing at herself. Then, by a stroke of luck, a sailor appeared who claimed to be able to speak the woman's language. Through this sailor the full story of Caraboo's origin was uncovered. The sailor explained that Caraboo was from the faraway island of Javasu, where she was a princess. Pirates had abducted her from her island home, but after a long voyage Caraboo had finally escaped by jumping overboard in the English Channel and swimming to shore.

The Worralls were overjoyed to learn that Caraboo was a princess. They announced to the newspapers that "Princess Caraboo" was living at their house, and soon all of England knew about her. For a few weeks the princess lived in a grand style. She spent her days dancing, fencing, climbing trees, praying to her god Alla Tallah, entertaining the numerous visitors who came to see her, and swimming naked in the lake when she was alone (gaining her enormous notoriety). The Worralls, meanwhile, basked in her reflected glory.

Unfortunately, Princess Caraboo's growing fame turned out to be her undoing. A woman named Mrs. Neale recognized a description of Caraboo printed in the *Bath Chronicle* and revealed that Caraboo had recently been employed at her house as a servant. Caraboo's true name was Mary Baker. She was actually the daughter of a cobbler in Witheridge, Devonshire. When presented with this accusation, Caraboo broke down in tears and admitted her deception.

But Mary Baker's natural charm, which had aided her so much in her portrayal of Princess Caraboo, continued to sustain her after her unmasking. Mrs. Worrall took pity on her and not only forgave her, but offered her enough money to allow her to sail to Philadelphia.

Princess Caraboo's fame preceded her to America, and upon her landing she was besieged by curiosity seekers. After seven years she tired of America and returned to England, where she occasionally responded to the continuing interest in Caraboo by giving public performances dressed as the princess. She died on January 4, 1865, and was buried in an anonymous grave in Bristol.

Princess Caraboo wearing the traditional dress of her island home, Javasu. A sketch by Edward Bird, 1817.   From J. M. Gutch, *Caraboo: A Narrative of a Singular Imposition Practiced Upon the Benevolence of a Lady Residing in the Vicinity of Bristol* (J. M. Gutch, 1817).

Sawing the Island Off

During the early 1820s a group of butchers and tradesmen used to meet every afternoon in the New York City neighborhood of Mulberry and Spring streets to talk about the news of the day. They discussed such topics as the construction of the Erie Canal, the recent yellow-fever epidemic, and Andrew Jackson's bid to become president. One afternoon during the summer of 1823 or 1824 they were mulling over a rumor they had heard about the island of Manhattan itself. It seemed all the new construction occurring around the battery end of the island had disturbed the island's weight distribution, causing it to begin tipping like a seesaw into the ocean.

For the next few weeks they couldn't stop talking and worrying about how Manhattan was sinking into the ocean. Eventually one member of the group, a retired carpenter who identified himself to strangers as Lozier, proposed an ingenious solution. He suggested that the island be sawed in half at Kingsbridge. Boats could then tow the lopsided half out to sea, turn it around, tow it back, and reconnect it to the secure half.

Soon Lozier began offering workers employment in this project. Given that the economy was not great, he easily found men eager to participate. Eventually so many workers were anticipating employment that Lozier felt obliged to set a date when the "sawing off" of the island would begin. He told half the men to meet on an appointed date at the "forks of the Broadway and Bowery" and the other half to meet at 1 Bowery, corner of Spring Street. When the day arrived, a large crowd of men presented themselves at the agreed locations, ready for work. But Lozier himself was nowhere to be found. He had gone into hiding rather than face the mob of angry, unemployed workers. Many of the men who had been duped swore that if they ever got hold of him they would "saw him off."

The story of the sawing off of Manhattan is one of the most popular tales about the early history of New York City. But when the author Joel Rose recently investigated the tale, he discovered that there had been no such hoax. Or rather, if there had been it had never been mentioned in a book, newspaper, or diary until almost forty years later, when the first recorded account of it appeared in a history of New York City's markets. Rose theorizes that a minor prank occurred during the 1820s, not worth recording at the time, and that decades later someone related a highly embellished account of it to the author of the market history. Once in the history book it became a permanent part of New York City folklore. Whether real or not the hoax has long served as an archetypal example of the humor of Yankee tradesmen.

The Great Moon Hoax

During the final week of August 1835 the *New York Sun* announced that life had been discovered on the moon. The *Sun* was one of the new "penny papers" turning the media industry on its head and ending the reign of the older sixpenny papers. It explained that the discovery had been made by the famous British astronomer Sir John Herschel, who had invented a new kind of telescope "of vast dimensions and an entirely new principle." This telescope was so powerful, the *Sun* declared, that it even allowed Herschel to examine the insect life of the moon.

Over the course of the next week the *Sun* printed new details about Herschel's lunar discoveries every day. The variety of life he spied through his telescope was truly astounding. Herds of lunar bison, unicorns, birds, and a host of other mysterious creatures all were sighted by him. The high point of the *Sun*'s coverage came when it revealed that Herschel had found evidence of intelligent life on the moon. He had discovered both a primitive tribe of hut-dwelling, fire-wielding biped beavers, and a race of winged humans that lived in pastoral harmony around a mysterious, golden-roofed temple. Herschel dubbed these latter creatures the "Vespertilio-homo," or "man-bat."

The American public was fascinated by the news of the lunar discoveries. Numerous papers reprinted the *Sun*'s articles, causing them to quickly spread throughout the nation, and everywhere the news was received it caused the same buzz of excitement. For a week almost nothing else was discussed. But eventually people began to grow skeptical. The rival penny papers had been cynical about the discoveries from the start, and they now demanded that the *Sun* admit to perpetrating a hoax. On September 16 the *Sun* responded by publishing a column in which it agreed that the discoveries might be a hoax, but it then disingenuously added that if they were, then the *Sun* was an innocent victim just like everyone else. This is the closest the *Sun* ever came to an admission of guilt.

Authorship of the hoax is usually attributed to Richard Adams

These prints showing lunar "man-bats" in their natural habitat were offered for sale by the *New York Sun* in 1835. The *Sun* made a large
profit from the sale of such prints.

Locke, a Cambridge-educated reporter who was working for the *Sun.* Locke never publicly admitted to being the author of the hoax, but it seems certain that he was—though an apparent confession made by him was itself a hoax perpetrated by a rival penny paper, the *New York Herald.* The other penny papers were beside themselves with jealousy at the publicity the hoax brought the *Sun,* but they also couldn't help being impressed at the skill with which it had fooled their sixpenny rivals. "Not one of the penny papers ever believed the moon hoax—one half the sixpenny were hoaxed," the *Herald* later crowed (October 27, 1835). The *Sun's* lunar discoveries became so famous that throughout the rest of the nineteenth century the term *moon hoax* was synonymous with fraud. Anyone who wanted to cast doubt on a claim simply had to say that it sounded rather "moon hoaxy," and everyone knew exactly what they were talking about.

To read the full text of the 1835 moon hoax go to
www.museumofhoaxes.com/moonhoax1.html

The Hoaxes of Edgar Allan Poe

Edgar Allan Poe (1809–1849) published six hoaxes during his brief life. He enjoyed playing games of rationality with his readers. Sometimes he cast himself as a master detective capable of discerning the truth behind any illusion or puzzle, a role that he expressed through the famous character of Chevalier C. Auguste Dupin. At other times Poe liked to display his ability to hide the truth from his readers, to force them to play detective. In fact, both detective and hoaxer were two sides of the same coin for Poe. Both roles manifested the power that he believed a rational mind could wield over reality. Poe was also fascinated by other hoaxes besides his own. He once referred approvingly to the age in which he lived as the "epoch of the hoax."

The Great Balloon Hoax

On April 13, 1844, a broadside, or "extra page," appeared in the midday issue of the *New York Sun* (the same penny paper that had perpetrated the Great Moon Hoax of 1835), announcing that the famous European balloonist Monck Mason had succeeded in flying across the Atlantic Ocean in seventy-five hours. If true, this would have been the first time the Atlantic had ever been crossed in a balloon—a remarkable achievement. The balloon, named the *Victoria*, had apparently taken off from England on a trip to Paris, but had been blown off course due to a propeller accident and ended up floating across the Atlantic and landing on Sullivan's Island, near Charleston, South Carolina. The entire report was a fiction created by Poe, but Poe later proudly described the enormous crowd that gathered to learn more about the historic news: "On the morning of its announcement, the whole square surrounding the *Sun* building was literally besieged, blocked up—ingress and egress being alike impossible, from a period soon after sunrise until about two o'clock P.M. . . . I never witnessed more intense excitement to get possession of a newspaper." But the excitement didn't last long. Word soon arrived from Charleston that the story was a hoax.

The Facts in the Case of M. Valdemar

The concept of mesmerism, or hypnosis, fascinated nineteenth-century readers. A quasi-scientific account written by Poe, which appeared first in the *American Whig Review* in December 1845, described an experiment involving a man on the verge of death, M. Valdemar, who was hypnotized just before he died. As a result his body perished, but his consciousness, still under the power of the hypnotist, survived. The patient could verbally respond to questions. This experiment allegedly continued for several months, at which point the patient began to beg for release from the hypnosis. When released, his body disintegrated as if it had been dead for some time. This story caused great excitement, especially in Europe, where it was widely reprinted. It also prompted many people to write to Poe requesting more information about the experiment. Poe warned one such correspondent, "Some few persons believe it—but I do not—and don't you."

Von Kempelen and His Discovery

In 1849 gold was discovered in California, prompting thousands of "forty-niners" to join the Gold Rush to California. Poe's account of the experiments of a German chemist, Baron von Kempelen, appeared in *The Flag of Our Union* on April 14, 1849. It described von Kempelen's discovery of an alchemical process to transform lead into gold. The account concluded by noting that news of the discovery had already caused a two-hundred-percent leap in the price of lead in Europe. Poe hoped that the story would cause some American readers to think twice before heading off to California in search of gold. He wrote to Evert A. Duyckinck, "My sincere opinion is that nine persons out of ten (even among the best informed) will believe the quiz (provided the design does not leak out before publication) and that thus, acting as a sudden, although of course a very temporary, check to the gold fever, it will create a stir to some purpose." The actual reaction to the hoax was somewhat less profound than Poe anticipated. It is not recorded that anyone delayed his departure to California on account of von Kempelen's spurious discoveries.

For more hoaxes by Edgar Allan Poe go to:
www.museumofhoaxes.com/hoaxes1800.html.

The Hoaxes of P. T. Barnum

Phineas Taylor Barnum (1810–1891) described himself as the "Prince of Humbug," an epithet he more than earned during his long and illustrious career. Barnum is best remembered today for the circus that still bears his name (and for the animal crackers named after him), but before his circus career he was for many years an internationally famous museum showman. His early career was marked by a variety of outrageous publicity stunts and hoaxes, which he used to attract attention to his bizarre exhibits. His promotional techniques often tested the boundaries of what the emerging middle class was willing to accept, but he was somehow able to convince audiences that he was selling them entertainment, not fraud. People viewed him as a kind of lovable con artist. The phrase *There's a sucker born every minute* will forever be attributed to him, even though he was not the man who originally said it.

Joice Heth

Joice Heth was a frail, elderly black woman whom a young Barnum put on display in 1835, advertising that she was the 161-year-old former nurse of General George Washington. Heth was the first exhibit that Barnum ever promoted, and in doing so displayed all the marketing skills that he would later become famous for. She immediately drew huge crowds of people eager both to witness her great age and to hear her stories about raising Washington (who had been dead for over thirty-five years). When the public's interest in her started to wane, Barnum rekindled its curiosity by spreading a rumor that Joice Heth was not a person at all, but was actually a mechanical robot cleverly designed to look like an old lady. This claim played off the popularity of another exhibit touring America at that time, the Great Chess Automaton (see Chapter Two). Barnum continued to display her until she died on February 19, 1836. But even in death Barnum found a way to exploit her. He allowed a public autopsy to be performed on her body in order to verify her age. Unfortunately for Barnum the doctor who performed the autopsy declared that she could not have been older than eighty.

The Feejee Mermaid

In August 1842 a traveling English naturalist named "Dr. J. Griffin" arrived in New York City. He had with him a spectacular curiosity—a mermaid supposedly caught near the island of Feejee. The body of the mermaid was put on display in Barnum's museum, and enormous crowds turned out to see it. Barnum hyped the exhibit by running advertisements in the major newspapers that showed a beautiful naked figure. The actual exhibit, however, was not so alluring. It was a small, taxidermically preserved creature with the withered upper body of a monkey and the dried tail of a fish. One critic described it as the "incarnation of ugliness." The genius of the exhibit was that there was absolutely nothing new about the mermaid. Before it arrived in New York City, it had previously been displayed in

Barnum lured visitors to see the Feejee Mermaid with advertisements such as this one, which ran in the *Charleston Courier* on January 24, 1843, while the mermaid was on a national tour following its New York debut.   Courtesy of Charleston Library Society, Charleston, South Carolina.

Boston for months by another museum without attracting any comment. But when Barnum applied his marketing magic to it, the mermaid became an overnight sensation. "Dr. J. Griffin" was part of the deception. He was actually Levi Lyman, one of Barnum's cronies.

The Feejee Mermaid was lost when Barnum's museum burned down during the 1860s. A similar mermaid, which some claim to be the original specimen but which is probably not, is owned by Harvard University and is located in the Peabody Museum of Archaeology and Ethnology.

The *New York Sunday Herald* published a more realistic depiction of the Feejee Mermaid. This image was republished by Barnum in the first edition of his autobiography.

The Free Grand Buffalo Hunt

New York City papers advertised that a free buffalo hunt would occur on August 31, 1843. The ads declared that dangerous wild buffaloes had been captured in New Mexico and transported in for the show. They were being kept behind thick double-rail fencing in an enclosure in Hoboken. Twenty-four thousand New Yorkers, enticed by the allure both of wild beasts and a free show, paid six cents each to take the ferry across the river to Hoboken, where they were met by a herd of malnourished, feeble, very tame buffaloes, hardly the dangerous beasts that had been promised. Barnum, who had secretly engineered the entire "free" show, laughed all the way to the bank, since he had cut a deal with the ferry operators to pocket half their net revenue for the day.

APRIL FOOLS' DAY HOAXES

Industrialization and urbanization made crowded city streets the center of activity on April Fools' Day during the first half of the nineteenth century. The throngs of homeless street urchins who inhabited the city centers claimed the day as their own, using it as an excuse to terrorize any gentlemen who dared to venture out. These gentlemen were on their guard to watch their wallets and coattails, and not to bend over to pick up any money lying on the pavement, as it was more than likely to be attached to a piece of string held by some young prankster hiding around a corner. Newspapers had not yet fully embraced the habit of April mirth, though a few examples of journalistic foolery can be found. It was really the lower classes who kept alive the day's traditions during this period, over the protests and complaints of the rich.

The Train to Drogheda

During the final week of March 1844 placards all around Dublin advertised that a free train ride would be offered on April 1 to all who desired it, ferrying passengers to the town of Drogheda and back. Early on the first of April a large crowd gathered at the station. As a train began to approach, the crowd surged forward, eager to secure their free seats. But the conductors and overseers intervened to keep the people away from the train, informing them that no free ride was being offered. The crowd would have none of this, and a riot soon broke out. The paper reported the next day that "the labourers on the road supported the overseers—the victims fought for their places, and the melee was tremendous." The following day a number of people went to the police station to lodge official complaints. But the police dismissed all complaints "in honour of the day." The prankster responsible for the placards is unknown.

The Great Cave Sell

A story appeared in the *Boston Post* announcing that a cave full of treasure had been discovered beneath Boston Common. It had, supposedly, been uncovered by workmen as they removed a tree from the common. As the tree fell, it revealed a stone trapdoor with a large iron ring set in it. Beneath the door was a stone stairway that led to an underground cave. In this cave lay piles of jewels, old coins, and weapons with jeweled handles. Word of the discovery quickly spread throughout Boston, and soon parties of excited curiosity-seekers were marching out across the common to view the treasure. A witness later described the scene: "It was rainy, that 1st of April, the Legislature was in session, and it was an animated scene that the Common presented, roofed with umbrellas, sheltering pilgrims on their way to the new-found sell. A procession of grave legislators marched solemnly down under their green gingham, while philosophers, archaeologists, numismatists, antiquarians of all qualities, and the public generally paid tribute to the Post's ingenuity." Of course, the common was empty of all jewelbearing caverns, as the crowd of treasure seekers eventually discovered to its disappointment.

Roorbacks

The term *roorback* refers to a fictitious claim that is invented in order to smear a political opponent. The term originated amid the rough-and-tumble politics of the pre–Civil War era in the United States, specifically during the presidential election of 1844. The Whig party couldn't find any dirt to spread about its famously clean-living Democratic party opponent, James K. Polk, so a few Whigs simply decided to invent some. They submitted a letter to the *Ithaca Journal* that alluded to a book titled *Roorback's Tour Through the Western and Southern States in 1836*, written by Baron von Roorback. According to them von Roorback had described encountering forty-three wretched slaves owned by Polk. The idea that Polk was a cruel slave owner shocked voters. When the truth came out—that Baron von Roorback and his book were both fictitious, as was the claim about Polk's slaves—the brazen lie ended up costing the Whigs the election. The word *roorback* came to refer to political dirty tricks of this kind though the term is no longer commonly used.

Railways and Revolvers in Georgia

A letter that appeared in the *Times* of London on October 15, 1856, detailed a list of bloody duels and murders that the correspondent had witnessed during a recent train ride through Georgia. According to the account the traveler had boarded a train in Macon and disembarked ten and a half hours later in Augusta, by which time six passengers had been slaughtered. The murders principally took the form of duels fought with "Monte Christo pistols." For each duel the conductor graciously halted the train so that the combatants could fight with greater freedom of movement. To the traveler's shock this level of violence was considered so normal that it barely warranted a raised eyebrow from the other passengers on the train. It was apparently an everyday fact of life in America. The *Times* offered the letter as proof of how violent American society had become.

When the American press learned of the letter, they were outraged. A transatlantic furor ensued in which American newspapers such as *The New York Times* vigorously denied the tale while the London *Times* continued to insist that it was true. The dispute dragged on for almost two months before the London *Times* finally admitted that it might have been duped. A London *Times* reporter traveling through the South a year later discovered that the term *Monte Christo pistols* was actually local slang used to refer to bottles of champagne—because of the popping sound the bottles made when opened. Empty bottles were referred to as "dead men." The reporter dryly noted that "encounters with the Monte Christo weapons in the baggage-wagons are, I understand, not uncommon on the line . . . [but] no fatal results have ever occurred."

The Civil War Gold Hoax

It was May 1864. Grant was closing in on Lee in Virginia, and Northerners were growing hopeful that the long, terrible ordeal of the Civil War would soon be over. Then, on Wednesday, May 18, New Yorkers read in two of their morning papers that President Lincoln had issued a proclamation ordering the conscription of an additional four hundred thousand men into the Union army on account of "the situation in Virginia, the disaster at Red River, the delay at Charleston, and the general state of the country." The implication of the proclamation was clear—the war might drag on for years to come.

Share prices on the New York Stock Exchange immediately plummeted, while gold, considered to be a safe, inflation-proof investment, rose in value. A few hours later a telegram arrived from the State Department in Washington declaring the proclamation to be "an absolute forgery." Evidently someone had delivered fake Associated Press dispatches to the papers, which had printed them without conducting adequate fact-checking. Unfortunately, by the time this was figured out, the damage to the stock market had already been done.

Detectives quickly tracked down the perpetrator of the crime, a newspaper editor named Joseph Howard, Jr. Armed with an intimate knowledge of the news business, he had forged the dispatches, invested heavily in gold, and then hired couriers to send the dispatches around to the city papers. When the stock market opened later that day, he simply waited for the bad news to hit, sold his investment, and pocketed a handsome profit. Upon being arrested at his residence in Brooklyn, Howard submitted quietly, made a full confession, and was shipped off to Fort Lafayette.

Remarkably enough, Howard ended up serving less than three months of his sentence before Lincoln ordered his release. The President was apparently moved by the appeal of Henry Ward Beecher, a friend of Howard's wealthy father, who pleaded that the young man was only guilty of "the hope of making some money."

Lincoln might also have exercised leniency since Howard's false proclamation turned out to be true. On July 18, two months after the hoax, Lincoln did issue a call for more men. Howard had only been wrong about the number. He had estimated that four hundred thousand would be needed. But Lincoln asked for five hundred thousand.

Vrain Lucas

Few accounts of forgery are as strange as the case of Vrain Lucas. His career as a forger began in 1851, when he met the esteemed French mathematician Michel Chasles. Lucas showed the mathematician a few letters he claimed to have found, writ-

ten by famous historical personages such as Joan of Arc and
Charlemagne. Chasles was intrigued, which inspired Lucas to
"find" more letters for him.

Lucas's letters were written by a broad spectrum of historical
celebrities, including Julius Caesar, Aristotle, Alexander the
Great, Lazarus, Mary Magdalene, and Shakespeare. And they all
shared a few things in common. Their content always reflected
favorably on France, and they were all written in French. This
appealed to Chasles, who was an ardent patriot. But most of
them were also written on the same watermarked paper, even
the ones supposedly from the early Roman empire before paper
had been invented. For some reason none of this ever caused
Chasles pause. He kept buying whatever Lucas produced, and
Lucas eventually produced thousands of these letters.

Suspicion was only raised when a scholar noticed that six-
teen of the letters had been copied from a 1761 manuscript. But
even then Chasles defended Lucas. It was only when Lucas
failed to deliver three thousand autographs, for which Chasles
had paid in advance, that Chasles finally brought charges against
him. This was in 1869, eighteen years after the two men had
first met. In February 1870 Lucas was sentenced to two years
in jail. As he was taken away to prison, it was discovered that
he had been preparing a special manuscript for Chasles before he had been interrupted by the trial. It was the text of the
Sermon on the Mount written by Jesus himself *in French*.

The Locals: The Hoaxes of Mark Twain, Dan De Quille, and Artemus Ward

The creation of the penny press during the 1830s completely
changed the character of the news business. The old six-cent
papers had confined themselves to business and political news,
but the penny papers discovered that there was a huge market
for local news: stories about neighborhood crimes, police reports, social gossip, and human-interest items. As a result, within

a few decades almost every major paper had a reporter specifically assigned to local coverage. Such reporters were referred to, logically enough, as the "locals." The local had to be able to amuse and entertain readers even on days when not much had occurred. This called for the skills of a humorist, and indeed many of America's best-known comedic writers got their start as locals. They spiced up slow news days with humor, satire, tall tales, and hoaxes. Three locals working on western papers proved to be particularly adept at their jobs. They were Samuel Clemens (aka Mark Twain), Charles Browne (aka Artemus Ward), and William Wright (aka Dan De Quille).

The Paulding County Hyena

On February 6, 1858, readers of the *Cleveland Plain Dealer* were shocked to learn that a hyena had broken loose from its cage in a circus and was terrorizing the residents of Paulding County. According to the report a band of men had set forth to recapture the predator, but with little luck. Following the trail of the enraged beast, the pursuers first discovered that it had disinterred a number of bodies from a local cemetery. Then, when they caught up to it and surrounded it, the hyena leapt on one of their number, killing the man instantly. Finally, it bounded off into the woods, killing another man along the way. Readers of the *Plain Dealer* anxiously waited to hear more about this vicious beast, but three days later, in a follow-up story, the paper apologetically noted that "a few errors" had occurred in the original article. No men had in fact been killed by the hyena. The paper admitted with embarrassment that the hyena had actually never escaped from its cage. It was quite certain of this because it had learned that there was no hyena at all. "He is not there now, never was there, and, it is firmly believed, never will be again," the author of the article stated with conviction. But the author boasted that there was one fact from the article that he was quite certain of: There was definitely a place named Paulding County! The reporting was the work of Artemus Ward.

The Empire City Massacre

In 1863 San Francisco newspapers were spearheading a campaign to convince investors to shift their money from mining ventures into utilities. According to a story that appeared in the *Territorial Enterprise* on October 28, 1863, this advice resulted in tragedy for at least one man. After losing all his money because the utility had fraudulently cooked its books, the man went insane and slaughtered his entire family (except for two young girls who miraculously survived). He then rode into town "bearing in his hand a reeking scalp from which the blood was still dripping," cut his throat, and collapsed dead in front of a saloon. The story was widely reprinted, and readers everywhere were horrified by the gruesome news. No one thought that it might be false. After all, who would make up something like that? Mark Twain, in fact. He wanted to get the San Francisco newspapers to print a story critical of the utility companies, so he made up the most sensational story he could think of to ensure that they would run it. He succeeded in this goal, but readers failed to see the humor in his hoax. Luckily for Twain his editor forgave him for the controversy that ensued and allowed him to keep his job.

Solar Armor

As anyone who has ever been to Nevada during the summer knows, its deserts can become scorchingly hot. In 1874 the *Territorial Enterprise* reported the "sad fate" of an inventor who had departed on foot from Virginia City toward Death Valley, determined to beat the desert's heat. He had clothed himself from head to foot in "solar armor": a sponge suit saturated with a "frigorific mixture" that cooled the wearer of the suit as it evaporated. The frigorific mixture was replenished through sacks located under the arms. Unfortunately, the inventor's solar armor worked too well, and he was found a day later frozen stiff in the middle of the desert, a foot-long icicle hanging from his nose. Newspapers throughout the world reprinted the bizarre story, but the *Daily Telegraph* of London had a reaction typical of the general response. It dryly noted that "we should require some additional confirmation before we unhesitatingly accept it." The story was the fanciful work of Dan De Quille, Mark Twain's colleague at the *Territorial Enterprise*.

The Traveling Stones of Pahranagat Valley

Dan De Quille published an article in the *Territorial Enterprise* on October 26, 1867, describing some unusual stones that could be found in the Pahranagat Valley of southern Nevada. When placed nearby each other, he claimed, the stones would move to come together. As he put it, "These curious pebbles appear to be formed of loadstone or magnetic iron ore. A single stone removed to a distance of a yard, upon being released at once started off with wonderful and somewhat comical celerity to rejoin its fellows." The article, which was written in a semiscientific style, seemed quite believable to its readers. It was so believable that as the years went by De Quille began to receive numerous inquiries about the stones from people all over the world. A German scientist wrote to De Quille and refused to believe him when informed that the stones were not real. Instead the scientist accused De Quille of trying to conceal the secret of the stones. A showman then offered De Quille "ten grand" if he would go on tour with his rocks. Eventually De Quille began referring inquiries to Mark Twain, who, he assured correspondents, "has still on hand fifteen or twenty bushels of various sizes." The matter got so out of hand that De Quille was forced to publish a retraction. "We solemnly affirm that we never saw or heard of any such diabolical cobbles as the traveling stones of Pahranagat," he declared in print on November 11, 1879, twelve years after the publication of the original article. But it was to no avail. Letters seeking more information about the miraculous stones still kept pouring in.

CHAPTER FOUR

1869–1913

Stone Giants and Antlered Rabbits

Broad social change occurred at an ever increasing pace during the late nineteenth century. Railroads connected far-flung regions. Skyscrapers rose in city centers. The first department stores appeared. Women entered the workforce in large numbers, and typewriters, telephones, and telegraphy revolutionized communications. But beneath these changes, which have been much celebrated, a more subtle cultural shift was occurring. It was the rise of the humble tall tale.

Tall tales, as discussed in the introduction, are defined as hoaxes that are promoted by entire communities, not just by individuals. They are communal deceptions. The genre of the tall tale had its roots in the ethnic folklores of Europe and Africa. When this style of fantastic storytelling was transplanted to America during the seventeenth and eighteenth centuries, it flourished, particularly in wilderness, farming, and frontier regions. But it was almost exclusively an oral form of storytelling and remained confined to the lower classes. It did not enjoy a great deal of cultural visibility. This changed during the nineteenth century.

The change that brought tall tales into cultural prominence was the democratization of American culture. As American society became more broad based and egalitarian, the culture of the common man rose in stature. Folk traditions such as tall tales were translated into print and disseminated to vast audiences through newspapers and books. Writers like Mark Twain helped to legitimate this folk culture by presenting it to elites in a way that they were willing to accept and even praise. Soon tall-tale telling had become an identifying mark of being an American, shared by rich and poor alike. The idiom of tall tales was translated into ever more forms, such as photography and architecture (think of Las Vegas, whose architecture is like a celebration of tall tales in the middle of the Nevada desert). Then as American culture spread to the rest of the world during the twentieth century, the practice of tall-tale telling spread with it.

Giants in the Earth

Digging in the earth was a highly popular pastime during the nineteenth century. People never knew what surprises the ground might offer up: dinosaur bones, human skeletons, gold, or artifacts of ancient civilizations. Beneath the surface of the earth seemed to lie hidden all the treasures of past ages, just waiting to be found. Which raised the tantalizing question—with all its biblical and scientific implications—of what existed back then during those past ages. What strange creatures once roamed the earth? What foreign civilizations flourished in the same landscapes where farmers now raised their crops? It was this sense of mystery that the petrified giants—which Americans began to routinely unearth during the late nineteenth century—spoke to. There was the Pine River Man, found in 1876; the "Solid Muldoon" found near Pueblo, Colorado, in 1877; the Taughannock Giant discovered in Ithaca, New York, in 1879; and the Forest City Man displayed at the World's Columbian Exposition in Chicago in 1893. They were all fake, of course—products of the public's fascination with prehistory joined with the desire of con artists to exploit that interest. But they were also all mere imitations of the first and greatest fake giant of them all: the Cardiff Giant, found on a small New York farm in 1869.

The Cardiff Giant

The Cardiff Giant emerged out of the ground and into American life on October 16, 1869, when he was discovered by some workers digging a well behind the barn of William C. "Stub" Newell in Cardiff, New York. Word of his presence quickly spread, and soon thousands of people were making the journey out to Stub Newell's farm to see the ten-foot colossus. Even when Newell began charging fifty cents a head to have a look at it, people still kept coming.

Speculation ran rampant over what the giant might be. The central debate was between those who thought it was a petrified man and those who believed it to be an ancient statue. The "petrifactionists" theorized that it was one of the giants mentioned in the Bible, Genesis 6:4, where it says, "There were giants in the earth in those days." Those who held to the statue theory followed the lead of Dr. John F. Boynton, who speculated that a Jesuit missionary had carved it sometime during the seventeenth century to impress the local indians.

The truth was somewhat more prosaic. It was the creation of an enterprising New York tobacconist named George Hull, who had been scheming of a way to strike it rich for quite some time. His idea of burying a stone giant in the ground turned out to be a stroke of genius. The entire venture cost him over $2,600 (all done with the collusion of the farmer Newell and the stonecutters who carved the giant), but the gamble paid off when a group of businessmen paid $37,500 to buy the giant and move it to Syracuse, where it could be more prominently exhibited.

In Syracuse the giant came under closer scrutiny. Othniel C. Marsh, a paleontologist from Yale, paid it a visit and declared it to be a clumsy fake. He pointed out that chisel marks were still plainly visible on it. These should have been worn away if the

giant had been in the ground for any appreciable length of
time. Sensing that the game was up (and having already cashed
out), Hull confessed. But the public didn't care. They kept coming to see it anyway. They even began referring to the giant affectionately as "Old Hoaxey."

Recognizing the giant's popularity, the great showman P. T.
Barnum offered the new owners $60,000 for a three-month lease
of it. When his offer was refused, he paid an artist to build an
exact plaster replica of it, which he then put on display in New
York City. Soon the replica was drawing larger crowds than the
original. This competition prompted the owners of the giant to
file a lawsuit against Barnum, but the judge refused to hear
their case unless the "genuineness" of the original could be
proven. Sheepishly they dropped their charges.

Many have declared the Cardiff Giant to be the greatest hoax
of all time. Whether or not this is the case, its huge size and mysterious presence certainly tapped into some element of the post–
Civil War American psyche. Although the massive public interest
in it gradually died down, it remained popular. Even today peo-

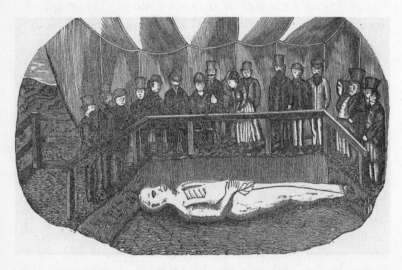

A sketch of the Giant on display in Cardiff, New York.   From *The American Goliath: A Wonderful Geological Discovery (Redington and Howe, 1869).*

ple still make the journey to visit it at its permanent home in the Farmer's Museum in Cooperstown, New York.

Tall-Tale Creatures

Amazing creatures of all varieties are a recurring feature in tall tales. There are so many of these animals that it is only possible to list a few of them here. Among those that will have to go un-explored are the upland trout (a fish that lives in trees), the treesqueak (another tree-living mammal, which can be heard squeaking whenever the wind blows), the snow snake (the bane of skiers), the gumberoo (which cannot be photographed be-cause its image will explode), the squonk (a morose creature known to literally dissolve into tears), and the rubberado (whose flesh, if eaten, will cause one to bounce). While the precise date of origin of many of these creatures is unknown, they all became widely familiar during the nineteenth century as folk culture made its way into the mainstream through the popular-ization of print.

The Jackalope

In the old West, when cowboys would gather around their campfires at night to sing, they would sometimes hear creatures singing back, mimicking their voices. The cowboys said that these were the jackalopes, a species of antlered rabbit possess-ing an uncanny ability to imitate human sounds. Jackalopes are also referred to as "warrior rabbits" because of their ability to fight with their antlers. When chased, jackalopes rely on their unique vocal abilities to elude capture. For instance, they will call out such phrases as "There he goes, over there," in order to throw pursuers off their track. In fact, it is said that the only way to catch a jackalope is to lure it with whiskey, a drink for which it has a particular fondness. Once it has drunk its fill of

the whiskey, it becomes slower and easier to hunt. The jackalope is now most commonly found in the states of Colorado,
Wyoming, and Nebraska. But it does have a German cousin
known as the *wolperdinger*. In Sweden a related species is
called the *skvader*. Douglas, Wyoming, has declared itself to be
the jackalope capital of America because, according to legend,
the first jackalope was spotted there around 1829. A large statue
of a jackalope now stands in the Douglas town center, and
every year the town plays host to Jackalope Day, usually held
in June. Jackalope hunting licenses can be obtained from the
Douglas Chamber of Commerce.

A pair of jackalopes scan the horizon of a field in Colorado.

The Fur-bearing Trout

When the first Scottish settlers emigrated to Canada during the seventeenth century, one of them wrote back home remarking about the abundance of "furried animals and fish" in the new land. Asked to provide more information about the furried fish, the settler duly sent home a specimen. This was likely the first European encounter with the fur-bearing trout, a species of fish that has evolved a thick coat of fur to keep itself warm in the cold waters of North American lakes and streams (though according to a rival theory, the furry trout owes its lush covering to an accident involving the spillage of four jugs of hair tonic into the Arkansas River). A few researchers suggest that as the weather grows warmer during the spring the fur-bearing trout sheds its coat, only to regrow it as winter returns. This may help explain why trout with full coats of fur are so seldom encountered. Fur-bearing trouts mounted as trophies can be found hanging on walls throughout the Great Lakes region of North America.

Ice Worms of the Klondike

In 1898 a young man named E. J. "Stroller" White was struggling to make it as a journalist in Dawson, Alaska. He got a job with the *Klondike Nugget* on the condition that he increase sales. To do so he wrote a story claiming that the recent cold weather was causing "ice worms" to emerge in huge numbers from a nearby glacier. They were squirming their way out of the glacier in order to "bask in the unusual frigidity." The worms became the talk of the town. People went out on expeditions to find them, carefully listening for the characteristic chirping that White had described. Bartenders in town began serving a drink called "ice-worm cocktails," which contained a piece of spaghetti frozen inside an ice cube. The search for the tiny creatures became such a tradition in the region that it inspired the town of Cordova, Alaska, to begin holding an ice-worm festival every year in their honor. This festival is still celebrated.

The irony is that for years everyone assumed that the ice worms were just a tall tale, but strangely enough, scientists have now documented the existence of real "ice worms" that actually do live inside Alaskan glaciers.

Imposters and Con Artists

The wealth of Europe and America grew dramatically during the final decades of the nineteenth century, fueled by the rise of massive corporations and far-reaching financial institutions. But the wealth was not evenly spread. A few became wealthy beyond their dreams, while others remained desperately poor. In such a situation it was inevitable that the have-nots would find ingenious ways of separating the most gullible haves from their money.

The Tichborne Claimant

In 1854 a wealthy young aristocrat named Roger Charles Doughty Tichborne disappeared at sea and was presumed dead. His distraught mother, refusing to believe that he was actually dead, placed ads in newspapers around the world, seeking information about his whereabouts. In 1866 she received a response from an Australian man who claimed to be her son. What followed was one of the most intriguing and debated cases of impersonation of all time. Roger Tichborne had weighed 125 pounds and spoke French as well as English when he disappeared. The Australian man, by contrast, weighed over 300 pounds and spoke no French. But their features were very similar. Lady Tichborne embraced him as her long-lost son, making him the full heir to her estate. When she died, the other heirs lost no time in bringing suit against him to stop him from gaining the inheritance. On the witness stand he proved unable to remember basic facts about the past of Roger Tichborne, and the court ruled that he was a fraud. But as he sat in jail for the

next ten years he lost a great deal of weight and began to resemble Roger Tichborne more and more. Many began to suspect that perhaps he really was the long-lost Roger. It seems
almost certain that he was a fraud, but when he died in 1898
the family allowed the name "Sir Roger Charles Doughty Tichborne" to be inscribed on his tombstone.

The Keely Motor Company

John Worrell Keely founded the Keely Motor Company in
1875 in order to develop and commercialize his invention, a
"vibratory generator" that required only a quart of water to produce the equivalent of the power needed to pull a fully loaded
train for over seventy-five minutes. Following successful demon-
strations of this miraculous device in his workshop, investors
rushed to give him money, even though the scientific community derided his claims. For fourteen years he kept working on
his engine, promising investors that the moment was just around
the corner when he would unveil it to the world. The investors
believed him and kept pouring money into his bank account.
When he died in 1898 investigators discovered the secret of the
engine: a compressed-air machine hidden in the basement of
his house that fed power to the engine located two floors directly above it.

Cassie Chadwick

Cassie Chadwick claimed to be the illegitimate daughter of
Andrew Carnegie. She said that Carnegie was paying her huge
sums of money in order to keep their relationship a secret. Based
upon this claim alone she managed to borrow almost $2 million
from Cleveland area banks and wealthy individuals between
1901 and 1904. Finally, when her debts grew too large, the banks
began to call in her loans, and at that point her entire scheme fell
apart. She was sentenced to ten years in prison. When Carnegie
was told about the fiasco, his only comment was "I have never
heard of Mrs. Chadwick."

The Case of the Miraculous Bullet

A fascinating Civil War medical case involving a unique example of artificial insemination was described in the November 1874 issue of *The American Medical Weekly*. The correspondent, Dr. LeGrand G. Capers, claimed that while serving as an army doctor for the Confederates during the Civil War, he saw an instance in which a bullet struck a soldier through the testicle and then carried on its flight, bearing with it particles of the soldier's semen, before it finally came to rest in the abdomen of a young woman standing nearby, thus impregnating her. A healthy baby was born to the woman nine months later. Dr. Capers reported that the soldier and the young woman, after meeting in this unusual manner, ended up marrying each other and produced two more children in a more conventional manner.

After appearing in the *American Medical Weekly* this Civil War story became something of a legend within the medical community. Its origin and details became obscured, but the basic outline of the tale was frequently repeated as true, even as late as 1959. But of course the story was not true. Dr. Capers had invented it to poke fun at the numerous highly embellished Civil War stories that were appearing everywhere during the 1870s. The joke, however, ended up being on him. As a highly respected doctor with a reputation to uphold he had submitted the story anonymously, not wishing his name to be forever attached to such a ridiculous tale. Unfortunately for him the editor of the journal recognized his handwriting and printed the story with Capers prominently listed as the author.

Journalism Hoaxes

By the end of the nineteenth century the upstart penny papers from the first half of the century had transformed into major newspapers, and as they did so, their owners generally became less willing to endorse outright hoaxes. But while officially frowning on hoaxes, the owners simultaneously encouraged a highly sensationalized, entertainment-driven style of reporting that often led journalists to fake or distort stories on slow news days. In the hands of Joseph Pulitzer and William Randolph Hearst, the news moguls who dominated the industry at the end of the century, this style became derisively known as "yellow journalism." Parallel with these developments a prominent space remained in the industry for "local" reporters (see Chapter Three), often writing for regional papers, who peppered their columns with humor and tall tales. Some of the most famous tall-tale tellers from this period were Joseph Mulholland of the *Philadelphia Public Ledger,* C. Louis Mortison of the *Waterbury Republican,* and Lou Stone of the *Winsted* (Connecticut) *Evening Citizen.*

The Central Park Zoo Escape

On November 9, 1874, the front page of the *New York Herald* warned in breathless prose that the animals had escaped from their cages in the New York zoo and were rampaging through the city. A lion had been seen inside a church. A rhinoceros had fallen into a sewer. The police and national guard were heroically battling the beasts, but already twenty-seven people were dead and two hundred injured. It was "a bloody and fearful carnival," the article despaired. And the animals were still on the loose! Many readers panicked when they read the article. Armed men swarmed into the streets, ready to defend their homes. It is said that the editor of *The New York Times* ran out of his home waving two pistols in the air and berating the police for not doing more. Of course, those who panicked hadn't read to the end of the article, where it stated quite clearly that "the entire story given above is a pure fabrication." The author of the piece was a reporter named Joseph Clarke, working in collusion with his editor, Thomas Connery. They had intended merely to draw attention to dangerous conditions at the zoo, not realizing that their article would provoke such a panic. The next day the *Herald* disappointed readers who were looking for an apology when it simply ran a short statement urging that safety precautions at the zoo be improved. Next to the Great Moon Hoax of 1835 the New York Zoo Escape probably ranks as the most notorious newspaper hoax of the nineteenth century.

The Winsted Wild Man

In August 1895 New York City papers received a story about a naked, hairy man who was terrorizing local residents in Winsted, Connecticut. Intrigued, the papers sent up reporters to find out what was happening. But with the arrival of the media in the small town and the excitement this provoked, people suddenly began seeing the wild man everywhere. With each new sighting he grew progressively fiercer. He seemed to gain a foot or so every day, and in some accounts he sprouted tusks. Then he became a massive gorilla with thick arms that hung all the way down to the ground. All these terrifying reports fanned a state of near hysteria in Winsted. People were afraid to leave their homes for fear of encountering the monster. A posse of over one hundred armed men was organized and sent out to hunt down and kill the creature. After days of searching the men finally succeeded in shooting a creature that was seen lurking in the undergrowth. But the fearsome beast turned out to be a local farmer's stray jackass. Eventually the truth came out. There never had been a wild man. The original report had sprung from the overly fertile imagination of Lou Stone, a young reporter for the *Winsted Evening Citizen*. From there mass psychology had done the rest. Over the succeeding years Stone became famous for the hundreds of stories he wrote about the strange flora and fauna surrounding Winsted, including his description of a tree that grew baked apples, a dog that talked, and a chicken that laid red, white, and blue eggs on the Fourth of July. He was affectionately known as the Winsted Liar. After his death the residents of Winsted named a bridge after him. The bridge spans Sucker Creek.

The Great Wall of China Hoax

On June 25, 1899, an interesting story about the Great Wall of China appeared in three Denver newspapers. It said that the Chinese were going to tear the Great Wall down and build a road in its place, and that they were taking bids from American firms to complete this project. The news supposedly came from a Chicago engineer, Frank C. Lewis, who was one of those bidding for the job. From Denver the story made its way to Chicago and the East Coast, where it appeared as front-page news in numerous papers. But not a word of the story was true. It had been created as a joke by three reporters working on separate Denver papers to spice up a slow news day. The story might have ended there, remembered as nothing more than a minor hoax, but many years later a rumor began to circulate about what happened when the news reached China. Supposedly the Chinese had been infuriated by the hoax and took up arms against Westerners in retaliation, thus starting the Boxer Rebellion. This rumor grew and grew until it reached the official status of fact. But in actuality the Great Wall of China hoax had nothing to do with the Boxer Rebellion. The idea that it did has been traced to a 1939 article by Harry Lee Wilber that appeared in the *North American Review.* Apparently Wilber was guilty of that old journalistic strategy of taking a good story and *"improving"* it.

William Randolph Hearst and the Spanish-American War

In 1895 a young William Randolph Hearst burst onto the national media scene when he purchased the *New York Journal* and began competing head-to-head with Joseph Pulitzer's *New York World.* Hearst went on to create a vast media empire that remains in existence today, but throughout his career he was rumored to be someone who never let the facts—or the lack of them—get in the way of a good story. The most famous anecdote about him stems from his involvement with the Spanish-American War. According to this famous tale, Hearst sent the illustrator Frederic Remington down to Cuba to draw pictures of the conflict between the Cuban rebels and the Spanish. Not finding much happening, Remington cabled Hearst asking permission to return home. Supposedly Hearst cabled back, "You furnish the pictures and I'll furnish the war." It is very doubtful that Hearst ever sent such a telegram, but the persistent belief that he did captures the popular conviction that he wasn't above faking the news in order to get what he wanted, which was a war in Cuba that he knew would increase his paper's circulation. Soon the United States did enter into a war with Spain over Cuba, and sure enough, the circulation of the *Journal* soared to record heights.

APRIL FOOLS' DAY HOAXES

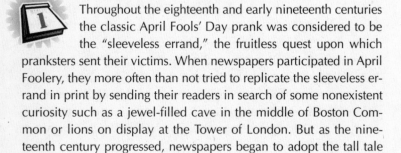

Throughout the eighteenth and early nineteenth centuries the classic April Fools' Day prank was considered to be the "sleeveless errand," the fruitless quest upon which pranksters sent their victims. When newspapers participated in April Foolery, they more often than not tried to replicate the sleeveless errand in print by sending their readers in search of some nonexistent curiosity such as a jewel-filled cave in the middle of Boston Common or lions on display at the Tower of London. But as the nineteenth century progressed, newspapers began to adopt the tall tale as their model for April Foolery. As a result today's journalistic April Fools are more likely to be tall tales than sleeveless errands.

Edison Invents Food Machine

After Thomas Edison invented the phonograph in 1877, Americans firmly believed that there were no limits to his genius. They were sure that he could solve any problem that he focused his powerful mind on. Therefore, when the *New York Graphic* announced on April 1, 1878, that Edison had invented a machine that could transform soil directly into cereal and water directly into wine, thereby ending the problem of world hunger, it found no shortage of believers. Newspapers throughout America copied the article, heaping lavish praise on Edison all the while. The conservative *Buffalo Commercial Advertiser* was particularly effusive in its praise, waxing eloquent about Edison's genius in a long editorial prompted by his most recent invention. The *Graphic* took the liberty of reprinting the *Advertiser*'s editorial in full. Above it the *Graphic* placed a single, gloating headline: "They Bite!"

The Monster of Deadman's Hole

In 1888 the *San Diego Union* reported that two hunters had killed a bizarre half-human, half-animal beast in an out-of-the-way location northwest of San Diego called Deadman's Hole. The creature was said to have the body of a bear, but it stood upright like a human and had a human face. There were hints that it was the product of an unnatural union between a man and some kind of carnivorous beast. The monster was also said to have been responsible for a string of gruesome murders. The hunters were able to fell the beast with a single shot, but when they located its lair they found it piled high with semi-gnawed human skeletons. The article concluded by reporting that the hunters planned to display the body in San Diego within a few days, causing a minor sensation in the city. Hundreds of people inquired about where the creature would be displayed. But of course, there was no monster of Deadman's Hole, outside of the imagination of the *Union*'s staff.

Photographic Fakes

When newspapers first reported Louis Daguerre's discovery of the photographic process in 1839, many readers found the news so incredible, they assumed it had to be a hoax. Of course, photography proved to be quite real. In fact, photography came to symbolize the scientific ideal of objectivity that gained force during the nineteenth century, because it seemed to be a way of capturing a direct impression of nature free from human interference. "The camera never lies," people said. The association of photography with truth and objectivity paradoxically made photographs an ideal tool for hoaxers.

The Silent City

In 1885 an Alaskan prospector named Dick Willoughby saw a fantastic mirage as he gazed out over Muir Glacier in southeastern Alaska. It was, he claimed, a vision of a sprawling city. He could even see the tops of houses and the spires of cathedrals, jutting up over the plain of the glacier. Unlike many who experience a vision and have no material proof to back up their claim, Willoughby was able to take a picture of the mirage. He took the photo back to Juneau and showed it around. The people there were intrigued. After all, photographs don't lie. Therefore, he must have really seen the "silent city," as he called it. He ended up selling thousands of copies of his photograph,

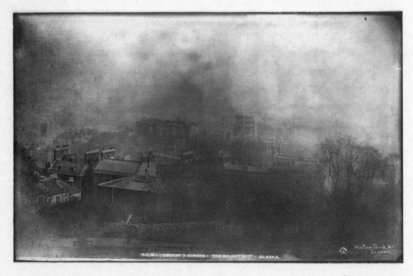

The "Silent City" shimmers into existence above Muir Glacier.   Photo by Dick Willoughby, 1885: Alaska State Library/Photo Number: PCA 87-2738

and he even conducted guided tours to Muir Glacier, though no one else was ever able to see the mirage. Eventually someone recognized that the "silent city" was simply a picture of Bristol, England, superimposed on top of blurry background scenery.

Sympsychography

An article by the famous scientist David Starr Jordan appeared in the September 1896 edition of *Popular Science Monthly*. It detailed the exciting discovery of a new form of photography called sympsychography. Starr explained that just as invisible

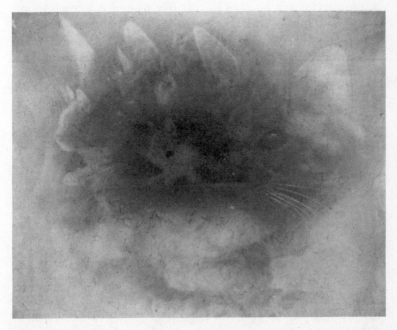

A sympsychographic image of a cat. Professor David Starr Jordan claimed this was an "impression of ultimate feline reality." From *Popular Science Monthly* 49 (September 1896).

For more photographic fakes go to
www.museumofhoaxes.com/photos/photos.html

X rays were able to produce a visible image on a photographic plate, invisible brain waves were, in the same way, able to do likewise. In other words, the thoughts of a man could be transferred directly to a photograph. This had supposedly been demonstrated by the experiments of Cameron Lee, who burned an image of a cat onto a photographic plate merely by thinking of a cat. The Astral Camera Club, which met on April 1, then took this concept one step further. Seven of its members simultaneously concentrated their minds on a photographic plate while thinking of a cat. What emerged was not one man's image of a cat, but rather a joint "impression of ultimate feline reality." The resulting picture was displayed in the article. Starr wrote that "it will be noticed that this picture is unmistakably one of a cat. But it is a cat in its real essence, the type cat as distinguished from human impressions of individual cats." Jordan thought that the educated readers of *Popular Science Monthly* would immediately recognize his spoof. Instead he received numerous letters from people who had taken the article at face value. One clergyman even confided to Starr that he had prepared six sermons on "the Lesson of the Sympsychograph."

The Protocols of the Elders of Zion

While the late nineteenth century produced many lighthearted tall tales, it also produced one notoriously vicious hoax that, in its long career, caused incalculable harm. This was the *Protocols of the Learned Elders of Zion*. The *Protocols* first appeared in Russia at the beginning of the twentieth century. It was said to be the text of a speech given by a Zionist leader outlining a secret Jewish plan to achieve world power by controlling international finance and subverting the power of the Christian church. The manuscript was then used to justify hate campaigns against the Jewish people throughout the twentieth century, from the Russian pogroms of the early twentieth century, through to the actions of the Nazis during the 1930s and '40s. Many copies of the *Protocols* are still in circulation today throughout the world. But the text of the *Protocols* actually derived from an 1865 work titled *Dialogue in Hell Between Machiavelli and Montesquieu,* which was written by Maurice Joly as an attack upon Emperor Napoleon III. It detailed how Napoleonic conspirators were plotting to undermine democratic institutions. The hoaxers simply substituted Zionist conspirators for Napoleonic ones. In other words, in its original form the *Protocols* had nothing to do with the Jewish people at all. It was only when Joly's work was recycled in Russia at the turn of the century that it was turned into evidence of a vast Jewish conspiracy.

First to the Pole

At the beginning of the twentieth century the North Pole beckoned as a challenge to explorers. Reaching the Pole was viewed as a measure of man's highest abilities, just as reaching the moon provided a similar challenge during the 1960s. But when Robert E. Peary and Frederick A. Cook both announced almost simultaneously, and independently, in 1909 that they had reached the Pole, it was the start of decades of bitter fighting and charges of fraud, rather than a moment of glory.

Peary claimed that he arrived at the Pole on April 6, 1909. By September he had made it back to civilization and was able to telegraph the proud announcement of his achievement to the newspapers. To his astonishment he learned that Cook had already laid claim to that victory just five days previously. Cook claimed to have reached the Pole on April 21, 1908, almost a year before Peary. Cook's explanation for his delay in announcing this achievement was that he had been lost in the Arctic wilderness for over a year.

Peary immediately launched into a campaign to discredit Cook. When Cook fired back, a heated, ugly dispute ensued. With the backing of the National Geographic Society, Peary succeeded in undermining Cook's claim, and he was generally credited with being the first to the Pole. Cook's problem was that his character was repeatedly called into doubt. Evidence indicated that he had lied about earlier achievements, and in 1925 he was thrown in jail for mail fraud. Therefore, people were unwilling to trust him. But over the years Peary's claim to the title has also come under withering assault, since he provided only weak documentation to back up his claim. It now seems possible that neither man reached the Pole (though each still has numerous supporters). If this is the case, the joint deception would certainly rank it as one of the greatest exploration hoaxes of all time.

The Captain of Köpenick

In his everyday attire as a down-on-his-luck shoemaker, Wilhelm Voigt commanded little respect in German society. But when he donned the secondhand captain's uniform that he had bought in a local shop, people's attitudes toward him immediately changed. On October 16, 1906, Voigt put on his uniform and effortlessly assumed control of a company of grenadiers as they were marching down the street. He proceeded with them over to the town hall of Köpenick, a small suburb of Berlin, arrested the mayor and the treasurer on charges of embezzlement, and took possession of 4,000 marks from the town treasury. He then told the soldiers to transport the officials down to Berlin headquarters, while he disappeared with the money. Hours later, and after much puzzlement down at headquarters, the military figured out what had happened. They tracked him down nine days later. Although his brazen stunt made him something of a popular hero, he was still sentenced to four years in jail. But he proved to be such a likable character that the kaiser himself pardoned Voigt after he had served less than two years. Voigt's subsequent fame allowed him to pursue a career in show business, where he entertained audiences by reenacting his stunt on the stage. In 1932 a movie was made about his hoax, titled *Der Hauptmann von Köpenick.*

The *Dreadnought* Hoax

On February 7, 1910, the prince of Abyssinia and his entourage were received with full ceremonial pomp on the deck of the HMS *Dreadnought,* the British navy's most powerful battleship. Although the commander-in-chief of the *Dreadnought* had only received a last-minute warning of the prince's arrival, he had the sailors standing at attention when the prince arrived. The Abyssinian party acknowledged the greeting with bows as they shuffled onto the ship, dressed in their long, flowing robes, and for the next forty minutes the commander gave them a personal guided tour. According to contemporary accounts the Abyssinians paused at each new marvel while murmuring the appreciative phrase "Bunga, Bunga!" in their native tongue. Finally the royal visitors departed as "God Save the King!" played in the background.

The next day the navy was mortified to learn that the party they had escorted around the warship had not been Abyssinian dignitaries at all. Instead it had been a group of young upperclass pranksters who had blackened their faces, donned elaborate theatrical costumes, and then forged an official telegram in order to gain access to the ship. Their ringleader was a man named Horace de Vere Cole, but the entourage also included a young woman called Virginia Stephen (later better known as Virginia Woolf).

By February 12 the British newspapers were full of the story of the stunt. "Bunga Bungle!" the *Western Daily Mercury* trumpeted. For a few days the navy was the laughingstock of Britain. Sailors were greeted with cries of "Bunga, Bunga" wherever they went. Humiliated and furious, the navy sent the warship out to sea until the episode blew over. It wanted to bring formal charges against the pranksters, but dropped the idea for fear that it would simply attract more publicity to the case. Finally it settled on a more informal punishment. Naval officers visited Cole and his co-conspirator Adrian Stephen and meted out to them six symbolic taps on their buttocks with a cane. Stephen submitted to this indignity grudgingly, while Cole insisted that the officers allow him to respond with an equivalent number of taps on their buttocks—a demand that remarkably enough was accepted. The other hoaxers were spared any retribution. This unusual punishment was seen as a face-saving way to settle a dispute between gentlemen of high social status. If Cole and Stephen had been lower class, the navy's response would certainly have been harsher. None of the participants went on to perpetrate any more hoaxes except for Cole, who was known throughout his life as an inveterate prankster.

The Piltdown Man

During the early twentieth century the scientific community was eagerly searching for the fossil "missing link" that would prove an evolutionary relationship between man and apes. In 1907 a jawbone was found in Germany that displayed characteristics of both species. This was the best evidence for a missing link yet, but scientists still wanted something better, something more definitive. Then in 1912 an amateur paleontologist named Charles Dawson appeared to have discovered the kind of artifact that was being sought: part of a skull that had the jawbone of an ape but the high forehead of a man. This seemed to show a clear linkage between the two species. But after decades of debate scientists finally concluded that Dawson's discovery did not represent the missing link. It represented instead one of the greatest scientific frauds of all time.

Dawson unearthed the skull and jawbone in a gravel pit near Piltdown, England, with the aid of Arthur Smith Woodward, keeper of the Department of Geology at the British Museum. This location gave the skull its name: the Piltdown Man. Woodward displayed the skull and jawbone at a meeting of the Geological Society of London and argued that they both came from a human who had probably lived half a million years ago, during the Lower Pleistocene period.

Woodward's claim immediately caused an enormous stir within the scientific community. Many felt that the jawbone and skull were simply too dissimilar to belong together. But Woodward's backers eventually won out and the new species entered the textbooks as *Eoanthropus dawson,* or "Dawson's Dawn Man."

Dawson died in 1916, leaving Woodward as the main defender of the Piltdown Man. For over three decades it was accepted as a legitimate, if unusual, piece of fossil evidence. But as more skeletons of early man were found, it became clear that the Piltdown Man was radically unlike anything else in the fossil record. Therefore in 1953 a team of researchers at the British Museum subjected the skull and jawbone to a rigorous series of scientific tests. What they found was shocking. The jawbone belonged not to a prehistoric man, but rather to a modern orangutan. It was only a few decades old and had been stained to give it the appearance of age. The skull, by contrast, actually was that of a prehistoric human, though only fifty thousand years old. Evidently someone had fraudulently planted these two artifacts together at the Piltdown site.

Having proven fraud, the question that remained was who had been responsible for the deception. Woodward had a strong reputation for honesty, and his innocence was generally acknowledged. Instead it was Dawson, motivated by a desire for scientific fame and recognition, who was fingered as the most likely culprit. Today many still agree with that verdict, but controversy simmers. Some argue that Dawson worked with an accomplice, perhaps Pierre Teilhard de Chardin, a young priest who briefly participated in the dig. Others place the blame elsewhere entirely. Martin Hinton, an employee at the British Museum whom Woodward once refused a job, has been implicated ever since a boxful of stained bones that may have belonged to him was discovered in 1975. Even Arthur Conan Doyle, the author of the Sherlock Holmes novels, has been named as a possible suspect. Whoever perpetrated the crime, it is considered to be one of the most damaging scientific hoaxes of all time, because it set the development of evolutionary theory back for years while researchers labored pointlessly to integrate a fake skull into the fossil record.

Alone in the Wilderness

On August 4, 1913, Joe Knowles took off his clothes and walked naked into the woods of Maine. For two months he lived by his wits alone, with no help from modern technology. He caught fish, made fire, strangled a deer, and vanquished a bear. He also kept a birch-bark record of his progress, which he periodically left in an predetermined drop-off site where an agent of the *Boston Post,* the sponsor of his adventure, then picked it up. Two months later he staggered out of the woods, dressed in the stinking skins of the animals that he had killed. When he made it back to Boston he was greeted by a crowd of two hundred thousand screaming, worshiping fans who had been eagerly following the reports of his adventure in the paper.

Knowles's adventure struck a strong chord with the American public. It was a time when the conservation movement was gaining ground, fueled by concerns about the closing of the frontier and the disappearance of wilderness areas. In addition, many feared that the comforts of urban living had made modern man weak. Knowles offered a testosterone-fueled rebuke to such fears. He proved that an American man still could survive unaided in the wilderness. The public loved the stunt, and the *Post,* which printed daily updates about his progress, saw its circulation rise by over thirty thousand.

But had Knowles really survived unaided for two months? Quite a few were doubtful. The rival *Boston American* claimed that it had found bullet holes in his bearskin, proving that he had not killed the bear with a club as he had claimed. Much later, in 1938, *The New Yorker* printed an article claiming that Knowles had simply holed up in a cabin in the woods with a conspirator, Michael McKeogh, who had written the birch-bark dispatches for him. According to McKeogh, Knowles had spent most of his time tanning in the sun and taking long, leisurely walks.

Whether or not Knowles really did survive unaided in the woods (most suspect he did not), he was certainly able to capitalize on his fame. He wrote a best-selling book about his experience, titled *Alone in the Wilderness.* He gave lectures in which he demonstrated survival skills and preached the gospel of self-reliance. And twice he convinced papers to send him on similar survival stunts, the final time in the company of an attractive young woman. But both times the sequels ended in failure when he emerged from the woods after only a few weeks.

Joe Knowles, naked, prepares to walk into the woods of Maine on August 4, 1913.

Game wardens escort Knowles as he exits the woods two months later.
From Joseph Knowles, *Alone in the Wilderness* (Small, Maynard & Company, 1913).

Tall-Tale Postcards

Around the turn of the century a new form of communication was born: the picture postcard. Postcards had been around since 1869, but it was not until 1894 that pictures began to be printed on them. The cards were an immediate success. Their popularity inspired a few photographers to experiment with ways to add more humor to them, and soon they had translated the idiom of the tall tale into visual form, creating so-called "freak" postcards. Customers loved them. Oversized crops and animals were a constant theme of the freak postcards, especially in the Midwest farming communities, where settlers got a kick out of sending cards to the relatives back east showing corn as big as trees and cabbages larger than barns. The fact that the Midwest was experiencing years of drought and pestilence made the joke all that much funnier. The era of the tall-tale postcard experienced its peak from 1905 to 1915. But cards of this kind are still being created and sent today, particularly in the Midwest.

"Bringing in the Sheaves." Photograph by William "Dad" Martin, 1908. Martin was a master of the art of tall-tale postcards. His work is instantly recognizable because of his fine attention to detail and the lifelike effects he achieved.

CHAPTER FIVE

1914–1949

New Jersey Martians and Van Gogh's Ear

The first half of the twentieth century was framed by the catastrophic conflicts of the two World Wars. The period in between the wars was a time of turbulence as well. Labor unrest, high crime rates, financial instability, and political upheaval all characterized these decades. But for some the deeper threat lay elsewhere, in the full coming of age of mass society and the mass media. Critics wondered whether Democracy, Freedom, and Truth could survive in an age of mass society, or whether these ideals would be beaten down beneath a mindless media cacophony of advertising, propaganda, and sensationalism. Many of the most famous hoaxes of this period related to this effort to come to terms with the implications of mass culture. They did so in three ways.

First, and most visibly, there was the ominous spectacle of the media being used to spread lies and propaganda in order to control the masses. This threat was amplified by the media's new power to disseminate both sight and sound. Radio brought music, news, and dramatic broadcasts directly into people's homes. Movies harnessed the hypnotic power of visual images. The state propaganda of Nazi Germany provided a disturbing example of how these new forms of media could be used for evil. And the mass panic following Orson Welles's 1938 *War of the Worlds* broadcast seemed to prove how susceptible the public was to media manipulation (even though the panic might not actually have happened, as discussed later in this chapter).

Second, there was the perspective of those who celebrated the new power of the media and actively tried to use it for their own ends. This was seen most clearly in the advertising and public relations industries. During the 1920s and 1930s advertisers began to adopt a far more aggressive approach. Instead of merely meeting the needs of consumers, they now sought to create consumer desire for products, even if the need for the products was questionable. This had long been done to a certain extent, especially by nineteenth-century showmen such as Barnum, but now the practice became far more organized and systematic. And it seemed to work. Consumer spending and debt rose dramatically. Encouraged by this success, advertisers began to blur the line between hoaxing and advertising to the point where the two often became indistinguishable. Many times the claims of advertisements were blatantly false. At other times publicists, such as Harry Reichenbach, who worked in the movie industry, creatively used hoaxes and stunts in order to generate free media exposure.

Finally, there were those who used hoaxes in order to defend the boundaries of elite culture against the encroachments of consumerism and experimental forms of art. The defenders of elite culture feared that aesthetic standards were being corrupted by a flood of mass-produced mediocrity. Therefore they struck back with hoaxes crafted in the style of the eighteenth-century Enlightenment, like Spectric Poetry and the Disumbrationist School of Art, which sought to expose the supposed lack of standards of those who were breaching the walls of High Culture.

World War I Hoaxes

World War I, or the Great War as it was called, was the most destructive conflict the world had ever seen. While the hoaxes listed below all related directly to it in some way, the greater impact the war had on the history of hoaxing was an indirect one. It left behind a Europe that was shattered and unstable. This proved to be a perfect breeding ground for a generation of con men and schemers who preyed upon the public.

World War I Armistice Signed

By November 1918 it seemed that the four-year-long conflict between the Allied and Axis powers might finally be coming to an end. Word leaked to the president of the United Press, who was in Europe at the time, that an armistice had been signed on November 7. Excitedly he cabled the news to America, where it then appeared as front-page news across the country and sparked nationwide celebrations. The only problem was that the armistice hadn't actually been signed. A German agent had planted the false news in order to demonstrate that the public in the Allied countries would welcome peace rather than a continuation of the conflict. The agent actually had read the political and public mood correctly. He was just a few days early. The real armistice was signed on November 11.

The Last German Prisoner of War

In September 1932 the soldier Oscar Daubmann finally made it home to Germany after a sixteen-year absence. As he told everyone he met, he had been captured by the French at the Battle of the Somme and was then shipped off to Africa after killing a guard. He spent the next twelve years locked in a squalid cell before finally escaping and making his way back home. The Germans treated him as a national hero. Everywhere he went his courage, bravery, and stamina were praised. He was asked to speak about the horrors he had suffered at the hands of the French. Newspapers wrote stories about his amazing escape. The Nazi party adopted him as one of their own and paraded him around as a poster boy for German strength and virtue. Then one day he arrived in a small town in Bavaria, where he got up on the podium to give his now customary speech about his imprisonment and escape. But before he could start talking an old man stood up in the crowd, pointed a finger at him, and said, "You are not Daubmann. You are my son, Alfred Hummel. Get down from that platform, you faker!" Daubmann, who wasn't really Daubmann at all, fainted. It turned out that he had been a prisoner for the past decade, but not a prisoner of war. He had been held in a German cell on a common burglary charge. Upon his release he bought a secondhand uniform in a shop and simply made up the wild story about a heroic journey home from an African cell.

The Veterans of Future Wars

In 1936 Congress decided to pay war bonuses to the veterans of World War I, ten years before those bonuses were due. This inspired a group of students at Princeton University to found an organization known as the Veterans of Future Wars. The premise of their organization was simple: its members, all young men who would probably participate in some future war for their country, should receive their war bonuses immediately before having done any military service, rather than having to wait to receive them until after they had fought and might be dead. After all, why shouldn't they have the money when they were young enough to enjoy it? The organization received national attention, and soon the movement had spread to other campuses, where fifty thousand other members signed up. They devised a special gesture by which they greeted each other: "hand outstretched, palm up and expectant." The members of the Veterans of Foreign Wars were not amused and referred to the young men as "insolent puppies." Within a year the joke had run its course and the organization had disbanded. But as it turned out, almost all the original members of the Veterans of Future Wars did live up to their organization's name by serving in World War II.

The Cottingley Fairies

By the end of World War I the English were emotionally bruised and battered from four years of unrelenting bloodbath and horror. They seemed to be in need of something that would reaffirm their belief in goodness and innocence, and they found it in a series of haunting fairy photographs taken by two young girls in a garden outside of a home in Cottingley, Yorkshire.

The two cousins, Frances Griffiths and Elsie Wright, initially took two photographs in 1917 to prove to their parents that they really had been playing with fairies, as they had claimed. The photographs showed the girls posing while delicate winged creatures danced around them. After a local photographic expert was shown the photos, they began circulating through upper-class British society. Then they came to the attention of Sir Arthur Conan Doyle, author of the Sherlock Holmes mysteries, who saw them as conclusive photographic proof of the existence of supernatural fairy beings. Doyle elaborated upon this belief in an article he wrote for *Strand* magazine in 1920, thus propelling the pictures into the national spotlight. When the girls provided him with three more fairy photographs, he wrote a second article. Doyle's passionate belief in the reality of the fairies helped to make the two girls famous, and it sparked an international controversy that pitted spiritualists against skeptics.

It was not until 1978 that a researcher noticed that the fairies in the pictures were almost identical to fairy figures in a children's book called *Princess Mary's Gift Book,* which had been published in 1915 shortly before the girls took the photographs. In 1981 the two cousins confessed that the fairies in four of the pictures were, in fact, paper cutouts from this book (though

they insisted that one of the photographs was real). They had
held the fairies in place with hatpins. To the modern eye the
fairies in the photographs seem quite obvious as paper cutouts,
making it all the more incredible that the controversy surrounding them lasted so long. But the photos still manage to project a
sensation of dreamy, childlike innocence. The five images remain one of the most famous photographic hoaxes of all time.

Elsie Wright accompanied by a leaping fairy. The fairy was held in
place with a hatpin.   Source: NMPFT, Bradford/Heritage-Images.

The Magic Turtle

The tale of the magic turtle is a classic prank that occurred
sometime in pre–World War II Paris. Its occurrence was recorded
by Hans Zinsser in his autobiography, *As I Remember Him*. It

involved the interaction between the owner of a small store and an American student who lived directly above her shop.

The shop owner kept, on her front windowsill, an aquarium that contained a small turtle. The student noticed that if he leaned out of his window, he looked directly down into the aquarium in which the turtle happily swam. Each day he watched as the woman diligently sprinkled breadcrumbs into the tank to feed her pet. Then one day he had an idea. He bought six turtles, ranging in size from very small to quite large, a fishing pole, and some netting. Early the next morning he leaned out of his window, scooped the woman's turtle out of its tank with the fishing pole, and replaced it with a slightly larger version. He repeated this exchange every morning for the next six days, always replacing the turtle in the tank with a slightly larger one. The woman noticed nothing until the second switch had been made. By the fourth switch she was excitedly telling all her neighbors about her miraculously growing pet. A vet sagely advised her to stop feeding it so much. By the sixth day, when the turtle was almost too big to fit in the tank, she had contacted the *Paris-Midi,* which ran the story of the turtle on its front page.

At this point the student had reached his maximum-size turtle, so he now began shrinking them back down to the first size. This caused even more excitement. The woman's store did record business as curiosity seekers came from all over to gaze at the remarkable reptile. Newspapers from throughout France interviewed her. Finally, when the turtle was back to its original dimensions, the student decided he had done enough and released the substitute turtles into the river. The woman, who never knew the real reason for her pet's sudden growth spurt, ended up donating her prized animal to the Jardin des Plantes so that the biologists there could observe it should it ever start enlarging again.

A Tale of a Tub

On December 28, 1917, H. L. Mencken published an article in the *New York Evening Mail* about the curious history of the bathtub. He noted that the first bathtub had appeared in America on December 10, 1842. But according to him, Americans were slow and cautious in accepting this innovation. Physicians denounced the devices as threats to the public health, and numerous cities passed ordinances restricting their use. The breakthrough came when Millard Fillmore installed a tub in the White House during the 1850s. This act of presidential endorsement swung public sentiment in their favor and soon tubs were widely used.

The joke was that nothing in Mencken's history was true, and he expected his readers to soon call his bluff. Instead, the exact opposite occurred. The history spread like wildfire throughout the country. References to it began appearing everywhere. Scholarly histories of public hygiene cited it. In 1926 a man named Fairfax Downey even wrote a serious history of the bathtub that drew largely on the false story. All of this dismayed Mencken. He wrote a number of follow-up articles in an attempt to check the spread of the story, but to no avail. It had acquired a life of its own. Mencken sadly concluded that "the American public will swallow anything."

In honor of Millard Fillmore's apocryphal adoption of the bathtub, the town of Moravia, New York, has held bathtub races down its main street every year since 1975. The races are part of a celebration that it calls Fillmore Days.

Art Hoaxes and Forgeries

The traditional art establishment faced threats from two directions during the early twentieth century: first, a challenge from upstart art movements such as Cubism, Dadaism, and Distortionism, all of which seemed determined to defy every convention of "classical" art; second, a problem from highly skilled forgers who were flooding the art market with increasingly skilled fakes. To counter the first threat the champions of traditional standards of artistic judgment crafted hoaxes that were designed to mock and discredit the experimental art forms (such as the "Disumbrationist School of Art" hoax described below). To counter the second threat art critics and scholars increasingly turned to high-tech science to unmask the forgers. But the forgers always seemed to stay one step ahead of those they were trying to fool (see Chapter Two, "Eighteenth-Century Literary Hoaxes," for more about the rivalry between scholars and forgers).

The Disumbrationist School of Art

In 1924 Paul Jordan Smith, a Los Angeles–based novelist and Latin scholar, painted a blurry picture of a South Seas islander holding a banana over her head. The picture was intended to be a spoof of abstract styles of modern art such as Cubism, and as a joke he entered it into an art exhibition, claiming that it was a work by the Russian artist Pavel Jerdanowitch (a name he had invented), who was the founder of the Disumbrationist School of Art (another invention of his). Smith used the foreign name because he figured that exotic-sounding painters always were a bigger hit with the critics. He titled the work "Exaltation" and made up something about how it represented the shattering of the bonds of womanhood. He said the woman had just taken a bite of a banana and was waving the banana skin over her head in triumphant freedom. To his chagrin, but not really to his surprise, the work was praised instead of being laughed at. This inspired Smith to paint and exhibit more pictures under Jerdanowitch's name, including one with a lot of squiggles and eyeballs that he named "Illumination." More praise followed. Smith finally tired of the deception and exposed the true identity of Jerdanowitch to the *Los Angeles Times.* Along with the unmasking he delivered a lecture about the declining standards of taste in the artistic community.

For examples of Disumbrationist art go to
www.museumofhoaxes.com/disumbrationist.html

Alceo Dossena

Alceo Dossena was a stonemason who lived in Northern Italy. He was also, inadvertently, one of the greatest forgers of all time. In 1916 he was making a living by carving reproductions of ancient sculptures. He never made any claim that these were actual antiques; he clearly described them as copies. But Dossena was so good at his craft that, without his knowledge, dealers began marketing his statues as the genuine article. When Dossena found out what was going on, he himself blew the whistle on the practice. After all, the dealers were earning far more from the sale of his works than they were paying him. But his work had spread so far and wide that it proved impossible to identify everywhere it had gone. Even today many of his pieces continue to circulate throughout the art world as genuine antiquities.

Hans van Meegeren

In 1947 Hans van Meegeren, a Dutch artist and art dealer, was arrested for collaborating with the Nazis. It was charged that he had sold a painting by Johannes Vermeer (1632–1675) titled "Christ and the Adulteress" to Reich Marshal Hermann Goering. This painting was considered a national treasure, making it a crime to sell it to the enemy. Van Meegeren defended himself by revealing that the painting was actually an imitation done in the style of Vermeer, an imitation that he had painted himself. His work had been so good that it had passed for an original, fooling Goering among others. Surely it wasn't a crime to cheat the Nazis, he asked. The authorities were reluctant to believe that van Meegeren was talented enough to produce a work of such quality, so he proved it by painting another imitation Vermeer while in his prison cell. It turned out that he had been churning out fakes for years, amassing a small fortune in the process, though he claimed that he had turned to deception only after the art world had spurned his legitimate efforts. He was convicted of forgery and sentenced to prison, but died of a heart attack before he served any time.

Literary Hoaxes

Conservative forces within the literary world fought against "modernist" influences, just as they did in the art community. To wage their losing battle they baited the modernists with a number of poetic parodies that subsequently became quite famous. The irony was that in hindsight these parodies don't seem that egregious at all. In fact, they seem considerably livelier and more spirited than the "real" literature that was being defended.

Spectric Poetry

In 1916 a slender volume of poetry titled *Spectra: A Book of Poetic Experiments* introduced the Spectric school of poetry to the world. It joined many other experimental schools of poetry currently in vogue, such as the Imagists, the Futurists, and the Idealists. The Spectric poems were rather bizarre and non-sensical, but were also fun, full of life, and decked out with colorful (albeit illogical) imagery. Lines such as these were typical: "I have seen the grey stars marching,/ And the green bubbles in wine,/ And there are Gothic vaults of sleep." The Spectric philosophy, as explained by its founders, Emanuel Morgan and Anne Knish, was to embrace the immediacy of experience, even if that experience could not be expressed rationally. Soon Spectrism had attracted a growing band of followers. The strange thing was that, despite repeated requests for meetings and interviews, the two founders, Morgan and Knish, never appeared in public. Rumors of a hoax began to circulate, and finally a poet named Witter Bynner admitted in 1918 that Spectrism was indeed a hoax, for which he and his friend Arthur Davison Ficke were responsible. He explained that their goal had been to parody the overly pompous experimentalism that was the fad of the moment, and so they had invented the free-spirited characters of Morgan and Knish. But many pointed out that the imposture appeared to have unleashed Bynner and Ficke's own inner creative energies, for the poetry that they published following the hoax was considerably changed in tone from their previous work. It had become lighter, freer—one could even say, rather Spectric.

Ern Malley

Max Harris was a glamorous young Australian poet who was making a reputation for himself as something of a rebel as editor of *Angry Penguins,* a cutting-edge literary magazine. Harris wanted to shake up the artistic community by exposing it to new ideas and new writers, and in 1944 he thought he had found a writer worth taking under his wing. That writer's name was Ern Malley. Harris never actually met Malley. Instead, he had received some of Malley's poems in the mail from a woman claiming to be Malley's sister. Ern himself had, it seemed, died of Graves' disease and his sister said that she had found the poems while going through his possessions after his death. The poems were strange, dark, brooding, and almost incomprehensible. They contained lines such as "I am still the black swan of trespass on alien waters." Harris loved them, and he arranged for a special edition of *Angry Penguins* to be devoted to Malley's work. There was just one problem. Ern Malley didn't exist. He was the cynical creation of two Australian poets, Harold Stewart and James McAuley, who were hostile to modernist poetry and wanted to see if they could get the literary world to accept "deliberately concocted nonsense." They had written the poems in one day by randomly picking out nonsequential lines from the *Oxford Dictionary of Quotations.* Harris's reputation and ego took a blow on account of the Ern Malley hoax. But Stewart and McAuley didn't come out of the hoax as heroes either. Many readers insisted that they enjoyed Malley's poems (they do make for an interesting read) and argued that the two poets had unintentionally produced better work than they were capable of when trying to be serious.

The Cruise of the Kawa

Books detailing real-life adventures to faraway lands were all the rage during the first decades of the twentieth century. Readers couldn't seem to get enough of these swashbuckling tales. *The Cruise of the Kawa,* published in 1921 by G. P. Putnam and Sons, tapped directly into this market.

It told the story of the adventures of Walter E. Traprock and his band of compatriots in the South Pacific. Before the book was published articles appeared in newspapers speaking of Traprock's important discoveries, foremost of which was a group of previously uncharted Pacific islands called the Filberts. But when the book appeared, it turned out that the geographical discovery was the least amazing of his finds, because on the Filberts Traprock had found a variety of fascinating new species, including plants that blushed, crabs that towed boats, and snakes that lived entirely on coconut milk. The most amazing of these new species was the fatu-liva, a bird that laid square eggs. A picture of these eggs (which remarkably resembled dice) was included in the book. Its caption read, "Skeptics have said that it would be impossible to lay a square egg. To which the author is justly entitled to say: 'The camera never lies.' "

The Cruise of the Kawa proved to be a hit with readers. Traprock even received a number of invitations to lecture across the country, including one invitation from the National Geographic Society. Needless to say, these invitations had to be turned down because neither Traprock nor the amazing fatu-liva bird actually existed. *The Cruise of the Kawa* was actually the work of George Shepard Chappell, a reporter for *Vanity Fair* magazine, who had been commissioned to write the book by the publisher George Putnam. Putnam intended it as a satire of the real-life travel genre. He wanted to see how ridiculous he could make a travel story before readers stopped believing it. Chappell later noted, "Far and wide *Cruise of the Kawa* was accepted as genuine, frequently even after it had been read."

Proof that the camera never lies. A photograph of a nest containing the square, spotted eggs of a fatu-liva bird.   From *The Cruise of the Kawa: Wanderings in the South Seas* by Walter E. Traprock, 1921.

Con Men and Pranksters

The interwar period was marked by violent financial turbulence, notably hyperinflation in Germany and, in America, the stock market crash of 1929 followed by the Great Depression. During these times it seemed that everyone was looking for a way to get rich quick. This produced a heady environment in which a long list of con men went to work. The gloom and doom of the era also made people grateful for the comic relief provided by pranksters such as Harry Reichenbach and Hugh Troy.

Charles Ponzi

Charles Ponzi (1882?–1949) was said by his worshipful followers to have "discovered money." He offered unbeatable interest rates on any money invested with him. He promised that he could make his investors a fifty percent return on their money in just forty-five days. At first people were skeptical, but then he actually began paying out interest and soon thousands of people were lining up to give him their cash. It is said that he had over forty thousand investors, which allowed him to finance a lavish lifestyle for himself, throwing cash around like it grew on trees. But then in 1920 rumors about his criminal past began to circulate and a number of big investors abruptly asked for their money back. This caused Ponzi's whole scam to go belly up. It turned out that he was simply paying early investors with the money obtained from new investors. As long as more and more new investors kept pouring in, his pyramid scheme worked, but as soon as the investment inflow stopped it all came crashing down like a house of cards. This type of scam has ever since been known as a Ponzi scheme. Ponzi was sentenced to five years in jail.

Stanley Clifford Weyman

Throughout his long career as a con man Stanley Clifford Weyman (1891–1960) proved as eerily adept at slipping on new identities as anyone else might be at putting on a new pair of clothes. By the age of thirty he had posed as a U.S. consul delegate to Morocco, a Serbian military attaché, a Romanian consul general (in which guise he was escorted around the USS *Wyoming*), a Peruvian doctor, and as Lieutenant Royal St. Cyr of the army air corps. He usually got caught and spent time in jail, but upon his release he always took up his old ways with no hesitation. In 1921 he perpetrated his most famous stunt when, posing as a State Department official, he arranged to have Princess Fatima of Afghanistan meet with President Harding. The State Department had actually, for political reasons, been ignoring the princess's presence in the U.S. When the government realized what had happened, they threw Weyman in jail for two years. Once again, he remained unrepentant and unreformed after his release. Throughout the remainder of his life he was caught posing as, among other things, a surgeon, a doctor, a psychiatrist, a lawyer, and even a Thai delegate to the United Nations.

Count Victor Lustig

Count Victor Lustig (1890–1947) was one of the most outrageous and colorful con men of all time. Of course, he wasn't really a count. This was simply the most famous of the over forty aliases that he employed throughout his career. He perpetrated his best-known con in 1925 when he managed to "sell" the Eiffel Tower. It had been widely reported in the papers that the tower, built in 1889, needed repairs. Posing as a civil servant, Lustig contacted various French scrap-metal dealers and informed them that the tower was to be torn down and that the French government was secretly accepting bids for the project. After the dealers had submitted their bids, Lustig quietly complained to one of them about the low salaries that civil servants had to subsist on. The dealer recognized the complaint as a request for a bribe and slipped Lustig $100,000 under the table, hoping thereby to secure the lucrative project. Lustig took the money and skipped town. The dealer was too embarrassed to ever report the crime. Lustig's scam might never have been known to the public if his success hadn't emboldened him to try to exact same con again. The second time, however, his victim went to the police. But in the meantime Lustig had fled to America. There he continued his criminal career. Some of his other exploits included selling a phony counterfeiting machine to criminals and scamming the gangster Al Capone out of $50,000. He was eventually caught and sentenced to Alcatraz, where he died.

Harry Reichenbach

During the 1920s public relations came into its own as a business, and Harry Reichenbach (1882–1931) was one of the great pioneers of the industry. Although he made his name promoting the movie industry, he got his start in the circus as a teenager, where he learned the promotional techniques of the carnival barkers. Around May 1913 a New York shopkeeper asked Reichenbach to help him sell a painting, two thousand copies of which were languishing in his shop. The picture, titled "September Morn," showed an attractive young woman discreetly bathing herself at the edge of a lake. Reichenbach displayed the painting prominently in the store window, then complained to Anthony Comstock, the infamous head of New York's antivice society, that the painting was corrupting the morals of young children who could see it from the street. Comstock filed an injunction to have the image banned. The court refused the injunction, but the resulting controversy eventually helped sell over seven million copies of "September Morn." Reichenbach received only $45 for this job. Later, to promote a movie called *The Return of Tarzan,* Reichenbach arranged for someone to check into a hotel under the name T. R. Zann. An actual lion was then delivered to the man's hotel room. The chaos that ensued at the hotel got wide press coverage. In all of the articles that were written about the event, the name T. R. Zann was prominently displayed, just in time for the release of *Tarzan* the next week.

Hugh Troy

By trade Hugh Troy (1906–1964) was an illustrator, but by nature he was a practical joker. As a young student at Cornell University he once used a rhino-foot wastepaper basket to leave tracks in the snow leading to the edge of a local lake. Half the campus, thinking that a rhino had escaped from a nearby zoo and fallen into the lake, refused to drink the campus water, convinced that it had become rhino tainted. Years later, as an artist working in New York City, Troy walked down to Central Park one day and brazenly carried away a public bench. He didn't get very far before a policeman stopped him, at which point Troy whipped out his sales receipt. He had purchased the bench at a store earlier in the day and left it in the park, just so that he could "steal" it later. In 1935 there was an exhibit of van Gogh's work at the Museum of Modern Art. Troy slipped into the exhibit and left a fake ear molded out of beef perched on one of the tables. Beside the ear he put a sign declaring, "This is the ear which Vincent van Gogh cut off and sent to his mistress, a French prostitute, Dec. 24, 1888." Pretty soon more people were crowded around the table staring at the ear than were looking at the paintings. Finally, during World War II Troy was given a desk job in the military. Finding his duties to be excruciatingly boring, he began to amuse himself by submitting "flypaper reports" to headquarters. These were reports, printed up on official-looking paper, that listed the number of flies trapped by flypaper during the last twenty-four hours. Soon he learned that other officers were being chastised by headquarters for not submitting their own flypaper reports.

Jim Moran

Jim Moran (1907–1999) was the all-time master of the publicity stunt. His stunts may not qualify as true hoaxes, since there was usually no deception involved. But in their outrageousness they share a kinship with hoaxes. His typical method of operation was to take a cliché and literalize it. For instance, he once sold an icebox to an Eskimo. During the 1944 presidential election he literally changed horses in midstream in the Truckee River in Nevada. He found a needle in a haystack (it took him ten days). He walked a bull through a china shop. But what was arguably his most famous stunt did not involve clichés and did not even work. He attempted to tie midgets to kites and fly them over Central Park in New York City. His idea was that the midgets could carry billboards on which he would sell advertising space. When told by the police that his scheme was illegal, he famously remarked, "It's a sad day for American capitalism when a man can't fly a midget on a kite over Central Park."

Sea Serpents

When dinosaur bones first began to be discovered during the eighteenth and nineteenth centuries, it led people to wonder whether such creatures still roamed the earth anywhere in an as yet unexplored region. Gradually all the earth's land masses were mapped and explored without turning up any sign of dinosaurs, but the great depths of the oceans still remained uncharted. As a result it was here that those who hoped to find a still-living dinosaur turned their scrutiny. Attention particularly focused on Loch Ness in Scotland, where during the 1930s many sightings of a mysterious creature began to be reported.

The Surgeon's Photo

Ancient Scottish legends spoke of a giant sea monster that lived in the waters of Loch Ness. But these were principally local legends, unknown to the outside world, until around 1933, when serpent sightings in the loch began to draw international attention. In 1933 the *Daily Mail* hired a famous big-game hunter, Marmaduke Wetherell, to travel up to the loch to investigate the sightings and to find the monster, if he could. Although he found no monster, in December 1933 he did locate what appeared to be its tracks—enormous footprints on the shore of the loch leading into the water. Unfortunately, when researchers from the Natural History Museum examined the tracks, they determined that they had been made with a dried hippo's foot, of the kind that were popularly used as umbrella stands. Humiliated, Wetherell retreated from public view.

A few months later the Loch Ness monster was again in the news. A highly respectable British surgeon, Colonel Robert Wilson, was driving along the shore of the loch on April 19, 1934, early in the morning when, he said afterward, he noticed something moving in the water. He happened to have a camera with him, so he quickly stopped his car and snapped a photo. The resulting image showed the slender neck of a serpent rising out of the loch. For decades this photo was considered to be the best evidence ever obtained of the existence of a sea monster in the loch. Wilson himself never publicized the image and refused to have his name associated with it. Therefore it came to be known more anonymously as "the Surgeon's Photo."

For years skeptics were sure that the photo was somehow a hoax. But no rigorous studies of the image were conducted until 1984, when Stewart Campbell analyzed the photo in an article in the *British Journal of Photography*. Campbell concluded that the object in the water could only have been two or three feet long, at most, and that it probably was an otter or a marine bird. He suggested that it was likely that Wilson knew this to be the case. But as it turned out, Campbell was wrong. The object in the water was not a form of marine life. It was a toy submarine outfitted with a sea serpent's head. This was revealed in 1994 when Christian Spurling, before his death at the age of ninety, confessed to reporters from the London *Sunday Telegraph* about his involvement in a plot to create the famous Surgeon's Photo. According to him the plot involved both Marmaduke Wetherell and Colonel Wilson. Spurling said that he had been approached by Wetherell, who asked him to build a convincing serpent model. This model was then taken to Loch Ness, photographed, and the pictures were given to Wilson, who Wetherell felt would be a credible front man. It appears that Wetherell's motive for concocting this elaborate plot was revenge, as he was still smarting from his humiliation over the earlier hippo-foot debacle.

Mauretania Sights a Sea Serpent

On February 11, 1934, an article in *The New York Times* stated that the passenger ship *Mauretania* had enjoyed multiple sightings of a sea serpent as it cruised through the Caribbean in late January. Reportedly the ship's crew first sighted a sixty-five-foot monster, which passed them in the ocean. Then, when anchored at the port of La Guayra, the creature was seen again, calmly sunning itself on the surface of the water. The *Times* theorized that the monster "appears from brief descriptions to be a relative of the 'monster of Loch Ness.' " The *Mauretania* was back in the *Times* two weeks later with more serpent sightings. The ship's captain was quoted as saying that the sightings were certainly accurate, since "sailors never lie." Then, on March 10, the *Mauretania* once again popped up in the columns of the *Times,* still with serpents in tow. But in actuality there were no sightings. The *Mauretania's* fantastic luck with sea serpents was the invention of reporter T. Walter Williams. Williams, it is said, is the only reporter whom the *Times,* famous for its adherence to facts, has ever knowingly allowed to spin tall tales in its pages. But in the case of the *Mauretania* and its sea ser-

THE NEW YORK TIMES, S

Mauretania Sights Sea Serpent; Entry in the Ship's Log Proves It

Senior First Officer Tells of 'Jet Black Monster,' 65 Feet Long and 6 Feet Broad Passed in the Caribbean—Sketched Picture of It on the Chart.

What Mauretania Officer Says He Saw in the Caribbean. Drawn From Data in Log and Sketch on Chart.

By T. WALTER WILLIAMS

It became known yesterday that the Cunarder Mauretania had passed a sea monster 65 feet long, | luncheon when the sea serpent was passed on Jan. 30." Captain Reginald V. Peel, com-

"Mauretania Sights Sea Serpent." Headline that appeared in *The New York Times* on February 11, 1934.   Source: *The New York Times.*

pents he may have gone a bit too far. On March 27 a brief, anonymous column in the *Times* warned that the *Mauretania* risked cornering the market on monsters and that it "may yet be haled into court for the violation of the anti-trust laws in the matter of sea serpents." This was evidently Williams's editor putting a brake on the fabulous career of the Caribbean passenger ship. After that the *Mauretania* and its sea serpents were never mentioned again.

Hugo N. Frye

In 1930 letters were mailed to Republican leaders throughout the United States inviting them to come celebrate the birthday anniversary of the esteemed Hugo N. Frye, the founder of the Republican party in New York State. Mr. Frye would have been 150 if he were still alive. None of the politicians could make it to the event, but almost all of them sent back letters expressing their sincere admiration for Frye's contributions to the Republican party. For instance, Secretary of Labor James Davis wrote, "It is a pleasure to testify to the career of that sturdy patriot who first planted the ideals of our party in this region of the country." Soon afterward the student editors of the *Cornell Sun,* the sponsors of the event, revealed that the great Hugo N. Frye was none other than "You Go and Fry." Red-faced Republicans in the New York Senate had to endure a week of humiliation as their Democratic colleagues reminded them, again and again, of the great example set by that "sturdy patriot" Hugo N. Frye.

The Milton Mule

Mayor Ken Simmons of Milton, Washington, was frustrated by the voters in his county. He suspected that that they often went to the polls with little understanding about whom they were voting for. This was especially true, he was convinced, during contests for low-profile positions. In these elections it appeared that most votes were cast mechanically along party lines. Simmons complained that people could be voting for a mule, for all they knew or cared.

To prove his point, in 1936 Simmons, who was a Democrat, took his mule down to the county courthouse, put its hoof-print on the official documents, and registered it to enter the next primary election. He had it run for the position of Republican precinct committeeman. Sure enough, at the next election Republicans turned out and voted 52–0 in favor of the mule (whose name was Boston Curtis). For Mayor Simmons the fact that the Republicans had unknowingly voted in the Democratic party symbol made the victory all that much sweeter.

Radio Panics

Radio technology was invented near the beginning of the twentieth century. By 1920 the first commercial radio broadcasts had begun, and by the end of the 1930s almost eighty percent of American households had sets. Most people considered radio to be a medium that was inherently trustworthy. Through it they heard political leaders such as Franklin Roosevelt talk directly to them, as well as live coverage of events such as the 1937 *Hindenburg* disaster. It provided them with a direct yet intimate connection to the broader world, and they tended to believe whatever they heard over it, because they had never been given a reason not to. This is why the great radio panics of the 1920s and '30s were considered so shocking. They dramatized a latent fear that the massive trust placed in radio was mistaken—that this new technology might actually represent a source of vulnerability that people had unthinkingly brought into their very homes.

The BBC Radio Panic

On January 16, 1926, BBC Radio abruptly interrupted a broadcast of a speech from Edinburgh to give this special announcement: an angry mob of unemployed workers were running amok in London, looting and destroying everything in sight. Listeners were stunned. Anxiously they gathered around their radios as the frightening news from London continued. They heard that the Houses of Parliament had been blown up with trench mortars. "The clock tower 320 feet in height has just fallen to the ground, together with the famous clock, Big Ben," the reporter excitedly informed them. "Fresh reports announce that the crowd has secured the person of Mr. Wurtherspoon, the minister of traffic, who was attempting to make his escape in disguise. He has now been hanged from a lamppost in Vauxhall."

The news was accompanied by the sounds of a mob in the background and explosions in the distance. At this point listeners began to panic. They must have thought of the relatively recent Russian Revolution of 1917 and worried that the same fate was now befalling England. Most of them somehow ignored the comically incongrous parts of the broadcast, such as the detail about the leader of the mob, Mr. Popplebury, who was also "secretary of the National Movement for Abolishing Theater Queues." Listeners in London poured out into the streets in an attempt to flee the city, while those outside the city rushed to their phones to find out what was going on. Authorities were swamped with frantic calls. Puzzled officials who swore that nothing was happening did little to placate callers who swore back that something had to be occurring, because they had heard about it *on the radio*. Finally, long after the situation had gotten well out of hand, the BBC eased tensions by reminding the audience that the events they had heard were simply part of Father Ronald Knox's comic skit titled "Broadcasting the Barricades." The fictitious nature of the skit had, indeed, been clearly announced at the top of Father Knox's show, but most listeners had forgotten about this warning when confronted with the realistic quality of the broadcast.

War of the Worlds

On October 30, 1938, CBS Radio was broadcasting the music of Ramon Raquello and his orchestra live from the Meridian Room at the Park Plaza in New York City when suddenly a reporter from Intercontinental Radio News interrupted the broadcast to deliver an important announcement. Astronomers had just detected enormous blue flames shooting up from the surface of Mars. The broadcast then returned to the music of Ramon Raquello. But soon more news flashes followed, and they began to grow increasingly ominous. Listeners heard that a meteor had fallen to earth near Grovers Mill, New Jersey. Then they heard that it was not a meteor at all, but rather some kind of spaceship from which a tentacled creature had emerged. At this point the broadcast began to get really strange. Listeners were told that the creature, now housed inside a gigantic, three-legged, armored contraption, was marching across New Jersey blasting everything in its path and releasing billowing clouds of toxic black gas against which gas masks proved useless.

Reportedly, it was around this point in the broadcast that some listeners began to panic. Some of them loaded blankets and supplies in their cars and prepared to flee the invader. One mother in New England, it is said, packed her babies and lots of bread into a car, figuring that "if everything is burning, you can't eat money, but you can eat bread." Other people hid in cellars, hoping that the poisonous gas would blow over them.

By the time the night was over almost everyone had learned that the news flashes were fictitious. They were simply part of the weekly broadcast of Orson Welles and the Mercury Theater, who, in honor of Halloween, had staged a highly dramatized and updated version of H. G. Wells's classic story *War of the Worlds,* which describes the invasion of the Earth by Martians.

Approximately six million people heard the broadcast, and out of this number it was long thought that almost one million people panicked. But more recent research suggests that the actual number is probably far lower. In fact, the idea that the broadcast touched off a huge national scare is probably

more of a hoax than the broadcast itself, which was never intended to fool anyone. At four separate points during the broadcast, including the beginning, it was clearly stated that what
people were hearing was a play.

Those who did panic tended to be those who had tuned in
late to the broadcast and missed the beginning. Also, there
were some who jumped to the conclusion that the alien invasion was actually a cleverly disguised German attack. As soon
as the national media caught wind of the panic, they jumped
on the news and hyped it out of all proportion. Ever since, the
event has been synonymous with the power that the media
wields over the gullible masses.

APRIL FOOLS' DAY HOAXES

The biggest innovation in April Foolery during the first
half of the twentieth century came from tall-tale photography. Since newspapers now had the capability to print
black-and-white photographs, pranksters at the papers took the opportunity this afforded to fool their readers with all manner of
strange images. Examples, crude by modern standards but effective
enough to hoodwink the less jaded viewers of those decades, included giant fish, deep-sea monsters, ocean liners docked in tiny
streams, and men flying by their own lung power.

For examples of some of these pictures go to
www.museumofhoaxes.com/aprilframe.html.

Wisconsin State Capitol Collapses

In 1933 the *Madison Capital Times* ran a picture on its front
page showing the dome of the Wisconsin State Capitol collapsing.
An accompanying article reported that the dome lay in ruins following a series of mysterious explosions, which luckily had not
harmed anyone. The article theorized that the explosions had been
caused by "large quantities of gas, generated through many weeks

of verbose debate in the Senate and Assembly chambers." Despite the fact that the story concluded with the words *April Fool,* many readers were initially taken in by it and grew very upset. One reader wrote to the editor complaining, "I was filled with indignation over your April Fool joke on the front page of the *Capital-Times* of April 1. There is such a thing as carrying a joke too far and this one was not only tactless and void of humor, but also a hideous jest."

World to End on April 1

On March 31, 1940, the Franklin Institute issued a press release stating that the world would end the next day. The release was picked up by radio station KYW, which broadcast the following message: "Your worst fears that the world will end are confirmed by astronomers of Franklin Institute, Philadelphia. Scientists predict that the world will end at 3:00 P.M. Eastern Standard Time tomorrow. This is no April Fool joke. Confirmation can be obtained from Wagner Schlesinger, director of the Fels Planetarium of this city." Local authorities were immediately flooded with frantic phone calls. The panic only subsided after the Franklin Institute assured people that it had made no such prediction. The prankster responsible for the press release turned out to be William Castellini, the institute's press agent. He had intended to use the fake press release to publicize an April 1 lecture at the institute titled "How Will the World End?" Soon afterward the Institute rewarded Castellini's efforts by firing him.

The New Zealand Wasp Swarm

In 1949 Phil Shone, a New Zealand deejay for radio station 1ZB, announced to his listeners that a mile-wide wasp swarm was headed toward Auckland. He urged his listeners to take a variety of steps to protect themselves and their homes from the winged menace. For instance, he suggested that they wear their socks over their trousers when they left for work and that they leave honey-smeared traps outside their doors. Hundreds of people who had dutifully heeded his advice were soon seen wandering around the city with their pants tucked firmly into their socks. As noon approached, Shone admitted that the wasp swarm was just a joke. But the New Zealand Broadcasting Service was not amused. Its director, Professor James Shelley, denounced the hoax on the grounds that it undermined the rules of proper broadcasting. From then on a memo was sent out each year before April Fools' Day reminding New Zealand radio stations of their obligation to report the truth and nothing but the truth.

Hitler Hoaxes

Spreading unsettling rumors about enemy leaders is a staple of government propaganda during times of war. But Adolf Hitler succeeded in inspiring far stranger propaganda than most other leaders.

Baby Adolf

In 1933 a picture began circulating throughout England and America purportedly showing Adolf Hitler as a baby. The child in the picture looked positively menacing. Its fat mouth was twisted into a sneer, and it scowled at the camera from dark, squinted eyes. A greasy mop of hair fell over its forehead. The image caused such a popular sensation that the German consul eventually felt obliged to denounce it. Then in 1937 Mrs. Harriet M. W. Downs, of Westport, Connecticut, recognized the image as an old baby picture of her own son, John May Warren (who by then was eight years old and didn't resemble Hitler at all). In the original image her son looked cute, bright, and wholesome. But an unknown hoaxer had darkened the shadows around the child's face to give him a more sinister look. In May 1938, Acme Newspictures, Inc., ran both pictures with an explanation of the hoax. How a photo of Mrs. Down's baby got caught up in this international hoax remains a mystery.

The Strange Death of Adolf Hitler

In March 1939 a book appeared titled *The Strange Death of Adolf Hitler*. It alleged that Hitler had died of poisoning in 1938, shortly before the Munich Conference. The book's anonymous author claimed to be one of four doubles who had immediately taken Hitler's place. Since Hitler appeared to be alive and well until 1945, this book was presumably a hoax. Oddly, the premature report of his death in 1938 was mirrored by consistent rumors about his survival after 1945.

Hitler's Silly Dance

In June 1940 Hitler accepted the surrender of the French government at a ceremony in Compiègne, France. After he signed the terms of the surrender, Hitler stamped his foot and stepped backward slightly. But this is not what the audiences in the Allied countries saw who watched the movie reel of the ceremony. They saw Hitler dance a bizarre little jig after signing the documents, as if he were childishly celebrating his victory. The scene was played over and over again in movie theaters. Of course, Hitler had not done a little dance. Allied propagandists had simply looped the footage of Hitler's step backward, so that it appeared as if he were dancing. The film clip served its desired purpose, which was to ridicule the Nazi leader.

CHAPTER SIX

1950–1976

Naked Animals and Swiss Spaghetti Trees

As World War II ended, the world finally achieved a kind of stability. But it was a stability based on the standoff between the two great superpowers, the United States and the Soviet Union. This apparent peace brought with it new and potentially even more unnerving tensions: the rise of big government, the creation of a massive military-industrial complex, the flare-up of border conflicts between the superpowers in countries like Korea, and the constant threat of nuclear war. Many felt that these were small prices to pay for peace. After all, the world, and particularly the United States, was growing prosperous. But soon a kind of paranoia crept into public discourse, expressed in talk of conspiracy theories, secret government programs, and visitors from outer space. This led to the belief, persistently expressed throughout this period, that the powers-that-be (governments and corporations) were hoaxing the people, that they were perpetrating massive disinformation campaigns to keep the masses in line. The flip side of this paranoia was defiance. As the conservatism of the 1950s gave way to the radicalism of the 1960s, hoaxing and tricksterism arose as ways to carve out a small niche of personal control in a world otherwise regulated by massive, impersonal bureaucracies.

The idea that the powers-that-be were lying to the people in order to further their own nefarious ends had many manifestations. There was the theory that secret forms of thought control were being beamed through television sets. There was the pervasive fear of communist infiltration. There was talk of top secret experiments involving hallucinogenic drugs. There were rumors, as the superpowers extended their reach into outer space, that governments were hiding the existence of extraterrestrial life. There were even concerns that instead of man conquering space, space beings were in reality conquering man. And what about that 1969 moon landing? Many were convinced (and still are) that it, too, was a lie.

A series of events added fuel to the atmosphere of conspiracy and paranoia: the quiz-show scandals of the 1950s, the flood of conflicting reports coming from Vietnam, and finally Watergate. But overall it was probably the sheer size of government and corporations, and their new presence in so many different aspects of life, that did the most to promote the distrust.

As if in response to the paranoia a new kind of cultural hero emerged during the late fifties: the trickster. The trickster defied the massive, overpowering system by committing small acts of rebellion that often took the form of hoaxes and pranks. Unlike the hoaxes of the eighteenth-century Enlightenment, whose goal was to promote the concept of reason, the hoaxes of the trickster were done in the name of creativity, freedom, and individual self-expression. They were forms of defiance against the relentless march of corporate, bureaucratic control.

The Great Monkey Hoax

On July 8, 1953, Cobb County police officer Sherley Brown and his partner were doing a routine patrol down rural Bankhead Highway near Austell, Georgia, when they pulled over to investigate a pickup truck that was stopped in the middle of the road. What they found was the most unusual scene they would ever encounter during their entire careers as officers. Three frightened, very sober young men were waiting nervously by the side of the road. And lying there on the tarmac in front of the truck, illuminated by the vehicle's headlights, was a bizarre two-foot-tall creature that looked for all the world like a space alien.

Nervously the young men spilled out their tale. They said they had been out "honkey-tonking" around. As they drove down the deserted highway, they came over a hill and suddenly spotted a brilliant light immediately ahead. It was a flying saucer, parked beside the highway and "glowing red all over." Three small aliens were wandering outside the craft, and as the truck approached, the aliens rushed toward their ship. The boys slammed on the brakes (long skid marks on the highway offered proof of this), but couldn't avoid hitting one of the aliens as it ran across the road. The other two creatures made it to the ship and took off.

The three young men were Ed Watters, Tom Wilson, and Buddy Payne. Two of them were local barbers, and the other was a butcher. They seemed credible enough. Plus, there *had* been talk just the day before of a UFO sighted in nearby Marietta. And finally, there was the incontrovertible proof of the alien itself lying lifeless in the road: a hairless, two-foot-tall humanoid creature with eerie, round, dark eyes. The police officers took the boys and the body of the alien back to town and notified their superiors. Just a few hours later, as word of the space alien quickly spread across the wires, sleepy Cobb County became the center of the nation's attention.

Reporters from Atlanta drove out to see what was going on. Journalists from other newspapers throughout the country frantically called, trying to get details about the alien. Even representatives from the air force arrived to survey the situation. The reporters had a local veterinarian examine the body, and his verdict was that it "looked like something out of this world." But then the officials from the Georgia Crime Lab showed up and carted the body off to Emory University, where an anatomy professor examined it. His verdict was slightly different. It was nothing more than a shaved capuchin monkey whose tail had been cut off.

After the professor had delivered his opinion, the boys quickly confessed. The prank had started as a bet made during a card game. Watters had wagered his friends that he could get himself featured in the local paper within a week. After buying a monkey at a local pet shop he gave it a lethal dose of chloroform, shaved it with depilatory cream, chopped its tail off, deposited it in the middle of the rural highway, and waited for the police to arrive. With all the ensuing media attention he handily won his bet. After all, he was profiled not only in the local papers, but also in *Life* magazine. Unfortunately he lost forty dollars when he was fined for obstructing the highway.

In 1998 Cobb County Police Colonel Sherley Brown posed with the creature that he found lying in the road on July 8, 1953. Many believed it to be an extraterrestrial being. It now resides in the Georgia Crime Lab. Source: Rich Addicks/*Atlanta Journal-Constitution*.

Television Hoaxes

Television technology existed as early as the 1930s, but it was not successfully commercialized by corporations until after World War II. It built upon the base established by radio and extended the trend of bringing entertainment directly into people's homes. Its critics have always charged that it is a perfect medium for disseminating disinformation and propaganda. This may be the case, but it has never proven to be a robust platform for hoaxes of a more traditional kind. Unlike radio and print, television doesn't leave a lot to the audience's imagination, which consequently makes it more difficult for a television hoax to appear realistic. There have been, nevertheless, a few very noteworthy exceptions to this rule.

Twenty-One

During the 1950s *Twenty-One* was one of the most popular quiz shows on TV, and its ratings soared even higher when Charles Van Doren, son of Pulitzer Prize–winning poet Mark Van Doren, appeared as a contestant on the show in late 1956. Van Doren seemed unbeatable. For week after week he answered every question correctly, winning a total of $129,000. But in 1957 a previous contestant, Herbert Stempel, revealed that the entire show was rigged. Van Doren, it turned out, was being fed the correct answers. A congressional investigation followed, and NBC, the producer of the show, issued an embarrassed confession.

Subliminal Advertising

The term *subliminal advertising* was coined in 1957 by the market researcher James Vicary. He used it to describe the flashing of hidden messages at viewers while they watched films or TV shows. Although the messages would appear on the screen only for fractions of a second, far too briefly for the conscious brain to see them, the theory was that the unconscious brain would perceive the messages and be triggered into action by whatever they suggested, much in the way a hypnotic command is said to work.

Vicary claimed that during a six-week period in the summer of 1957 he had exposed over forty thousand moviegoers to subliminal ads (without their knowledge) while they attended a theater in Fort Lee, New Jersey. The ads he flashed were "Drink Coca-Cola" and "Hungry? Eat Popcorn." His results were startling. He reported that sales of popcorn rose 57 percent and drink sales rose 18.1 percent. Of course, Vicary's results were not published anywhere, but even anecdotal evidence of this kind made the advertising industry pay attention, and scared consumer advocates.

Advertisers immediately rushed to place subliminal ads in TV shows and films. This prompted Congress to investigate whether the practice needed to be regulated. But skeptics denounced the entire concept as a fraud. When Vicary was challenged to repeat his results, he was unable to do so. Finally, in 1962, Vicary admitted that he had simply made up his data. Some suspected that he had never even performed the tests. No subsequent research has ever shown that subliminal messages have any measurable effect on audience behavior whatsoever.

The Swiss Spaghetti Harvest

On April 1, 1957, the British news show *Panorama* broadcast a segment about a bumper spaghetti harvest in southern Switzerland brought on by an unusually mild winter. The audience heard Richard Dimbleby, the show's highly respected anchor, discussing the details of the spaghetti crop as they watched a rural Swiss family pulling pasta off spaghetti trees and placing it into baskets. "The spaghetti harvest here in Switzerland is not, of course, carried out on anything like the tremendous scale of the Italian industry," Dimbleby informed the audience. "For the Swiss . . . it tends to be more of a family affair."

The narration then continued in a tone of absolute serious-
ness. "Another reason why this may be a bumper year lies in
the virtual disappearance of the spaghetti weevil, the tiny creature whose depradations have caused much concern in the
past." Some viewer questions were anticipated. For instance,
why does spaghetti always come in uniform lengths? "This is
the result of many years of patient endeavor by past breeders
who succeeded in producing the perfect spaghetti." Finally
Dimbleby assured the audience, "For those who love this dish,
there's nothing like real, home-grown spaghetti."

Soon after the broadcast ended, the BBC began to receive
hundreds of calls from puzzled viewers. Did spaghetti really
grow on trees, they wanted to know. Others were eager to
learn how they could grow their own spaghetti tree. To this
the BBC reportedly replied that they should "place a sprig of
spaghetti in a tin of tomato sauce and hope for the best." To be
fair to the viewers, spaghetti was not a widely eaten food in
Britain during the 1950s and was considered by many to be
very exotic. Its origin must have been a real mystery to most
people. Even Sir Ian Jacob, the BBC's director general, later admitted that he had to run to a reference book to check on
where spaghetti came from after watching the show. The pres-
tige of the *Panorama* show itself, and the general trust that was
still placed in the medium of television, also lent the claim
credibility. The idea for the segment was dreamed up by one
of the *Panorama* cameramen, Charles de Jaeger. He later said
that the idea occurred to him when he remembered one of his
grade-school teachers chiding him for being "so stupid he
would believe spaghetti grew on trees."

"There's nothing like real, home-grown spaghetti." A Swiss worker harvests the crop from a spaghetti tree. From *Panorama*, April 1, 1957. Source: *BBC Photo Archive.*

Jesters and Tricksters

The Trickster is a difficult figure to categorize. He (or she, though most often they seem to be men) can be mischievous, subvervise, annoying, obnoxious, heroic, and noble—all at the same time. The trickster refuses to be bounded by the rules and limitations created by others, and in struggling against these limits he ends up transforming the world around himself. Almost every world mythology has a tricksterlike character. There is Coyote in Native American myth, Loki in Nordic myth, and Hermes or Prometheus in ancient Greek myth. During the Cold War period tricksters (and their close cousin the jester) proliferated. They symbolized the struggle of the counterculture

against "the system." Two of the most famous literary representations of tricksters were the characters of Yossarian in Joseph
Heller's *Catch-22* and McMurphy in Ken Kesey's *One Flew Over
the Cuckoo's Nest.* Kesey himself, in real life, was quite a trickster. He and a bunch of his friends, calling themselves the
Merry Pranksters, traveled around the country in a psychedelic
bus. One of these Merry Pranksters, Wavy Gravy, was also master of ceremonies at Woodstock in 1969 and later spearheaded
the "Nobody for President" campaign (a highly successful campaign, as Wavy Gravy points out, since in America the majority
of the population consistently votes for nobody). Another well-
known trickster was Abbie Hoffman, author of *Steal This Book,*
who once threw dollar bills onto the floor of the New York
Stock Exchange in order to watch as traders greedily scrambled
to pick them up. The jesters and tricksters to follow all pre-
ferred hoaxing as the specific tool for their mischief.

Alan Abel

During the early fifties Alan Abel headed to New York City,
hoping to establish himself as a comedian. Unfortunately, he
had little luck getting work, so he had to take a desk job at
the American Automobile Association. Bored to tears, he soon
found himself playing pranks on unsuspecting customers by
giving them bizarre driving instructions. It was around this time
that he began to realize that he was more suited to a career as a
full-time prankster than anything else. Still frustrated from trying to break into comedy by traditional routes, he also realized
that hoaxing offered a great way to take matters into his own
hands and gain media exposure that was otherwise being denied to him. His big breakthrough came with the "Society for
Indecency to Naked Animals" hoax that began in 1959 (described more fully later in this chapter). This launched him onto
his career as a hoaxer. A few of his subsequent antics from this
period included orchestrating a campaign to elect Yetta Bron-
stein, a Bronx housewife (but really his wife in disguise), for
president of the United States. He also whipped the media into

a frenzy when he announced the first International Sex Bowl competition in 1969. By the mid-seventies he had succeeded in becoming a well-known public figure. His offbeat career continued on during the eighties and nineties (see next chapter).

Dick Tuck

Dick Tuck was a legendary political trickster who made a career out of making life miserable for Richard Nixon. In 1950, when both men were near the start of their careers, Tuck offered to help organize a campaign rally for Nixon at UC Santa Barbara. But, unbeknownst to Nixon's staff, he booked the largest auditorium possible, on a day when few students were able to attend. As a result, when Nixon showed up to speak, there were forty students waiting to hear him in a four-thousand-seat auditorium. As Nixon's political star began to rise, Tuck continued to torment him. When the 1956 Republican Convention was held in San Francisco, Tuck, learning that the city garbage trucks drove right past the convention hall on their way to the dump, paid the drivers to put signs on the sides of their vehicles that read, "Dump Nixon." Once when Nixon was delivering a speech from the rear platform of a train, Tuck dressed up as a conductor and signaled the train to leave the station, while Nixon was still talking. In 1962 Tuck hired pregnant women to attend Nixon rallies carrying signs that read, "Nixon's the One!" Nixon was infuriated but also inspired by Tuck's pranks. He finally told his staff that they needed to develop a "Dick Tuck capability" of their own. Subsequently Nixon hired Donald Segretti to conduct a dirty tricks campaign against Democratic opponents. Unfortunately, Segretti's pranks tended to be just mean, not funny. This led Nixon to muse once that it "shows what a master Dick Tuck is . . . Segretti's [dirty-tricks campaign] hasn't been a bit similar."

Joey Skaggs

As a young art student in New York City during the mid-sixties, Joey Skaggs aspired to a career as a fairly conventional kind of artist—that is, an artist who created works that are conventionally thought of as art (i.e., things you can hang on a wall or stand in a corner). But as he grew impatient with the rigidity of the art establishment, he began to turn toward performance art. He raised eyebrows when he dragged a skeleton attached to a crucifix around New York City on Easter Sunday in 1967. The public reaction to this stunt proved rather unpleasant, but the manner in which the media discussed the event gave him an idea. Instead of passively allowing the media to report about him, he wondered, why not actively take a role in manipulating what the media said? In other words, why not make the media the canvas he would work on, using hoaxes as his paintbrush? With this idea in mind he set to work. The next year he packed a group of long-haired hippies into a Greyhound bus and led them on a "hippie bus tour" through suburban Queens as part of a satire of middle-class tourism. Then in 1969 he stretched an enormous fifty-foot bra across the steps of the U.S. Treasury building on Wall Street in order to force the media to talk (if only briefly) about the intersection between sex, money, and power in American life. His fame as a hoaxer steadily rose throughout the seventies. At the end of the period covered by this chapter he achieved notoriety with his "Cathouse for Dogs" hoax—a satire of the pet industry in which, much to the consternation of the ASPCA and the NYPD vice squad, he posed as a "dog pimp" running a bordello for dogs. He has continued to hoax the media up to the present day (see next chapter).

I, Libertine

When Jean Shepherd (best known as the author of the 1983 movie *A Christmas Story*) was starting out as a deejay in New York in the mid-'50s, the only time slot he could get was the graveyard shift from twelve to five in the morning. But that didn't bother Shepherd. In fact, he enjoyed it because it gave him the freedom to experiment. Alone in the studio at night, he threw out the scripted, highly packaged format that had been the norm in radio up until that time, and began talking off the top of his head, delivering dark, comedic monologues about whatever was on his mind that day.

Soon he had developed a devoted following. People called in with comments of their own. His listeners, all night-owls, enjoyed a sense of belonging to a secret, close-knit community that existed on the margins of normal society. Shepherd even gave his community of fans a special name. They were the "night people."

One day Shepherd was musing on air about how people let the media and advertising industries control what they thought and did. He commented that people wouldn't even buy a book unless the media told them it was okay to do so by putting it on a best-seller list. This gave him an idea. Could his listeners, working together as a community, manipulate the media to create demand for a nonexistent book? What if they all spread the word about a hot new title? Could they make people want it simply by generating enough word-of-mouth and media buzz?

Shepherd's listeners embraced his plan with a passion. One of them came up with the name for the fake novel: *I, Libertine*. Someone else invented an author: Frederick R. Ewing. They made him an expert on eighteenth-century erotica. The next day legions of the night people trekked out to bookstores to order the book. Puzzled bookstore owners began contacting publishers, inquiring when this novel that everyone was talking about would be released. Before long the book was appearing on soon-to-be-published lists. It was mentioned in magazine and newspaper articles. The archdiocese of Boston even took the proactive step of banning it. Everyone was dying to get their hands on a copy of it.

The news of the night people's hoax was eventually broken by *The Wall Street Journal*. But the story didn't end there. Ballantine Books decided that there was such demand for the novel that it would be a shame not to give the public what it wanted. So it commissioned writer Theodore Sturgeon to pen an actual book titled *I, Libertine*. It came out in 1956 and quickly became a best seller, thereby proving that the right publicity really can sell anything, even a nonexistent product.

Unusual Animals

Strange creatures featured prominently in the tall tales of the nineteenth century. They continued to play a starring role in the hoaxes of the twentieth century. The only difference between the two centuries was that the nineteenth-century tall-tale creatures were typically of indeterminate origin. The human source of their twentieth-century brethren was usually easier to identify.

The Bare-Fronted Hoodwink

Ornithologist M. F. Meiklejohn first described the existence of the mysterious bird known as the bare-fronted hoodwink (scientific name: *Dissimulatrix spuria*) in a 1950 article in the journal *Bird Notes*. Meiklejohn surmised the existence of the hoodwink after a long and careful study of birds "partially seen or indeterminately heard." He determined that all such partial sightings could be attributed to a single species—the hoodwink. According to him the hookwink exhibited a unique talent for being almost seen or almost captured. He advised that bird watchers in the field could recognize the species by its "blurred appearance and extremely rapid flight away from the observer." Amateur bird watchers appeared to have more luck spying it than did more experienced observers. Despite this creature's skill at evasion a specimen of this remarkable species was actually acquired and put on display in the Royal Scottish Museum at Edinburgh on April 1, 1975. Visitors to the exhibit remarked that it looked oddly like a stitched-together patchwork of otherwise unidentifiable bird parts. Accompanying the exhibit were photographs of the hoodwink taken in the field. Unfortunately, in all frames the hoodwink had been "just missed."

Snouters

Snouters, also known as rhinogrades, are an unusual class of creatures best known for the highly specialized development of their noses. The snouters were described for the first and only time in 1957 by a German naturalist named Dr. Harald Stümpke. He found them on the Hi-yi-yi Islands in the Pacific Ocean. There are many different species of snouters, but as a group they have evolved to use their noses for virtually every imaginable function. For instance, the sniffling snouter catches fish with the long, delicate threads that emerge from its nostrils. The perfumed honeytail snouter stands rigidly upright on its thick nose and catches insects with its sticky tail. The suctorial snout leaper uses its long, flat nose to spring itself backward great distances. Unfortunately, the Hi-yi-yi island chain sank into the ocean during the 1950s as a result of an earthquake triggered by an atomic bomb test. When the islands sank, they took with them not only the remarkable snouters, but also Dr. Stümpke himself, who had returned to the islands to further study their unique wildlife. His book, widely considered a classic, is all that remains of the snouters.

Bigfoot

Reports of a large, bipedal, humanoid creature living in the woods of North America have long existed. Native Americans called the creature Sasquatch. But the existence of such a creature could never be confirmed. Then, in October 1967, Roger Patterson and Bob Gimlin claimed to have seen a bigfoot while riding on horseback through the forests of northern California, and they had film footage of the encounter to prove it. The footage showed a large, hairy, upright creature striding along a riverbank before it disappeared into the woods. The film electrified the bigfoot debate. Bigfoot supporters insisted that here was finally the conclusive, undeniable proof of the creature's existence. But skeptics almost immediately cried hoax. They argued that the film showed nothing more than a man in a monkey suit, though they conceded that Patterson may have believed he was filming an actual bigfoot. But who could have made such a convincing monkey suit? All evidence trails led to one of Hollywood's leading special-effects artists, John Chambers, who just happened to be designing the monkey costumes for the movie *Planet of the Apes* in 1967 when Patterson shot his film. Rumors swirled around Hollywood for years linking Chambers to the hoax. The researcher Mark Chorvinsky tracked down and recorded many of these rumors. But Chambers stonily denied everything. The biggest break in the case came in 1997 when the director John Landis (of *Animal House* fame) revealed that Chambers had once confessed the hoax to him. Landis's claim does not close the book on the debate, but it certainly adds fuel to the fire of the hoax theory. Chambers died in August 2001, still denying that he had anything to do with the 1967 bigfoot footage. In the meantime, the debate about the film rages on, and likely will for the foreseeable future

The Society for Indecency
to Naked Animals

G. Clifford Prout was a man with a mission, and that mission was to put clothes on all the millions of naked animals throughout the world. To realize his dream he founded an organization called the Society for Indecency to Naked Animals, abbreviated as SINA (it was left unexplained why the society was "for indecency" not "against indecency"). Prout first appeared before the American public to promote his organization on May 27, 1959, as a guest on NBC's *Today Show*. His appearance generated a huge viewer response, and soon thousands of letters were pouring in to SINA's headquarters (Prout had provided a New York mailing address).

More interviews followed on the success of this first appearance. Wherever he could, Prout expounded on his anti–animal nudity philosophy and repeated his society's catchy mottos:

"Decency today means morality tomorrow" and "A nude horse is a rude horse." Prout urged SINA members (he claimed there were over fifty thousand of them) to take an active role in their communities by confronting people who shamelessly walked their naked pets down the street.

SINA was actually the creation of Alan Abel, who played the role of SINA's vice president while actor Buck Henry performed as Prout. The SINA hoax ran on for years. People were either outraged by the SINA philosophy, or quite taken with it. But surprisingly few called the bluff of Abel and Henry. On August 21, 1962, SINA reached a high point when it was featured on the CBS news with Walter Cronkite. As the segment was airing, some CBS employees recognized that Prout was actually Buck Henry. Henry was, after all, a CBS employee. This brought a formal end to the hoax. But Abel managed to keep the joke going for a few more years by means of a SINA newsletter mailed to the faithful. The newsletter included features such as press releases and sewing patterns for pet clothes.

APRIL FOOLS' DAY HOAXES

The most famous April Fools' Day hoax from this period was, by far, the Swiss Spaghetti Harvest of 1957 (listed in this chapter under *Television Hoaxes*). It set the standard of gentle, tall-tale style humor, which other April Fools' Day hoaxers then sought to follow. A special relationship between the British media and April Fools' Day also began to emerge. But this relationship really reached its peak during the 1980s when British tabloids decided to lay special claim to the day.

Around the World for 210 Guineas

The year 1972 was the hundred-year anniversary of Thomas Cook's first round-the-world travel tour. To commemorate the occasion the *Times* of London ran a full article about Cook's 1872 tour, in which it noted that the vacation had cost the participants only

210 guineas each, or approximately $575. Of course, inflation had made a similar vacation quite a bit more expensive by 1972. A few pages later the *Times* noted that in honor of the hundred-year anniversary, the Thomas Cook travel agency was offering a thousand lucky people the chance to buy a similar package deal at 1872 prices. The offer would be given to the first thousand people to apply. The article noted that applications should be addressed to "Miss Avril Foley." The public response to this bargain-basement offer was swift and enthusiastic. Huge lines of people formed outside the Thomas Cook offices, and the travel agency was swamped with calls. Belatedly the *Times* identified the offer as an April Fools' joke and apologized for the inconvenience it had caused. The people who had waited in line for hours were, to put it mildly, not amused. The reporter who wrote the article, John Carter, was fired (though he was later reinstated).

The Spiggot Metric Boycott

In 1973 Westward Television, a British TV studio, produced a documentary feature about the village of Spiggot. As the documentary explained, the stubborn residents of this small town were refusing to accept the new decimal currency recently adopted by the British government, preferring instead to stick with the traditional denominations they had grown up with. As soon as the documentary was over, the studio received hundreds of calls expressing support for the brave stand taken by the villagers. In fact, many of the callers voiced their intention to join in the antidecimal crusade. Unfortunately for this burgeoning rebellion, the village of Spiggot did not exist.

The Eruption of Mount Edgecumbe

Residents of Sitka, Alaska, were alarmed in 1974 when the long-dormant volcano neighboring them, Mount Edgecumbe, suddenly began to belch out black smoke. Thousands of terrified people spilled out of their homes and onto the streets to gaze up at the volcano, fearful that it was active again and would soon erupt.

Anxious calls poured into the local authorities. Luckily it turned out that man, not nature, was responsible for the smoke. A local prankster named Porky Bickar had flown hundreds of old tires into the volcano's crater and then lit them on fire, all in an attempt to fool the city dwellers into believing that the volcano was stirring to life. Six years later when Mount St. Helens erupted, a Sitka resident reportedly wrote to Bickar to tell him, "This time you've gone too far!"

Planetary Alignment Decreases Gravity

In 1976 British astronomer Patrick Moore announced on BBC Radio 2 that at exactly 9:47 A.M. Pluto would pass behind Jupiter, and that this alignment of the planets would result in a stronger gravitational pull from Jupiter, counteracting the Earth's own gravity and making people momentarily weigh less. He told listeners that they could experience this astronomical phenomenon for themselves by jumping in the air at 9:47. If they did so, he said, they would experience a strange floating sensation. When 9:47 A.M. arrived, BBC2 began to receive hundreds of calls from listeners who claimed that they had felt the sensation. One woman said that she had been seated around a table with eleven friends, and that all of them, including the table, had begun to float around the room. Another caller complained that she had risen from the ground so rapidly that she had hit her head on the ceiling. If the callers did indeed experience this floating sensation, it must be chalked up to the power of suggestion, since the pull of gravity had remained quite constant throughout the day.

Report from Iron Mountain

In 1967, as the war in Vietnam was escalating and race riots were breaking out in many U.S. cities, a book appeared titled *Report from Iron Mountain on the Possibility and Desirability of Peace*. The book, which was described in an introduction as a leaked government document, appeared to confirm what many had feared—that the U.S. government had no desire for peace, ever. Quite the opposite, in fact. The writers of the secret report had concluded that peace "would almost certainly not be in the best interest of stable society" because war was simply too vital a part of the world economy.

The report had apparently been written by a "Special Study Group" (SSG) whose members had convened in 1963 at a nuclear hideout called Iron Mountain. Just in case peace did break out, the SSG had compiled a list of suggestions for the government to follow. Top of the list was the invention of "alternate enemies." The SSG also suggested that the government keep the population in line by scaring citizens with reports of extraterrestrial threats, massive global environmental pollution, and "an omnipresent, virtually omnipotent international police force."

The publication of the report caused a sensation. So many copies of it were sold that it made its way onto *The New York Times* best-seller list, and it was eventually translated into fifteen languages. President Johnson supposedly "hit the roof" when he learned of it. He ordered that cables be sent to U.S. embassies throughout the world instructing them to play down public discussion of the report. If asked directly about it the embassies were to emphasize that the report had nothing at all to do with official U.S. policy.

In 1972 a freelance writer named Leonard Lewin confessed that he had penned the entire thing. In other words there was no Special Study Group and no government plot to maintain a constant state of war. It was all a hoax. The idea for the book had come to him when a friend, Victor Navasky, showed him a *New York Times* article reporting that the stock market had dipped because of a "peace scare." E. L. Doctorow, an editor at the Dial Press, agreed to collaborate in the hoax by publishing the report as nonfiction. Despite Lewin's confession a number of ultraconservative groups continue to insist that the report was real and that Lewin's confession was the actual hoax.

Paul Is Dead

On November 9, 1966, the singer Paul McCartney, band member of the Beatles, died in a fiery car crash. After the accident Paul was surreptitiously replaced by a double known as Billy Shears. But Paul's band mates, who couldn't help trying to share their secret with the world, placed all kinds of clues about Paul's death in their subsequent albums such as *Sgt. Pepper's Lonely Hearts Club Band,* the *White Album,* and *Abbey Road.*

This scenario (of Paul's death in 1966 and subsequent replacement) was the bizarre rumor that swept around the world during the fall of 1969. Beatles fans spent countless hours searching for the clues that supposedly appeared in the albums. The most famous clue could be seen on the cover of *Abbey Road,* which showed John, Ringo, Paul, and George walking across a zebra crossing. Fans argued that this obviously represented a funeral procession. John (in white) was the priest, Ringo (in black) was the undertaker, Paul (barefoot) was the corpse, and George (in jeans) was the gravedigger. A license plate on a car in the street behind the four read "28 IF." This was taken to mean that Paul would have been twenty-eight *if* he were alive.

The researcher Andru Reeve has traced the origin of the "Paul Is Dead" rumor to a song that appeared in May 1969 titled "Saint Paul." The song spoke of Paul being in heaven and may have suggested the idea of his death to some fans. Then in October 1969 the Detroit deejay Russ Gibb played the song "Revolution 9" from the *White Album* backward on the air. As he did so, he claimed that he could distinctly hear the words *Turn me on, dead man* spoken repeatedly. This was the spark that ignited the fire. Soon the rumor of Paul's death had spread to college campuses throughout the world, and then it reached the mainstream media. Hundreds of articles appeared in various magazines pondering the possibility of Paul's death, and John Chancellor even discussed the issue on the NBC evening news. McCartney only inflamed the rumor by refusing to appear in public for almost two months. Finally *Life* magazine tracked him down to his Mull of Kintyre country house and took a photo of him that it ran on its cover, thereby squelching the rumor.

Reeve notes that Lennon and McCartney owned the record company that published the "Saint Paul" song that started the whole ball rolling. This suggested to him the intriguing possibility that the Beatles purposefully planted the rumor. Whether or not they did, they certainly benefited from the massive record sales that the rumor of Paul's death promoted.

The Autobiography of Howard Hughes

Throughout history it's been quite common for forgers to fake diaries and biographies of people who are already dead. After all, the dead tell no tales and can't pop up to deny the work. It's far less common to fake the biography of a living person, for obvious reasons. But this didn't deter the writer Clifford Irving. In one of the boldest forgeries of all time Irving forged an "autobiography" of the eccentric billionaire Howard Hughes— while Hughes was *still alive*. And he almost walked away with $1 million for his efforts.

Hughes had famously retreated from public life in 1958, thereafter refusing to be photographed or interviewed. This behavior created an enormous amount of curiosity about his life. Publishers were dying to print the inside story of how Hughes spent his days, knowing that such a book would be an instant best seller. But unfortunately neither Hughes nor any of his closest associates were talking. Until Irving came along, that is.

In 1971 Irving told his publisher, McGraw-Hill, that Hughes had contacted him after reading and enjoying one of his earlier books. Hughes, he said, wanted to write an autobiography in order to set straight all the lies and rumors that were circulating about his life, and he wanted Irving to ghostwrite the work. Irving produced letters from Hughes (all forged, of course) to prove that the offer was real. McGraw-Hill completely fell for

Irving's story. They eventually gave him almost $1 million in or-
der to secure the rights to the work, and in return Irving handed
them Hughes's "autobiography" a few months later.

The scheme almost worked, until something happened that
Irving hadn't counted on. Hughes actually broke his long media
silence in order to come forward and publicly deny all knowledge of Irving and the autobiography. Irving had figured that
the famous recluse would never break his self-imposed exile.
After returning the money he had taken, Irving spent a short
time in jail. When he got out he wrote the *true* account of how
he had almost gotten away with writing the *fake* autobiography
of Howard Hughes. The fake autobiography itself never saw
the light of day until it was published on the Internet in 1999.

The Stone Age Tasaday

In 1971, as war was raging in Vietnam, the world was introduced to a gentle tribe of Stone Age people known as the
Tasaday who had recently been discovered living in a remote
Philippine rain forest. The Tasaday had apparently never before
had contact with the outside world. In fact, until their discovery
they had believed themselves to be the only people in the
world. Even more intriguingly, the Tasaday were entirely peaceful. It was said that they possessed no words in their language
for enemy, war, or conflict. They were an innocent people living in a primitive Garden of Eden. Their example offered a
sharp contrast to the horrors of modern warfare on display in
Vietnam.

Manuel Elizalde, Jr., a Philippine cultural minister, appointed
himself the protector of the Tasaday and made it his duty to
make sure that they were shielded from the modern world, particularly the media. The media, of course, were clamoring to visit
them. But Elizalde insisted that all interaction with the tribe occur
only under strictly supervised conditions and for limited periods
of time. Nevertheless, reporters were able to obtain numerous

images of the cave-dwelling Tasaday, and these images, which appeared in hundreds of magazines and newspapers throughout the world, captivated war-weary audiences. Then the Marcos government declared martial law in the Philippines in 1972, and all contact with the Tasaday was lost.

Fourteen years later the Marcos government was overthrown. A Swiss journalist named Oswald Iten, who also possessed a doctorate in anthropology, seized the opportunity to trek into the jungle and visit the Tasaday. What he found astounded him. The Tasaday's caves were empty, and the tribe members were living nearby, dressed in western clothing and living a simple, but certainly not primitive, lifestyle. They admitted to Iten that Elizalde had pressured them into posing as a primitive tribe. "He gave us money to pose as Tasaday," they said, "and promised us security from counterinsurgency and tribal fighting."

Images of the peaceful Stone-Age Tasaday captivated war-weary audiences in 1972. But the Tasaday were actually paid to pose as a primitive tribe.   Source: *Bettmann/CORBIS.*

The revelation that the Tasaday were a hoax shocked the world just as much as their initial discovery had. Elizalde continued to insist that the tribe was real. He even flew some of the tribe members to Manila to file a lawsuit against their detractors. While in Manila the Tasaday piously declared that not only had they no word for *war* in their language, they also had no word for *fake*. But anthropologists had become more skeptical. It is now generally agreed that while the Tasaday may have represented an actual ethnic group living in the rain forest, they were certainly not isolated, nor were they primitive. The motive for the elaborate hoax appears to have been political. The Marcos government wanted to use the tribe to promote tourism as well as to project an idyllic view of the Philippines to the outside world.

CHAPTER SEVEN

1977–1989

Australian Icebergs and Cockroach Pills

As the 1970s neared their end, an economic shift began to transform the industrial societies of the world. The stable, centralized control of the Cold War status quo gave way to decentralized, competitive frenzy. This change triggered a wide range of social effects. First of all, it decreased the economic emphasis placed on manufacturing, while increasing the importance of information work and service-sector jobs. It also challenged the power of the massive corporate and government institutions that had provided a sense of stability and order during the middle decades of the twentieth century. Smaller, more nimble institutions arose to take their place. The giant corporate behemoths of the American automobile industry, for example, suddenly faced stiff competition from more agile Japanese firms. Likewise IBM, which had once single-handedly dominated the computer industry, had to completely reinvent itself in order to stay competitive with high-tech start-ups such as Microsoft, Apple, and Intel.

For individuals this economic shift was a double-edged sword. It created opportunities as well as challenges and uncertainties. Young, ambitious college-educated workers (dubbed "yuppies") profited from the rapidly growing information economy and the booming stock market. But many blue-collar workers were shunted out of the relative security of unionized manufacturing jobs and into less stable, lower-paying careers in the service industry. Even for high-paid information workers the idea of lifetime job security became a thing of the past.

The most famous hoaxes of this decade (Rosie Ruiz, Janet Cooke's journalistic inventions, the Hitler diaries, the various stock market frauds) reflected this mood of insecurity and uncertainty. The atmosphere of risk and rapid change fostered what academics refer to as a postmodern sensibility, which basically means that people began to believe that nothing could be taken for granted, not even the most widely assumed truths. All kinds of cultural representations from the 1980s reflected this sensibility. Pop icons such as Boy George challenged basic social assumptions about what it meant to be masculine or feminine, and popular movies such as *Blade Runner* even raised questions about the stability of human identity itself.

The Cloning of a Man

In 1978 David Rorvik made a startling claim—that the world's first human clone had been born. Rorvik was not just a random eccentric whose claim could be dismissed. He was a respected medical reporter for publications such as *Time* and *The New York Times*. He presented the full story of the birth of the clone in a book titled *In His Image: The Cloning of a Man*.

Rorvik's story read like a medical thriller. He told how a team of top scientists had been flown to a secret island location in order to fulfill a millionaire's warped dream of creating a clone as his heir. After five years they succeeded, and the first human clone was born.

Before Rorvik's book even appeared it print it generated controversy. The *New York Post* proclaimed the birth of the clone on its front page on March 3, 1978. The next day it was all over the news. But when scientists were asked what they thought about the claim, they were uniformly skeptical, arguing that such a feat was simply beyond the capabilities of current medical science.

Months later Lippincott and Rorvik found themselves in court when J. Derek Bromhall, a British scientist, sued them for defamation after learning that his research had been cited as the basis for the cloning experiment. The court asked Rorvik to provide concrete evidence of the existence of the cloned boy. He failed to do so. Therefore, the court ruled that Rorvik's book was a "fraud and a hoax." A year later, in 1982, Lippincott agreed to pay an unspecified amount of damages to Bromhall.

Rorvik's motivations for perpetrating the hoax remain unclear. Money might have been a factor, although he lost a great deal of what he earned to legal fees. Alternatively, he might have hoped to draw attention to the ethical issues raised by the startling advances in the biological sciences. During the 1980s these advances spawned the biotechnology industry and in 1997 allowed the (true) cloning of a mammal, a Scottish sheep named Dolly. In this sense, although Rorvik's story was not true, it was, at least, prescient.

Alan Abel

As discussed in the previous chapter, Alan Abel got his start during the 1950s as a jester and hoaxer. During the late 1970s and '80s he continued to practice his irreverent brand of public humor. Ideas for new hoaxes seemed to flow continually from his brain. He even managed to establish himself as something of a professional hoaxer. For a fee he appeared at business conventions posing as a serious speaker whose presentation gradually grew stranger and stranger as it progressed. His stunts succeeded in amusing many and angering others, but they almost always commanded attention.

Omar the Beggar's School for Panhandling

During the 1980s homelessness and panhandling became visible problems in the downtown regions of many major American cities. Part of the problem stemmed from economic conditions, while others attributed it to a decline in government programs for the poor. Whatever the cause, one person seemed to be profiting from the situation: Omar the Beggar. Omar was an ex-executive who had fallen on hard times and found himself living on the street. But apparently, even though life had handed him lemons, he had found a way to "make lemonade" by establishing a school to teach others how to maximize their profits while panhandling on the street. He was profiled on TV, on radio talk shows, in newspapers, and in magazines. He even published a book containing the stories of some of his successful students. But Omar was actually a character created and played by Alan Abel. The idea occurred to Abel after he witnessed a man begging for money in New York City who then drove away in a Mercedes parked around the corner. Abel hired professional actors to portray graduates of his school.

The Death of Alan Abel

On January 2, 1980, *The New York Times* announced the death of Alan Abel on its obituary page. It provided a flattering account of his career, describing him as "a writer, musician, and film producer who specialized in satire and lampoons." It also noted that he "made a point in his work of challenging the obvious and uttering the outrageous." Abel, the column said, had died of a heart attack while at a ski resort. Unfortunately for the *Times* Abel was not actually dead. The news of his death was yet another hoax engineered by Abel and a team of twelve accomplices. It is reported that the editor of the *Times* was so mad at the deception that he vowed never to print Abel's name again. Of course, given Abel's skill at gaining publicity, this was a vow that the editor was unable to keep.

Rosie Ruiz Wins the Boston Marathon

On April 21, 1980, Rosie Ruiz, a twenty-three-year-old New Yorker, was the first woman to cross the finish line in the Boston Marathon. She had achieved the third fastest time ever recorded for a female runner (two hours, thirty-one minutes, and fifty-six seconds), which was made all the more extraordinary by the fact that she looked remarkably sweat free and relaxed as she climbed the winner's podium to accept her wreath. Race officials almost immediately questioned her victory.

The problem was that no one could remember having seen her during the race. Monitors at the various race checkpoints hadn't seen her, nor had any of the other runners. Numerous photographs taken during the race failed to contain any sign of her. It was as if she had never run the race. Finally, a few members of the crowd came forward to reveal that they had seen her jump into the race during its final half-mile. Apparently she had then simply sprinted to the finish line.

As race officials prepared to announce her disqualification, they discovered evidence that she had also cheated during the earlier New York marathon, where she had earned the time that had qualified her to participate in the Boston marathon. Her New York time, it turned out, had been achieved by taking a shortcut on the subway. Officials stripped her of the Boston victory and awarded the title to the real winner, Jackie Gareau.

Ruiz has not been the only marathon contestant to earn a victory dishonestly. In 1904 Fred Lorz won a bronze medal in the Olympics with a little help from an eleven-mile ride in a truck, and in 1991 spectators noticed that the winner of the Brussels marathon, Abbes Tehami, had somehow shaved his moustache off during the race. It turned out that Tehami had only finished the race. His coach had started it for him.

APRIL FOOLS' DAY

 The media has always been a proud upholder of the tradition of April Fools' Day, but throughout most of the nineteenth and twentieth centuries there was no expectation that newspapers or radio stations would always do something in honor of the day. The jokes and pranks, when they did appear, were usually the work of mischievous reporters or editors acting on their own initiative. Expectations began to change during the 1980s, at least in Britain, as an April Fools' Day craze swept the media. It became the norm for media outlets to offer some spoof story in honor of the day, often leading to cases in which serious stories were mistaken as jests. The heightened British enthusiasm for April 1 quickly spread to America and the rest of Europe, but it remained strongest among the British, who produced many of the most memorable April Fools of the decade.

San Serriffe

In 1977 the British newspaper the *Guardian* published a special seven-page supplement to honor the tenth anniversary of the independence of San Serriffe, a small island republic located in the Indian Ocean. A series of articles affectionately described the geography and culture of this obscure nation. It was said to consist of only two islands: Upper Caisse and Lower Caisse. Its capital was Bodoni, and its ruler was General Pica. Included in the supplement were paid advertisements by prominent companies. For instance, Texaco offered the public the chance to compete to win a two-week trip to Cocobanana Beach in San Serriffe, and Kodak asked readers to send in their favorite pictures from vacations spent there. The *Guardian*'s phones rang off the hook all day as readers phoned to get more information about the idyllic island. Unfortunately, the island didn't exist. Typographically astute readers might have noticed that the island's geography and leadership were all named after fonts and other printing terminology. The success of this hoax is generally credited with inspiring the enthusiasm for April Foolery that the British media displayed throughout the 1980s. San Serriffe itself proceeded to become a running gag in the *Guardian*, re-appearing in subsequent years. Part of the joke was that it surfaced in a new location each time it was featured, supposedly because of a bizarre, geological phenomenon that caused the fictitious island to drift slowly around the world.

The Sydney Iceberg

On April 1, 1978, a barge appeared in Sydney Harbor towing a giant iceberg. Sydneysiders were expecting it. Dick Smith, a local adventurer and millionaire businessman (owner of Dick Smith's Foods), had been loudly promoting his scheme to tow an iceberg from Antarctica for quite some time. Now he had apparently succeeded. He said that he was going to carve the berg into small ice cubes, which he would sell to the public for ten cents each. These well-traveled cubes, fresh from the pure waters of Antarctica, were promised to improve the flavor of any drink they cooled. The cubes would be marketed under the brand name Dickciles. A radio station reporter kept up a live broadcast from the iceberg (christened the Dickenberg 1) as it made its way into the harbor. Excitedly the entire city waited to catch a glimpse of the curiosity. Boaters who traveled out to meet the berg were given complimentary cubes. Then it began to rain. The water washed away the firefighting foam and shaving cream that the iceberg was really made of, exposing the white plastic sheets beneath. In this degraded condition the Sydney Iceberg sailed proudly on, floating past the opera house and city skyline. Boaters who now joined the procession were still given free cubes, though the ice actually came from the onboard beer refrigerator.

Dick Smith's Iceberg enters Sydney Harbor on April 1, 1978. When this picture was taken, rain had already washed away most of the "berg."   Source: Dick Smith/Dick Smith Foods.

Operation Parallax

In 1979 a London radio station known as Capital Radio announced that the British calendar had become dangerously out of sync with the rest of the world. Apparently the practice of switching the clocks ahead during British Summer Time had caused the island's time to gradually advance forty-eight hours in front of all other countries. Therefore, the government had decided to institute Operation Parallax, which mandated the cancellation of the fifth and twelfth of April that year, thus resynchronizing Britain with the larger world. Capital Radio received numerous calls as a result of this announcement. One employer wanted to know if she had to pay her employees for the lost time. Another woman was curious about what would happen to her birthday, since it fell on one of the canceled days.

The Eruption of Mount Milton

In 1980 Channel 7 news in Boston concluded its nightly broadcast with a special bulletin announcing that a 635-foot hill in Milton, Massachusetts, known as the Great Blue Hill, had erupted, and that lava and ash were raining down on nearby homes. Stock footage was shown of lava pouring down a hillside. The announcer explained that the eruption had been triggered by a geological chain reaction set off by the recent eruption of Mount St. Helens. After making this announcement he held up a sign that read "April Fool." But it was too late. Panicked residents were already overwhelming the local authorities with frantic phone calls. One man, believing that his house would soon be engulfed by lava, rushed outside carrying his sick wife in his arms. The Milton police continued to receive worried phone calls well into the night. Channel 7 was so embarrassed by the reaction that they later apologized to their viewers and fired the executive producer responsible for the prank.

The British Weather Machine

In 1981 the Manchester *Guardian* reported that scientists at Britain's research labs in Pershore had invented a machine capable of controlling the weather. The article explained that "Britain will gain the immediate benefit of long summers, with rainfall only at night, and the Continent will have whatever Pershore decides to send it." Readers were assured that Pershore scientists would guarantee that it snowed every Christmas in Britain. Accompanying the article was a picture of a disheveled scientist surrounded by scientific equipment. The caption beneath the picture read, "Dr. Chisholm-Downright expresses quiet satisfaction as a computer printout announced sunshine in Pershore and a forthcoming blizzard over Marseilles."

The Interfering Brassieres

In 1982 the London *Daily Mail* reported that a local manufacturer had recently sold ten thousand "rogue bras" that were causing a unique and unprecedented problem, not to the wearers but to the public at large. According to the article the support wire in these bras had been made out of specially treated copper originally designed for use in fire alarms. When this copper came into contact with nylon and body heat, it was producing static electricity, which, in turn, was interfering with local television broadcasts. Apparently the chief engineer of British Telecom became so concerned upon reading the article that he immediately ordered all his female laboratory employees to disclose what type of bra they were wearing.

Sidd Finch

The April 1985 edition of *Sports Illustrated* contained a story about a new rookie pitcher who planned to play for the Mets. His name was Sidd Finch (short for Siddhartha Finch), and he could reportedly throw a ball with pinpoint accuracy at 168 mph, almost fifty percent faster than any previously recorded pitch. Surprisingly, Sidd Finch had never played baseball before. Instead, he had learned the "art of the pitch" in a Tibetan monastery under the guidance of the "great poet-saint Lama Milaraspa." His pitching style was eccentric but extremely effective. With one foot bare he twisted his body backward until he looked "like a pretzel gone loony" and then let fly with the ball, or whatever else he was throwing. Unfortunately, the article noted, there was still some uncertainty about whether Finch would actually play for the Mets. He was still trying to decide between becoming a pitcher or pursuing a career as a French horn player. Nevertheless, Mets fans everywhere rejoiced at the thought that their team might soon acquire this extraordinary pitcher. Almost two thousand readers wrote in to comment on the story. On April 15 the magazine admitted that the story was a hoax, although this was technically unnecessary since its author, George Plimpton, had left an obscure clue within the article itself that revealed the hoax. The subheading of the story read, "He's a pitcher, part yogi and part recluse. Impressively liberated from our opulent life-style, Sidd's deciding about yoga—and his future in baseball." The first letter of these words, taken together, spelled "Happy April Fools' Day! Ah Fib!"

Sidd Finch warms up his pitching arm by throwing a javelin.
Source: Lane Stewart/*Sports Illustrated*.

Jimmy's World

The article that appeared in the *Washington Post* on September 29, 1980, told a heart-wrenching tale. It detailed the life of "Jimmy," a young boy who had become a victim of the thriving heroin trade that was devastating the low-income neighborhoods of Washington, D.C. Caught in a cycle of addiction, violence, and despair, Jimmy had become a heroin addict after his mother's live-in boyfriend introduced him to the drug. As Janet Cooke, the author of the article, described him, "Jimmy is eight years old and a third-generation heroin addict, a precocious little boy with sandy hair, velvety brown eyes, and needle marks freckling the baby-smooth skin of his thin brown arms." She noted that Jimmy aspired to be a heroin dealer when he grew up.

The story immediately generated controversy. Many demanded that Cooke reveal where the boy lived so that he could be helped. But Cooke refused to disclose his location, claiming that she needed to protect her sources and that her life would be in danger from drug dealers if she failed to do so. Meanwhile, the city government launched an intensive search to find him.

As the popular outrage about Jimmy grew, rumors began to swirl around the city suggesting that he didn't exist, that Janet Cooke had simply made him up. The *Post* stood by her and denied these rumors, but everything came to a boil on April 13, 1981, when Cooke was awarded the Pulitzer Prize on account of her story. The editors of the *Post,* who had learned that Cooke had lied about various academic credentials on her résumé, confronted her and demanded that she provide proof of Jimmy's existence. Unable to do so, Cooke finally admitted that she had never met Jimmy and that much of her story was fictitious. Cooke offered her resignation, and the *Post,* humiliated by the incident, returned the Pulitzer Prize.

A year later Cooke appeared on *The Phil Donahue Show* to offer her take on what had happened. She blamed her decision to invent Jimmy on the high-pressure environment of the *Post,* which was still riding high from the journalistic coup it had scored in the early seventies with the Watergate story. She claimed that numerous street sources had hinted to her about the existence of a boy such as Jimmy, but unable to find him, she eventually penned a fictitious story about him in order to satisfy her editors at the *Post,* who were pressuring her to produce something.

In a way the story of Jimmy did convey a truth about conditions that existed in many inner-city regions of America, even though it did not actually tell the truth. Nevertheless, Cooke was disgraced as a journalist and dropped out of the public eye for many years. She briefly reemerged in 1996 to tell her story to the magazine *GQ*. The movie rights from that interview were subsequently sold for $1.5 million.

Joey Skaggs

Joey Skaggs had been perpetrating hoaxes and designing media stunts ever since he was a young artist living in New York City in the late 1960s (see the previous chapter). But it was really in the late 1970s, while teaching at New York's School of Visual Arts, that he began to gain national attention for his work. His pranks have a constant theme: to illustrate the ways that the media functions (or fails to function) in modern life. One of the more obvious lessons of his work is that the media feeds on sensationalism. By simply offering up bizarre, sensational stories Skaggs has been able to hoax the media time after time. In this sense Skaggs stands in the tradition of eighteenth-century hoaxers such as Jonathan Swift and Benjamin Franklin, who also used hoaxes as self-conscious tools for social criticism and enlightenment.

Dr. Gregor's Cockroach Pills

The remarkable physical abilities of cockroaches are well known. They can survive for weeks without food or water; they're incredibly strong for their size; and legend has it that they're impervious to radiation. Therefore, there was a certain logic to the amazing health cure that Dr. Josef Gregor unveiled at a press conference held on May 22, 1981: cockroach-hormone pills. According to him the pills had been proven to remedy a variety of ills, including acne, anemia, allergies, menstrual cramps, and radiation sickness. He even produced seventy patients who were willing to attest to the remarkable curative power of the pills. Over 175 papers printed articles about the new pills, and Dr. Gregor appeared on a variety of TV shows. Finally, in September of that year, Joey Skaggs revealed that he was Dr. Gregor. Surprisingly, no one had noticed that Dr. Josef Gregor was a reference to Gregor Samsa, the main character in Franz Kafka's novel *The Metamorphosis,* which is about a man who turns into a giant cockroach.

The Fat Squad

Americans turned on to fitness during the 1980s. An aerobics craze swept the nation, sending millions of women to the gym to get into shape. Jane Fonda workout videos flew off the shelves, and suddenly it seemed like everyone was going on a diet. The health craze reached a bizarre extreme in 1986 with the founding of the Fat Squad, by Joe Bones, an ex–drill sergeant. The staff of this organization was dedicated to helping their clients lose weight by standing guard beside them twenty-four hours a day. Should a client ever be tempted to snack, the fat squad member would be right there to prevent it. Joe Bones boasted, "Once you hire us, you cannot fire us." This new diet aid received international coverage. It was only exposed as a hoax when Joe Bones appeared on *Good Morning America* and viewers called in who recognized that the fat-hating drill sergeant was actually Joey Skaggs in disguise.

Cold War Hoaxes

By the 1980s the United States and the Soviet Union had been locked in Cold War rivalry for decades. The struggle had simply become a fact of life for those who had grown up knowing no other political reality. But President Reagan's newly aggressive stance toward the Soviet Union raised the rivalry to a new level of cultural awareness, which was reflected in a number of hoaxes. As it turned out, the Cold War was actually progressing through its endgame, culminating in the spectacular collapse of the Berlin Wall in 1989, followed soon afterward by the disintegration of the Soviet Union.

Tass Expands into American Market

On April 1, 1982, the *Gazette* and *Compass*, two weekly newspapers serving the Old Lyme area of Connecticut, both announced that they had been bought out by *Tass*, the official news agency of the Soviet Union. On their front pages they declared that this was "the first expansion of the Soviet media giant outside of the Iron Curtain." They also revealed that after *Tass* had finalized the sale, the publishers of both newly purchased papers had unfortunately been killed in "simultaneous hunting accidents," in which they had shot each other in the back of the head with "standard-issue Soviet army rifles." An accompanying picture showed *Gazette* and *Compass* staff members wearing winter coats and fur hats, and carrying hockey sticks and bottles of vodka. In response to the news the offices of the *Gazette* and the *Compass* received numerous calls offering condolences on the deaths of the publishers. One caller also confessed that he had long suspected the two papers of harboring communist tendencies and offered the opinion that it was only a matter of time before all the papers in the country were communist controlled. When the publishers tried to explain that the article had actually been an April Fools' prank, the caller replied, "You expect me to believe a bunch of Commies?"

Kremvax

In 1984 the Internet was in its infancy. Techie enthusiasts communicated via a text-based, online messaging community called Usenet. Around April 1 a message was distributed to the members of this community announcing that the Soviet Union would soon be joining their network. The message purported to come from Konstantin Chernenko (from the address chernenko @kremvax.UUCP), who explained that the Soviet Union wanted to join Usenet in order to "have a means of having an open discussion forum with the American and European people." The announcement prompted a flood of incredulous responses from the members of Usenet, who had assumed that national security concerns would have forbid such a linkup. Two weeks later the real author of the message, a European named Piet Beerma, revealed that it was all a hoax. Kremvax, as the stunt came to be called, is credited with being the first April Fools' Day prank on the Internet. Six years later Moscow really did join Usenet and mischievously named its domain site Kremvax, after the fictitious predecessor.

Soviet Missile Lands on Air Force Base

On April 1, 1986, an unknown prankster planted a sixteen-foot missile decorated with the hammer-and-sickle symbol of the Soviet Union outside of Andrews Air Force Base near Washington, D.C. The missile was nose-down in the ground, as if it had landed and become embedded in the dirt. It was clearly visible to commuters on their morning drive into work. A sign near the missile read, april fools . . . courtesy of mothers against missiles. Park police quickly cleared the missile away.

California High School Announces War with Soviet Union

On October 31, 1986, the students of Dominguez High School were sitting calmly in their classrooms when a woman's voice came over the intercom to announce that the Soviets had shot down two American planes over the Mediterranean Sea, that war between the two countries had been declared, and that President Reagan had authorized missiles to be launched against the Soviet Union. "This can be the beginning of the end of the world," she warned. The students panicked, fleeing out of their classrooms in terror. A few minutes later the woman made another announcement. The previous news flash had just been a joke. The United States was not at war. The person behind the prank, which gained national media coverage, turned out to be none other than the school's principal, who had authorized it as a Halloween/Homecoming joke.

Aliens and Abductions

During the 1970s and '80s speculation about the existence of UFOs, extraterrestrials, and secret government cover-ups became an accepted part of everyday popular culture. Events such as the widely reported November 1986 sighting of a UFO by the crew of a Japan Air Lines cargo plane helped to fuel interest in the phenomenon, while books such as *Communion* by Whitley Strieber and *Intruders* by Budd Hopkins introduced the concept of alien abductions to mainstream audiences. But inevitably some of the UFOs flying through the night sky were less real than others.

Alternative Three

On June 20, 1977, a documentary called *Alternative Three* was broadcast on British television. The show purported to document a vast global conspiracy reaching to the very highest levels of the American and Soviet governments that involved an effort to abduct the Earth's best and brightest citizens and secretly transport them to a colony on Mars. Scientists had learned during the 1950s that the Earth was facing an unavoidable environmental catastrophe that would result in the almost certain extinction of humanity itself. Faced with this inevitability, the world's governments had decided to create a "Noah's Ark" colony on Mars. The plan to create this colony was referred to as "Alternative Three." The stony-faced earnestness of the show's narrator convinced many that the documentary was real, and after the show concluded local TV stations received numerous calls. But if viewers had watched a little more closely they would have seen that the copyright notice for the show was dated April 1—April Fools' Day (although it was not broadcast on April 1). The producers of the show eventually declared that it had been a joke, but this failed to deter those who by then had become true believers in the documentary. These faithful few continued to insist that "Alternative Three" was real. They argued that, by making the documentary appear to be a fanciful hoax, the world's governments had actually insured that no one would suspect that it had, in fact, disclosed the frightening truth.

UFO Lands Near London

On March 31, 1989, astonished British policemen were sent to investigate a glowing flying saucer that had settled down in a field in Surrey. As the policemen approached the craft with their truncheons held out before them, a door opened in the bottom of the ship and a small figure wearing a silver space suit walked out. The policemen immediately fled in the opposite direction. The alien turned out to be a midget, and the flying saucer was a hot air balloon that had been specially built to look like a UFO by Richard Branson, the thirty-six-year-old chairman of Virgin Records. The stunt combined his passion for ballooning with his love of pranks (and publicity). Branson had taken off in the balloon the day before, planning to land in London's Hyde Park on April 1. But a wind change had blown him down a day early in the Surrey field. The police reported that they had received a surge of phone calls from terrified motorists dialing from roadside emergency phones as the balloon passed over the highway. One of the policemen who approached the craft later admitted, "I have never been so scared in twenty years of being a policeman."

Richard Branson, dressed in an ET costume, poses in front of his UFO balloon.   Source: Simon Townsley/The Times/NI Syndication Ltd.

The Hitler Diaries

The fall of the Third Reich created a thriving market in Nazi memorabilia. On April 22, 1983, the German magazine *Der Stern* announced that it had made the greatest Nazi memorabilia find of all time: a diary kept by Adolf Hitler himself. And this was not just one thin journal. It was a sixty-two-volume mother lode, covering the crucial years of 1932–1945.

The diaries caused a buzz of excitement to sweep through the media. Magazines and news agencies bid for the right to serialize them. Journalists, historians, and World War II buffs eagerly anticipated the insights they would offer into the mind of the twentieth century's most infamous man. Of course, voices of skepticism were raised. Many historians pointed out that Hitler was notorious for not liking to write down his thoughts, but *Der Stern* insisted that it was not possible that the diaries were a fraud. The Cambridge historian Hugh Trevor-Roper, who was given a chance to examine the diaries where they lay in a Swiss Bank, backed the magazine up by declaring his confidence in their authenticity.

The explanation of where the diaries had come from, and why they had remained hidden for so long, was appropriately roundabout. Apparently during the last days of the Third Reich an airplane carrying many of Hitler's personal effects had crashed near Dresden. The diaries were pulled out of the wreckage of the crash and preserved for the next three decades by an East German general. In the early 1980s they were smuggled out of East Germany, one at a time, by the brother of a West German memorabilia dealer named Konrad Kujau. They were then sold to *Der Stern* through the efforts of their reporter Gerd Heidemann for the astronomical price of 9.9 million marks.

Anticipation continued to build about what the diaries would reveal, until a greater number of experts had a chance to examine them and delivered their unanimous verdict: the diaries were clumsy, almost amateurish forgeries. Physically it was clear that the diaries were fake. The whitener and fibers in their paper were of postwar manufacture. The content of the journals was also a dead giveaway. The entries were stupefyingly dull and trivial, not revealing anything novel about Hitler's state of mind. Moreover, most of the entries had simply been plagiarized from a book called *Hitler's Speeches and Proclamations* written by Max Domarus, a former Nazi federal archivist. Even historical errors that Domarus had made were sedulously repeated in the diaries.

Faced with this evidence *Der Stern* grudgingly admitted that it had been duped. The source of the forgery was soon traced to Konrad Kujau, the West German memorabilia dealer. He had written the diaries himself, after having perfected the art of imitating Hitler's handwriting. Heidemann was also accused of having skimmed off over 1.7 million of the marks that had been paid for the diaries. Kujau and Heidemann were both convicted of fraud and sentenced to over four years in prison each.

Talk-Show Hoaxes

During the 1980s people who stayed at home during the day had access to more sources of high-tech entertainment than ever before (TVs, radios, VCRs, compact discs, and personal computers), but simultaneously their access to interpersonal contact was often limited. Daytime TV talk shows began to cater to this audience by offering them a steady diet of talk and gossip that explored the most outrageous aspects of human behavior. Although these shows claimed to be providing a public service by delving into important social issues, critics charged that they more often degenerated into carnival-like spectacle.

FAINT

The January 21, 1985, edition of the *Donahue* show was devoted to a typically unusual subject—gay senior citizens. But few people would later remember the topic of that day's show, because as the live broadcast progressed seven members of the audience proceeded to faint. Concerned by the bizarre outbreak of swooning, Donahue canceled the rest of the show and sent everyone home. The producers theorized that the hot temperature inside the studio might have caused the people to collapse, but a few days later Deborah Harmon, one of the fainters, admitted that she had been paid to do so by the well-known prankster Alan Abel. He had also paid the six other audience members who had fainted. Abel later explained that the stunt was designed as a protest against the deteriorating quality of daytime talk shows. He claimed that a group called FAINT (Fight Against Idiotic Neurotic TV) had spearheaded the protest. "We want to raise the consciousness of the public by going unconscious," he said. This stunt attracted more censure than any of Abel's other pranks because critics charged that it could have inspired panic at a time when there was public concern over the possible spread of Legionnaire's disease.

The Fake Guest Scandal

In November 1987 Tani Freiwald appeared on *The Oprah Winfrey Show* claiming to be a wife married for fourteen years who hated sex. Wes Bailey accompanied her as her unfortunate husband. Then in May 1988 the couple were featured on the *Sally Jessy Raphael* show. But this time Bailey claimed to be a husband afflicted with impotence, and Freiwald posed as a sex worker hired to cure him of his affliction. Finally, in July 1988 the two appeared on *Geraldo*. Now Bailey claimed to be a thirty-five-year-old virgin, and Freiwald accompanied him as a sex surrogate hired by a therapist to ease him out of this condition. In August 1988 the two finally admitted to their serial deception, explaining that their motivation had been the thrill of appearing on national television. The revelation sent shock waves through the media. After all, the deception seemed to confirm what many viewers had long suspected—that a good number of the outrageous guests who appeared on such shows were simply paid actors. The talk shows defended their integrity by pointing out that they had been the ones who had been deceived. After all, in each case the couple had been referred to the shows by a licensed psychologist. The scandal temporarily threatened to damage the credibility of the shows, but only temporarily. Soon everyone was watching and enjoying them again. After all, the tension between reality and deception has long been a staple of American entertainment, dating all the way back to P. T. Barnum (see Chapter Three).

The Tawana Brawley Case

Racial tension, inflamed by economic uncertainty, simmered beneath the surface of 1980s America. All this latent anger came to a boil around an incident that occurred toward the end of the '80s in upstate New York.

On November 28, 1987, a fifteen-year-old black girl named

Tawana Brawley was found lying inside a trash bag. She was covered in feces and racial insults had been scrawled on her body. When questioned by police she claimed that a group of white men, including police officers, had raped and beaten her. The black community rallied around her, and a prominent black leader, the Reverend Al Sharpton, appointed himself her spokesman. Support for Brawley reached its peak on June 15, 1988, when her advisers held a meeting at the Bethany Baptist Church in Brooklyn that was broadcast to an audience of ten million viewers.

However, the material evidence did not back up Brawley's claims. Her body displayed no signs of rape or assault. She was not frostbitten, even though she had supposedly been kept naked in the freezing woods for days. The feces on her body turned out to be from a neighbor's dog, and even more damningly, a local resident of the apartment community where she was found claimed to have seen her climb into the trash bag alone and lie down of her own accord.

In October 1988 a grand jury issued a report following a seven-month investigation, in which it concluded that Brawley's claims were a hoax. Many speculated that Brawley had made up a wild story in order to avoid punishment at the hand of her stepfather for having run away from home for three days. But Brawley herself insisted that she was telling the truth, a stance that she has maintained to this day. More than anything else, the episode and its bitter aftermath displayed the deep racial divisions that still haunted American society.

Financial Hoaxes

The 1980s were a boom time in the stock market. Hollywood captured this mood of rampant speculation in movies like *Wall Street,* in which the character of Gordon Gecko (played by Michael Douglas) declared that "greed is good." Stocks rose to dizzying heights, then crashed back down again on October 19, 1987 (aka Black Monday), when the Dow Jones Industrial Average plunged twenty-two percent in one day. During this decade efforts to scam the markets proliferated (though in hindsight such deceptive financial activity seems a mere prelude to the excesses of the 1990s). For instance, in 1988 a bogus claim of a large investment in General Cinema Corporation caused a temporary spike in that company's stock price, while in 1989 false rumors halted trading in a number of stocks including IBM, Pan Am, and NWA. These were fairly straightforward instances of manipulation through misinformation, but a number of other cases from this decade were slightly more unusual.

Dayton Hudson

On June 23, 1987, P. David Herrlinger, a forty-six-year-old investment adviser working out of Cincinnati, called up the Dow Jones News Service and informed them that he represented a large private investment firm that was about to offer to buy the retailer Dayton Hudson for $6.8 billion. The news immediately triggered a $9 spike in the company's stock price. Unfortunately the news was completely bogus. The sad part was that Herrlinger was not your run-of-the-mill scam artist. On the contrary he was diagnosed as suffering from manic depression and was no longer making rational decisions. When his co-workers asked him what he was doing, he gleefully replied, "We're going to make some money," and when confronted with the obvious fact that he lacked the financial resources necessary to make a $6.8 billion offer on Dayton Hudson, he commented, "An offer is really an intangible thing." Herrlinger, who was subsequently hospitalized that same day, later argued through his lawyer that Dow Jones bore the responsibility for disseminating the fake takeover bid, on the logic that they should never have believed him in the first place. In the aftermath of the hoax many expressed concern at the ease with which a single irrational individual had been able to manipulate the market.

Savings and Loan Branch Opens on the Moon

American savings and loan banks (S&Ls) were created to offer low-interest loans to home buyers. But during the early
1980s the federal government began easing regulations that had
controlled the sort of clients to whom the S&Ls could loan
money and at what interest rates. The result was a rapid expansion of the S&L industry, financed through the extension of numerous questionable loans. The Lamar Savings and Loan in
Austin, Texas, was one of the most aggressive in its expansion,
and in 1984 it set a standard for overly optimistic growth that
has never since been topped. It announced that it would be
opening a new branch on the moon, and it submitted a formal
application with the Texas Banking Commission to obtain permission to do so. It even boasted that the science-fiction writer
Ben Bova had become the first person to open an account in its
moon branch. Unfortunately the commission denied its request.
In 1988 the Lamar S&L became a victim of its own aggressive
growth. It collapsed along with many other insolvent S&Ls,
thereby contributing to a widespread financial disaster that ulti-
mately cost taxpayers over $200 billion.

CHAPTER EIGHT

1990–1999

Crop Circles and Cross-Dressing Ken

The 1990s represented the full coming-of-age of the age of information. Increased computing power, combined with technologies such as fiber-optic phone lines and communications satellites, translated into a new wealth of information that became available to a broad segment of society. This information explosion occurred with startling rapidity. At the start of the decade few people beyond a handful of academic and military researchers used e-mail or any form of Internet service (the World Wide Web hadn't even been created yet), but by the decade's end all of these technologies had become mainstream. As more and more people plugged into the "information superhighway," the amount of data flowing along it increased exponentially. But the sheer amount of facts, figures, and competing claims thus made available also created a paradox. There was more data there than anyone could meaningfully process, and the bewildering array of resources and points of view floating around in cyberspace meant that it was extremely difficult to distinguish the worthwhile from the irrelevant.

The decentralized, decontextualized nature of the Internet proved to be the feature most advantageous to hoaxers. Because the Internet allowed communication over large distances from diverse inputs, it often stripped away contextual information that would allow people to weigh the credibility of its sources. All that remained were the naked claims themselves, devoid of identifying features. Hoaxers and criminals used this anonymity to ensnare victims. They posted fake information on Internet message boards, used multiple aliases to make it appear that information was coming from many sources, adopted fake personae when logging on to chat rooms, created bogus Web sites designed to imitate legitimate enterprises, and barraged victims with misleading e-mails. They could do this because it was impossible to see who was really behind that screen name or that e-mail address. The broader identifying context had been removed.

Although the nineties started out with a wave of optimism stemming from the introduction of all the new technologies, the cultural mood became considerably darker as the problem of establishing trust and reliability in the free-wheeling environment of the Internet became apparent. People began to realize that the information avalanche was meaningless without a way to distinguish good information from bad. Anxieties were expressed about whether technology and the Internet had made our culture vulnerable in new ways. Loss of privacy, cyberterrorism, and identity theft became new problems to worry about. Throughout the decade hoaxes both dramatized and made light of such concerns, while also prompting discussion about what appropriate solutions to the dilemma of information overload should be.

Crop Circles

Apart from the Internet the phenomenon that was most consistently associated with hoaxing during the nineties was the repeated discovery of crop circles in fields throughout the world, particularly in southern England. Fierce debate swirled around the question of who or what had created these circles. Were they signs left by extraterrestrials, marks left by unusual weather phenomena, or the handiwork of hoaxers? It seemed that the only thing that everyone agreed on, no matter what position they adopted in the larger debate, was that the phenomenon definitely included a healthy dose of humbug.

Operation Blackbird

Crop circles really began to seize the imagination of the public during the late 1980s. By 1990 a full-fledged media frenzy surrounded them. In the summer of 1990 a group of researchers, who described themselves as "cerealogists," set out to solve the mystery once and for all. They camped out on a hillside in Wiltshire, the world capital of crop circles, and waited with banks of recording equipment for a crop circle to form. Operation Blackbird, as it was called, was a high-tech affair sponsored by British and Japanese television networks and aided by the British army. On July 25 the operation seemed to meet with success. The lead researcher, Colin Andrews, excitedly announced to the waiting media that a circle had formed during the night in an adjacent field. Unfortunately he spoke too soon. When the researchers examined the circle more closely, they realized that it was extremely crudely made. Hardly the sophisticated work one would expect from an alien spaceship. In addition, a board game called Horoscope and a wooden crucifix had been suggestively left behind in the middle of the swirled stalks. In other words it appeared that someone was deliberately playing games with the cerealogists. The identity of the prankster has never been determined, but the event seriously undermined the efforts of the cerealogists to be taken seriously. Conspiracy theorists insisted that the army itself had perpetrated the hoax in an effort to undermine the credibility of the researchers.

Doug and Dave

In September 1991 two Englishmen, Doug Bower and Dave Chorley, stepped forward to take credit for the entire crop-circle phenomenon. According to this pair, who were both in their sixties, their activities had begun as a lark back in the late 1970s. They had wanted to fool people into thinking that UFOs had landed. Their hobby had then gradually evolved into an obsession, involving night after night of circular toil in the fields of England. The tools of their trade were disarmingly simple, being nothing more than wooden planks and string. Armed with this equipment the two were able to demonstrate the ability to fashion crop circles similar to many that had been found. But cerealogists noted that it strained credibility to think that the pair had created all the hundreds of circles that had been discovered in the past decade, and they certainly could not have been responsible for the circles outside of England. The media hyped Doug and Dave's revelation, and as a consequence many dismissed the entire phenomenon as their work. But over time even circle skeptics began to question Doug and Dave's confession. What evidence was there to support their claim of having created hundreds of circles throughout the '80s? Were they themselves just publicity seekers? To this day these questions have not been answered, leaving it unclear how many circles Doug and Dave were actually responsible for.

The BMW Crop Circle

Demonstrating the international nature of the crop-circle phenomenon, a circle appeared in a field of rye located outside of Johannesburg, South Africa, during the first week of February 1993. The South African media excitedly speculated whether it was the work of a UFO. Newspapers and TV and radio shows all discussed it, fanning interest in the phenomenon, until February 14, when a small detail was pointed out that had previously escaped almost everyone's notice: the circle formed a BMW logo. The circle turned out to be the work of the Hunt Lascaris ad agency, working on behalf of BMW. TV commercials soon followed, showing aerial views of the circle accompanied by the tag-line "Perhaps there is intelligent life out there after all." All in all, Hunt Lascaris reckoned that it garnered over $1 million worth of free publicity from the stunt.

The BMW crop circle that appeared outside of Johannesburg, South Africa, in 1993.   Source: BMW South Africa.

Cross-dressing Ken

In July 1990 Carina Guillot and her twelve-year-old daughter, Jocelyn, were visiting relatives in Florida when they wandered into a Toys "R" Us store and spotted something very unusual. Standing there inside a sealed cardboard package among the ranks of Ken dolls dressed in their standard-issue outfits was one very unique Ken decked out in a purple tank top and sporting a lace apron on top of a polka-dotted skirt. Mrs. Guillot immediately thought, *Oh, my God, now we have a cross-dressed Ken.*

Being avid collectors of Ken and Barbie dolls, Carina and Jocelyn Guillot knew that this was no run-of-the-mill Ken. They immediately took the doll up to the front of the store, where the employees examined it and confirmed that the packaging and seal were intact. This appeared to be a valid, untampered Mattel product. Excitedly, the Guillots bought the doll and took it home.

Within days news of the cross-dressing Ken had reached the

national media. It was featured everywhere: in national newspapers, on the radio, and even on TV programs such as *The
Arsenio Hall Show* and *The Joan Rivers Show*. Mattel was at a
loss to explain how this one doll had managed to break ranks
and shine forth in his true colors. Pundits theorized that Ken
had finally gotten sick of living in Barbie's shadow and had
come out of the closet once and for all. This truly appeared to
be a Ken doll for the nineties. The Ken frenzy reached a peak
when a collector offered the Guillots $2,000 for the doll, quite a
markup from the $8.99 they had paid a few days before. Re-
portedly someone else then bid $4,000. The Guillots turned the
offers down.

The speculation finally came to an end when a Toys "R" Us
night clerk, named Ron Zero, admitted that he had dressed up
the Ken doll as a prank and had then carefully resealed the

Ken comes out of the closet. The Guillots display their
cross-dressing find.   Source: Marianne Barcellona, 1990.

package with white paper glue. "We always did crazy things like that," Zero explained. "We'd hang dolls in the aisle or put Ken and Barbie in the Barbie house with Barbie spanking Ken." Toys "R" Us found Zero's prank so amusing that they fired him four days after he confessed.

Milli Vanilli

In 1988 the German record producer Frank Farian discovered Robert Pilatus and Fabrice Morvan (Rob and Fab) while they were living in Munich. Impressed by their charisma and chiseled good looks, Farian formed them into a pop group that he dubbed Milli Vanilli. Their success was almost instantaneous. They rocketed to stardom on the strength of their hit singles, "Girl You Know It's True" and "Blame It on the Rain." Their debut album sold over seven million copies, and they won a 1989 Grammy as best new artist.

But there was an ugly truth lurking behind the attractive façade presented by Rob and Fab: they possessed almost no musical abilities whatsoever. They couldn't play instruments, write music, or even sing. All of their songs had been created in a studio by professional musicians. Whenever Rob and Fab performed onstage, they simply lip-synched the words. Embarrassed by the situation, Rob and Fab confronted Farian and insisted that he allow them to sing on their next album. Farian, however, had no interest in agreeing to this, so on November 14, 1990, he revealed in an interview that their act was a sham. The news rocked the music industry, and the media latched on to the story with a passion. For many critics Rob and Fab's deception seemed to be a perfect representation of the artificial, prepackaged nature of the pop music industry itself.

Rob and Fab bravely tried to soldier on after the revelation. They recorded an album using their own names, but the effort failed miserably. Scorned by the music industry and ridiculed by the public, they drifted into the half-light of notoriety. In

1998 Rob Pilatus apparently succumbed to the cloud of censure hanging over him. He was found dead in a hotel room due to a drug overdose. He was only thirty-two years old.

APRIL FOOLS' DAY HOAXES

For centuries pundits have been predicting the imminent demise of April Fools' Day. For instance, as early as 1874 *The New York Times* declared that the April Fool custom "dies out apace, and if it has any tangible existence at all, it is among small boys." The 1990s proved such critics wrong. April Foolery became more popular than ever and spread to a wider audience than ever before, aided by the rise of the Internet, which proved to be a perfect medium for disseminating pranks. In addition, corporations newly embraced the event as a tool for generating free publicity, and as the economic barriers between communist and capitalist states began to erode, April foolery flourished in China and Russia. All in all the centuries-old custom produced some of the most memorable hoaxes of the decade.

Nixon for President

In 1992 National Public Radio's *Talk of the Nation* program reported that former president Richard Nixon had declared his candidacy for the Republican presidential nomination. Accompanying the announcement were audio clips of Nixon delivering his candidacy speech. He was heard declaring, "I never did anything wrong, and I won't do it again." NPR also played reactions to Nixon's announcement, including a clip from Torrie Clarke, press secretary of the Bush-Quayle campaign, in which she said, "We are stunned and think it's an obvious attempt by Nixon to upstage our foreign policy announcement today." Listeners reacted viscerally to the announcement, flooding NPR with calls expressing shock and outrage. It was only during the second half of the program that host John Hockenberry revealed the announcement to be a joke. Nixon's voice had been impersonated by comedian Rich Little.

China Ends One-Child Policy . . . for PhDs

China's state-imposed limit of one child per couple, designed to curb the nation's rapid population growth, had long been the subject of controversy and international condemnation. So it caused excitement when, in 1993, the *China Youth Daily*, an official state newspaper of China, announced that the draconian policy was being lifted, even though only for holders of PhDs. Apparently the state had decided that encouraging highly educated couples to breed would, in the future, reduce the need to invite foreign experts into the country to help with the state's modernization efforts. The startling announcement was immediately picked up and disseminated by Hong Kong's *New Evening News* and the *Agence France-Press*. Unfortunately these news agencies had not noticed the small disclaimer at the bottom of the article identifying it as a joke. The Chinese government responded to the *China Youth Daily*'s hoax by condemning April Fools' Day as a dangerous Western tradition. Speaking through the *Guangming Daily*, Beijing's main newspaper, it declared that April Fools' jokes were "an extremely bad influence," and added, "Put plainly, April Fools' Day is Liar's Day."

Drunk Driving on the Internet

A 1994 article in *PC Computing* magazine described a bill numbered SB 040194 going through Congress that would make it illegal to use the Internet while drunk or to discuss sexual matters over a public network. The article warned that the bill would grant the FBI the power to tap the phone line of anyone who "uses or abuses alcohol" while accessing the Internet. It also cautioned that passage of the bill was a near certainty because "who wants to come out and support drunkenness and computer sex?" The author of the article, John Dvorak, offered this explanation for the bill's origin: "The moniker 'Information Highway' itself seems to be responsible for SB 040194. . . . I know how silly this sounds, but Congress apparently thinks being drunk on a highway is bad no matter what kind of highway it is." The article generated so many outraged phone calls to Congress that Senator Edward Kennedy's office had to release an official denial of the rumor that he was a sponsor of the bill. Clues that the article was a hoax included the bill's number, 040194 (i.e., 04/01/94). In addition the name of the contact person listed at the bottom of the article was Lirpa Sloof, "April Fools" spelt backward.

The Taco Liberty Bell

In 1996 the fast food chain Taco Bell took out a full-page ad in *The New York Times* to announce that they were purchasing the Liberty Bell and renaming it the Taco Liberty Bell. Their reason for doing this was to "do their part to reduce the country's debt." In a related release the company pointed out that corporations had been adopting highways for years, and that Taco Bell was simply "going one step further by purchasing one of the country's greatest historic treasures." Thousands of people called the National Historic Park in Philadelphia, where the Liberty Bell was housed, to angrily protest the selling of the bell. Taco Bell kept a straight face until noon, at which point it revealed that the earlier press releases were jokes. Soon afterward Mike McCurry, the White House spokesperson, responded to the jest by declaring that the federal government would also be "selling the Lincoln Memorial to Ford Motor Company and renaming it the Lincoln-Mercury Memorial." The hoax paid off for Taco Bell. Their sales during the first week of April shot up by over half a million dollars.

TACO BELL BUYS THE LIBERTY BELL.

IN AN EFFORT TO HELP THE NATIONAL DEBT, TACO BELL IS

PLEASED TO ANNOUNCE THAT WE HAVE AGREED TO PURCHASE THE

LIBERTY BELL, ONE OF OUR COUNTRY'S MOST HISTORIC TREASURES.

IT WILL NOW BE CALLED THE "TACO LIBERTY BELL" AND WILL

STILL BE ACCESSIBLE TO THE AMERICAN PUBLIC FOR VIEWING.

WHILE SOME MAY FIND THIS CONTROVERSIAL, WE HOPE OUR

MOVE WILL PROMPT OTHER CORPORATIONS TO TAKE SIMILAR ACTION

TO DO THEIR PART TO REDUCE THE COUNTRY'S DEBT.

TACO BELL
NOTHING ORDINARY ABOUT IT.

Taco Bell's full-page ad in *The New York Times* announcing its purchase and renaming of the Liberty Bell, April 1, 1996. Source: Taco Bell Corp.

The transfer of the bell. The CEO of Taco Bell (left) accepts ownership of the Liberty Bell from Benjamin Franklin, April 1, 1996. Source: AP/Wide World Photos.

Life Discovered on Jupiter

The Internet-based service America Online grew rapidly throughout the 1990s, demonstrating the power of the Internet to serve as a new basis for mass communication. By 1996 it had gained five million subscribers. When these subscribers logged on to the service on April 1 they were greeted with a news flash that read, "Government source reveals signs of life on Jupiter." This headline was backed up by statements from a planetary biologist and an assertion by Ted Leonsis, AOL's president, that his company was in possession of documents proving that the government was hiding the existence of life on the massive planet. The story quickly generated over 1,300 messages on AOL. When it turned out to be a prank, many questioned whether the service had risked losing its credibility by perpetrating such a stunt, but AOL dismissed these concerns. A spokeswoman for the company later explained that the hoax had been intended as a tribute to Orson Welles's 1938 Halloween broadcast of the *War of the Worlds* (see Chapter Five).

Left-handed Whoppers

In 1998 Burger King published full-page advertisements announcing the introduction of a new item to their menu: "Left-Handed Whoppers" specially designed for the 32 million Americans who are left handed. According to the advertisement the new sandwich included the same ingredients as the original Whopper (lettuce, tomato, hamburger patty, etc.), but these ingredients had been "rotated 180 degrees, thereby redistributing the weight of the sandwich so that the bulk of the condiments will skew to the left, thereby reducing the amount of lettuce and other toppings from spilling out the right side of the burger." The advertisement noted that the left-handed Whopper would initially be available only in the United States, but that Burger King was "considering plans to roll it out to other countries with large left-handed populations." According to the company thousands of customers visited its stores on April 1 to request the new sandwich. In addition there were many who wanted to know if a right-handed version was available.

Alabama Changes Value of Pi

In 1998 an article appeared on the Internet claiming that the Alabama legislature had voted to change the value of the mathematical constant pi from 3.14159 . . . to the "Biblical value" of 3.0. According to the article NASA engineers in Huntsville were up in arms about the decision. The story first appeared as a posting on the Usenet group "talk.origins." It also ran in the April issue of the *New Mexicans for Science and Reason* newsletter. But before long it had spread across the country, forwarded by people who received it in their e-mail. Soon the Alabama legislature was receiving calls from angry citizens protesting the legislation. Thankfully there was no truth to the story. It had originally been posted by a New Mexico physicist named Mark Boslough, who had intended to parody legislative attempts to circumscribe the teaching of evolution in classrooms. The Indiana House of Representatives actually had once considered changing the value of pi, back in 1897. But being that it's a mathematical constant, pi is quite beyond the power of any state legislature to change.

Webnode

In 1999 a press release was issued over Business Wire announcing the creation of a new company called Webnode. This company, according to the release, had been granted a government contract to regulate ownership of "nodes" on the "Next Generation Internet." Each of these nodes (there were said to be over 50 million of them) represented a route that data could travel. The company was licensed to sell each node for $100. Nodes would increase in value depending on how much traffic they routed, and owners would also receive usage fees based on the amount of data that flowed across their section of the Internet. Therefore, bidding for the nodes was expected to become quite intense. Although Webnode was not yet a publicly traded company, the press release declared that shares in the company could be reserved for later purchase, although no money would presently be accepted. Readers were directed to the company's Web site, webnode.com, for more information. The "Next Generation Internet" was a real government project, leading many to assume that Webnode was a legitimate enterprise. But in actuality it was not. It was a prank created by a group of investors who had met on the Silicon Investor financial Web site. Business Wire didn't find their prank amusing. It filed a suit against them alleging fraud, breach of contract, defamation, and conspiracy.

Russia Sells Lenin's Body

Following the collapse of the Soviet Union in 1989, the Russian government struggled to mend its ailing economy, but the nation's financial situation remained dire. In November 1991 *Forbes FYI*, an American business magazine, revealed just how hopeless the Russian economic situation had become: The Russian government, desperate for foreign currency, had apparently decided to sell the embalmed body of Vladimir Lenin to the highest bidder. The body had been on public display in a Red Square mausoleum for decades. It was said that the Russians would start the bidding at $15 million. ABC News and *USA Today* both repeated the story before the editor of *Forbes FYI* revealed that it was a hoax. Russian interior minister Viktor Barannikov denounced the joke as "an impudent lie."

Grungegate

In the early nineties grunge was the musical fad of the moment: greasy-haired, lumberjack-shirted garage bands playing punk-metal guitar rock. Groups such as Nirvana, Soundgarden, and Mudhoney epitomized this new Seattle-based sound. On November 15, 1992, *The New York Times* published an article analyzing the roots and evolution of the grunge movement. It theorized that grungers had embraced greasy hair and lumberjack shirts as a way to rebel against the vanity and flashy style of the eighties. The *Times* also reported that, just like any self-respecting subculture, the grungers had developed their own lexicon of "grunge speak." Grunge terms, according to the *Times*, included literary gems such as *cob nobbler* (a loser), *lamestain* (an uncool person), *wack slacks* (old, ripped jeans), and *swingin' on the flippity-flop* (hanging out).

Three months later, a small Chicago-based magazine called *The Baffler* revealed that the *Times* had been the victim of a hoax. The grunge terms didn't exist. Megan Jasper of Seattle-based Caroline Records, whom the *Times* had used as its source for the glossary, had simply made the words up. *The Baffler* gloated that "when the Newspaper of Record goes searching for the Next Big Thing and the Next Big Thing piddles on its leg, we think that's funny." As if to rub it in, members of the grunge band Mudhoney began using the fake terms during interviews. The *Times* responded that the prank was "irritating."

Microsoft Buys the Catholic Church

In 1994 a press release began circulating around the Internet claiming that Microsoft had bought the Catholic Church. The press release, which bore a Vatican City dateline, noted that this was "the first time a computer software company has acquired a major world religion." The release then quoted Microsoft chairman Bill Gates as saying that he considered religion to be a growth market and that "the combined resources of Microsoft and the Catholic Church will allow us to make religion easier and more fun for a broader range of people." Under the terms of the deal Microsoft would acquire exclusive electronic rights to the Bible and would make the sacraments available online.

Most of the release was clearly parody. For instance, it compared the business practices of Microsoft to the Catholic Church's historical conversion efforts, claiming that throughout history the Church, like Microsoft, had been "an aggressive competitor, leading crusades to pressure people to upgrade to Catholicism, and entering into exclusive licensing arrangements in various kingdoms whereby all subjects were instilled with Catholicism, whether or not they planned to use it." Despite the parody, a number of readers were apparently confused and telephoned Microsoft's public relations agency to inquire if the news was true. This prompted Microsoft to issue a formal denial of the release on December 16, 1994.

This was the first Internet hoax to reach a mass audience. Its success signaled the enormous power of the new online technology to disseminate information, or misinformation, in ways that sidestepped the traditional gatekeepers of the media. A follow-up release announced that, in response to Microsoft's acquisition of the Catholic Church, IBM had bought the Episcopal Church.

The Sibuxiang Beast

On the evening of September 19, 1994, a stark warning was repeatedly broadcast to the TV viewers in Taiyuan, a city in northern China. A message scrolled across an otherwise blank screen warning people that the horrifying Sibuxiang beast, a mythical creature whose bite was said to be fatal, was not only real, but on the loose and heading toward the city. "It is said that the Sibuxiang is penetrating our area from Yanmenguan Pass and within days will enter thousands of homes," the message read. "Everyone close your windows and doors and be on alert."

The residents of Taiyuan panicked. Many of them barricaded themselves inside their homes, fearing to go out. Others called the local authorities to find out what was happening.

As it turned out, the Sibuxiang beast was quite real, but it was not an animal. It was a new brand of liquor. The TV message, in other words, had been an advertisement. The panicked viewers had failed to realize this, even though the message had ended with the phrase "Plotted by Jinxin Advertising."

The confusion stemmed from the relative novelty of TV commercials in China. Most Chinese commercials involved little more than a product shot and a voice-over. The Sibuxiang commercial, because it did not fit this mold, was not recognized for what it was.

Foreign commentators excitedly heralded the ad as evidence of the growing presence of capitalist innovation in China. Chinese authorities were not so pleased. They fined Jing Huiwen, its creator, 5,000 yuan (about $590) for causing a public panic. But Jing figured that paying the fine was a bargain considering the amount of publicity the ad generated. The commercial and ensuing panic were discussed on all the news shows throughout China, causing Sibuxiang liquor to become a well-known brand overnight. Three months after the ad aired, Jing reported that his client base had quadrupled.

A Call to Queen Elizabeth

On October 30, 1995, the citizens of Quebec were scheduled to vote on whether Quebec would separate from Canada. Naturally Canada's politicians were extremely nervous about this possibility, and it was in this context that Queen Elizabeth, sovereign of Canada as well as of England, accepted a call a few days before the referendum from Jean Chretien, the Canadian prime minister.

Chretien and the queen spoke for approximately seventeen minutes. During the call Chretien repeatedly referred to how nervous he was about the upcoming referendum, and he asked the queen if she would consider speaking on Canadian television in favor of a united Canada. The queen replied that she would consider doing so, if Chretien would fax her a sample of what he would like her to say.

It was at this point that the call began to grow a little odd. Chretien commented that the queen should keep her comments as short "as the ingredients on a cornflake box." He then began to inquire about the queen's plan for Halloween. "You are not going so far as to wear a costume?" he asked. "No, no," the queen replied.

Unbeknownst to the queen she wasn't talking to Jean Chretien at all. The man on the other end of the phone was Pierre Brassard, a deejay at a Montreal radio station famous for his ability to impersonate Canadian politicians. Brassard later broadcast a shortened version of the conversation over the air.

News of the hoax stunned the Canadian and British publics. Angry questions were raised about the lack of security precautions surrounding the queen. Brassard, however, noted that security was not that loose. He had only succeeded in contacting her with the help of a team of seven researchers, and even then a large measure of luck had been needed to pull it off.

Ironically, the hoax ended up playing in the queen's favor because the public rallied to her defense. In addition, listeners were fascinated simply to hear the queen in a rare, unscripted situation of this kind. The *Sunday Mirror* commented that she sounded like "a cross between a busy housewife and a multi-lingual, clued-up businesswoman."

The Sokal Hoax

An article in the spring 1996 issue of *Social Text,* a journal of cultural studies, bore the turgid title "Transgressing the Boundaries: Toward a Transformative Hermeneutics of Quantum Gravity." It was authored by Alan Sokal, a professor of physics at New York University. *Social Text* articles didn't usually receive coverage in the mainstream media. After all, the journal catered to a relatively small group of intellectuals. But this particular article created an international whirlwind of controversy that resulted in the names of both Alan Sokal and *Social Text* being plastered across the front pages of newspapers worldwide.

What created the controversy was not what the article said, but rather what it didn't say. Sokal argued that the traditional concept of gravity was a capitalist fiction. He urged that it be replaced by a new theory, called "quantum gravity," that was more compatible with the ideologies of socialism, feminism, and relativism. He also noted that science for too long had been burdened by its pursuit of absolute truth. What Sokal didn't mention was that he was joking.

On the day that the spring issue of *Social Text* appeared in print, Sokal simultaneously published a letter in the academic trade publication *Lingua Franca* revealing that his article was a parody. He skewered the editors of *Social Text* for their apparent failure to recognize this. "Any competent physicist or mathematician (or undergraduate physics or math major) would realize that it is a spoof," he asserted. He suggested that their uncritical acceptance of his piece pointed to "an apparent decline in the standards of rigor in certain precincts of the academic humanities."

At heart Sokal seemed to be offended by the radical ideas about science bandied about by the editors of *Social Text* and their generally left-wing readers. In this sense his hoax recalled the tactics used to discredit radical influences in art and poetry during the early decades of the twentieth century (see the Spectric poetry and Disumbrationist art hoaxes in Chapter Five). But many, especially those who enjoyed watching intellectuals get taken down a notch, applauded Sokal's actions. The editors of *Social Text,* meanwhile, squirmed and blushed, and then grew angry, vocal, and indignant. By doing so, it is widely agreed, they only succeeded in digging themselves deeper down the hole into which they had fallen.

Allegra Coleman

Esquire magazine's November 1996 cover featured Allegra Coleman, the hot new star said to be taking Hollywood by storm. "Forget Gwyneth, Forget Mira," the cover trumpeted. "Here's Hollywood's next Dream Girl."

The feature article inside gushed about the buzz building around her. David Schwimmer, star of *Friends,* was said to be her on-again, off-again boyfriend, although he was getting some competition from Quentin Tarantino, who had apparently dumped Mira Sorvino to go out with her. It was even rumored that Woody Allen had completely overhauled his next movie so that she could star in it. "The real thing," the article asserted. "She has it."

The source of Allegra's appeal was not entirely clear. "Her nature is spongy and luminescent," the self-help guru Deepak Chopra was quoted as saying by way of explanation. Excerpts from her diary didn't clarify matters either. "I am having thoughts," one entry read. "Really getting into thinking." She seemed to be a mystery. Or, as Allegra herself put it, "It's like Stonehenge, you know? The biggest mystery, totally unsolved."

Nevertheless, Hollywood was intrigued. After *Esquire* ran the article, the magazine began receiving calls from talent scouts, desperate to get in touch with the new star. But not all readers were taken with Allegra. The *St. Louis Post-Dispatch* denounced *Esquire* for celebrating her obvious brainless vapidity.

As it turned out, Allegra really was a mystery, principally because she didn't exist. *Esquire* had made her up in order to spoof the fawning puffery that most magazines shower on movie stars. The woman shown on the cover and in the photos inside was a little-known actress named Ali Larter. After posing as Allegra Coleman, Larter went on to develop a real career in Hollywood, acting in movies such as *House on Haunted Hill, American Outlaws,* and *Legally Blonde.*

World Wide Web Hoaxes

The World Wide Web (as opposed to e-mail and news groups) came into existence around 1991 as a subset of the larger Internet. It made it easy for almost anyone to reach a potential audience of millions. This proved to be a boon for hoaxers. Newspapers, radio, and television, by contrast, had never been as democratic and open in their access. Web-based hoaxes really began to come into their own toward the end of the decade as the Web became more a mainstream part of everyday life.

Ourfirsttime.com

The concept behind this Web site was simple. Mike and Diane, two wholesome eighteen-year-olds, had announced their intention to lose their virginity together at 9:00 P.M. on August 4, 1998. But unlike most teenagers, they had invited the entire world to watch this intimate moment unfold live over the Web. It would all happen at www.ourfirsttime.com. Once the mainstream media got hold of the story, it spread to an international audience within a day. So many people visited Mike and Diane's Web site to read more about the story that the site crashed and went offline. But it didn't take long for Internet sleuths to sniff out a hoax. The mastermind behind the event turned out to be Ken Tipton, a former video-store owner and small-time entrepreneur. His plan was first to hype the "Internet deflowering" as a free, educational event, but then to impose a five-dollar viewing fee shortly before the event and compound this by having "Mike and Diane" choose to abstain at the last minute. The notoriety that the hoax achieved earned it the status of being the first widely disseminated Web-based hoax. The "Microsoft Buys the Catholic Church" hoax of 1994, by contrast, was the first *Internet* hoax to achieve mass recognition.

Ron's Angels

It's perfectly legal for women to sell their eggs to infertile couples. But Ron Harris, an erotic photographer, proposed taking this process one step further. He established a Web site called Ronsangels.com at which nubile supermodels auctioned off their eggs to the highest bidders. The concept sent shudders of horror down the spines of the members of the infertility industry. News of the Web site was broken by reporter Carey Goldberg of *The New York Times* on October 23, 1999. In her words the Web site melded "Darwin-based eugenics, Playboy-style sensibilities, and eBay-type commerce." A wave of press attention followed. Suspicions were finally raised when other reporters noticed that no bids were being logged on the site, and that over half the supposed egg donors were also employed as models at Harris's other endeavor, a pornographic Web site called Eroticboxoffice.com. It turned out that no eggs were being sold. The online egg auction was just a publicity stunt designed to attract visitors to Harris's real business, the pornography site.

eBay Auctions

The online auction site eBay, which brings together buyers and sellers of all manner of merchandise, has been one of the most successful Web-based commercial ventures. But pranksters

soon realized that there was little to stop them from either posting bogus merchandise or placing false bids. The result was a
steady stream of sham auctions. In June 1999 $2 million worth
of "pure, uncut cocaine" was put up for sale. In September 1999
bidding on a human kidney reached $5.7 million before eBay
halted the auction, followed a few weeks later by a million-dollar
auction for an unborn child, which was also halted. Other notorious items falsely put up for sale have included London's Millennium Dome and a man's soul. The most famous fake bid
was a January 2000 offer to pay $10 million for the domain name
"Year2000.com."

Y2K Hoaxes

The nineties started out with a mood of almost hysterical
optimism. Internet evangelists proclaimed that the new communication technologies would bring the world together and solve
all of humanity's problems (similar claims were made when
telegraphy, radio, and television were first introduced). But by
the end of the decade darker notes of paranoia were being expressed. These fears coalesced around the concept of
Y2K, the upcoming calendar change from 1999 to 2000. Prophets of doom predicted that, despite the efforts of governments
and corporations to address the technological issues raised by
the changeover (specifically, the inability of many computers
to interpret dates past 1999), the event would cause the self-
implosion of computer systems worldwide, throwing mankind
back into a premodern dark age. Inevitably a number of pranksters (especially April Fools' Day pranksters) took advantage of
this preoccupation with the year 2000.

Guinness Mean Time

On March 30, 1998, the Guinness brewery issued a press release announcing that it had reached an agreement with the

Old Royal Observatory in Greenwich, England, to be the official beer sponsor of the observatory's millennium celebration. According to this agreement Greenwich Mean Time would be renamed Guinness Mean Time until the end of 1999. In addition the famous observatory would refer to seconds as "pint drips." The *Financial Times*, not realizing that the release was a joke, broke the news in an article in which it discussed how some companies were exploiting the millennium excitement in order to promote their own brand names. It declared that Guinness, with its Greenwich tie-in, was setting a "brash tone for the millennium." When the *Financial Times* learned that it had fallen for a joke, it printed a curt retraction, stating that the news it had disclosed "was apparently intended as part of an April 1 spoof."

Y2K Solved

In 1999 the *Singapore Straits Times* reported that a seventeen-year-old high school student had one-upped all the major software corporations of the world by creating a small computer program that would easily solve the Y2K bug. The camera-shy C student had supposedly devised the program in twenty-nine minutes while solving an algebra problem for his homework. His family and a technology consulting group were reportedly forming a joint venture named Polo Flair in order to commercialize his discovery. They anticipated achieving revenues of $50 million by the end of the year. Numerous journalists and computer specialists contacted the *Straits Times*, seeking more information about the boy genius and his Y2K cure. One journalist even wanted to know if the boy would be willing to appear on TV, despite the fact that he was camera shy. Unfortunately the boy and his ingenious program did not exist. Quick-witted readers would have noticed that *Polo Flair* was an anagram for "April Fool."

The Y2K CD Bug

On April 1, 1999, a Canadian radio station, in conjunction with Warner Music and Universal Music Group, informed listeners that the arrival of Y2K would render all CD players unable to read music discs created before the year 2000. Luckily, the deejay said, there was a solution. Hologram stickers were available that would enable CD players to read the old-format discs. These stickers would be sold for approximately two dollars apiece. Furious listeners, outraged at the thought of having to pay two dollars for the stickers, immediately jammed the phones of both the radio station and the record companies, demanding that the stickers be given away for free. They continued to call even after the radio station revealed that the announcement was a joke.

CHAPTER NINE

AFTER 2000

Bonsai Kittens and Monster Cats

As the information explosion of the past two decades continues to expand, two implications have become clear.

First, the growth in information has ironically placed a heavier burden on individuals to do the work of differentiating true claims from false ones. People have been forced to become savvier navigators of the information universe. Claims and counterclaims flood in from all sides, not only from traditional sources—newspapers, radio, television, advertisements, books, and magazines—but also from e-mail, and novel Internet sources like Weblogs (Web-based journals). Sensing which sources are reliable, and which are not, has become a fine and highly inexact art. Inevitably, not everyone succeeds. But not only the "gullible" fail. The new millennium has seen such respected institutions as *The New Yorker, National Geographic,* and Slate.com all taken in by hoaxes.

Second, the advance of communications and information technologies has led not only to the expansion of the public but also to its globalization. The continents interact with each other in more immediate ways than ever before. What this means is that hoaxes, along with other foreign influences wanted and unwanted, increasingly travel unchecked across international borders. The Piltdown Chicken hoax, which began in China and moved to America, provided an excellent example of this.

From a cultural standpoint the hoaxes of the new millennium have often reflected the darker themes and tensions that the world has grappled with after the inflated hopes and expectations of the 1990s evaporated. The millennium began with the apocalyptic fears of Y2K. When the lights failed to go out at the stroke of midnight, many grumbled that Y2K, and the billions spent on it, had been the greatest hoax in history. The mood of doubt and negativity continued to predominate as the dot.com bubble fully burst, the world economy slid into recession, and America experienced one of the most bitterly contested presidential elections in its history. Then the events of September 11 occurred. There were many patches of levity, but quite a few of the most notable hoaxes from 2000–2002 displayed a preoccupation with these themes of death, doubt, apocalypse, and disaster.

The Piltdown Chicken

On October 15, 1999, the National Geographic Society cranked its publicity machine into high gear to announce the amazing discovery in northeastern China of a 125-million-year-old fossil that appeared to be the long-sought missing link between dinosaurs and birds. For over twenty years paleontologists had debated whether birds were descended from dinosaurs. This fossil seemed to provide conclusive proof of that connection.

The dino-bird in question, dubbed *Archaeoraptor liaoningensis,* was unveiled for reporters at a press conference held at the National Geographic's corporate headquarters. The society simultaneously published a glossy article about the find in its well-known magazine.

The fossil bird, when living, would have been about the size of a large chicken or a turkey. But it would have been a turkey that bore the long tail of a dinosaur. It was this mixture of dinosaur and bird parts that made researchers believe they had found the dinosaur-bird missing link. As Christopher Sloan, author of the *National Geographic* article, enthusiastically wrote, "Its long arms and small body scream, 'Bird!' Its long, stiff tail . . . screams, 'Dinosaur!'" What Sloan didn't realize at the time, was that the body and tail together should have screamed, "Fake!"

Xu Xing, a Chinese scientist who had initially helped to identify the fossil, was the one who eventually blew the whistle on it. He announced that he had found a second fossil containing an exact, mirror-image duplicate of the *Archaeoraptor*'s tail, but attached to a different body. Fossil stones, when taken from the ground, often cleave in two, producing two mirror-image sets of fossil slabs. Evidently someone had taken one of the slabs bearing the tail fossil and affixed it to a fossil of a bird, thereby producing a hybrid dinosaur-bird creature.

National Geographic published an admission of its mistake in March 2000 and a fuller analysis of how it had been duped in October of that year. It admitted that red flags had been raised about the discovery at various points, but that it had failed to see them. More seriously, it acknowledged rushing its find into publication before more scholarly journals had the chance to peer-review the data.

U.S. News & World Report was the first to refer to the *Archaeoraptor liaoningensis* forgery as the case of the Piltdown Chicken, alluding to the infamous and quite similar Piltdown Man hoax of 1912 (see Chapter Four).

The Ultimate Lie

Every year the Donside Paper Company, based in Aberdeen, holds a competition for graphic design students. Its competition for the year 2000 was a little different. Entrants were challenged to respond to one of three challenges: 1) promote the Bermuda Triangle as a holiday destination; 2) design a welcome pack for a shopaholics' association; or 3) tell a lie convincingly.

Many entries had already arrived when the participating schools received a letter on Donside stationery explaining that the contest had regrettably been canceled. Obediently the schools began to turn away new entries. In a panic Donside called to ask what they were doing, and only then did the schools realize their mistake. The cancellation letter had itself been an entry from a contestant who had taken the challenge to tell a convincing lie to heart.

Reeling from this embarrassment, the schools hastily sought to wrap up the contest, but they were delayed when they received a fax from Donside announcing that the closing date had been moved back a month and all entries were required to be resubmitted. Wearily, the schools began to contact all the contestants, until they realized that they had been tricked again.

Donside announced that it had no intention of punishing the mischievous contestants. In fact it was quite willing to judge their entries alongside the others. Unfortunately the pranksters never revealed their identities.

APRIL FOOLS' DAY HOAXES

They say that on the Internet every day is April Fools' Day, but at the start of the new millennium many of the best April Fools' Day hoaxes continued to appear on radio and in print.

The Fifteenth Annual New York City April Fools' Day Parade

A news release sent to the media shortly before April 1, 2000, stated that the fifteenth annual New York City April Fools' Day Parade was scheduled to begin at noon on Fifty-ninth Street and would proceed down to Fifth Avenue. According to the release, floats in the parade would include a "Beat 'Em, Bust 'Em, Book

'Em" float created by the New York, Los Angeles, and Seattle police departments. This float would portray "themes of brutality, corruption, and incompetence." Also, a "Where's Mars?" float, reportedly built at a cost of $10 billion, would depict lost Mars missions; and finally, the "Atlanta Braves Baseball Tribute to Racism" float would feature John Rocker "spewing racial epithets at the crowd." CNN and the Fox affiliate WNYW sent television news crews to cover the parade. They arrived at Fifty-ninth Street at noon only to discover they were the only ones there. Reluctantly they realized that they had been hoaxed. The prank was the handiwork of Joey Skaggs (see chapters Six and Seven), who had issued press releases about nonexistent spoof parades every April Fools' Day for the past fifteen years.

FatSox

In April 2000 the *Daily Mail* (London) announced that Esporta Health Clubs had launched a new line of socks designed to help people lose weight more easily. Dubbed "FatSox," this revolutionary hose could actually suck body fat out of a person's feet as they sweated. As the person's body heat rose and their blood vessels dilated, the socks drew "excess lipid from the body through the sweat." After having sweated out the fat the wearer could then simply remove the socks and wash them, and the fat, away. The *Daily Mail* gushed that the invention promised to "banish fat forever."

IPO for F/rite Air

By April 2000 the dot.com bubble was rapidly deflating. This didn't deter hundreds of Dutch investors from lining up to buy shares in F/rite Air, which was billed as being a hot new technology company backed by supporters such as Bill Gates, Paul Allen, and George Soros. The announcement about the company's IPO was posted on iex.nl, a financial Web site for Dutch investors. Shares in the IPO could be reserved for $18 each by e-mail, although it was said that analysts anticipated the stock soaring to above $80 on the first day of its filing. The company seemed like a sure thing, and almost immediately orders worth over $7 million flooded in. The orders didn't stop coming in even after the newspapers had revealed the IPO to be an April Fools' Day joke. *F/rite air* means "hot air" in Dutch.

An Interview with President Carter

In 2001 Michael Enright interviewed former President Jimmy Carter on the Sunday edition of the Canadian Broadcasting Corporation's radio program *This Morning.* Carter had been invited on the show to discuss the softwood lumber trade, since he had recently written an editorial piece in the *The New York Times* criticizing Canada's heavily subsidized lumber industry. The interview took a turn for the worse when Enright began telling Carter to speed up his answers. Suddenly Enright said, "I think the question on everyone's mind is, how did a washed-up peanut farmer from Hicksville such as yourself get involved in such a sophisticated bilateral trade argument?" Carter seemed stunned by the insult. He stammered and then replied, "Excuse me? A washed-up peanut farmer? You're one to talk, sir. Didn't you used to be on the air five times a week?" The tone of the interview did not improve from there. Carter eventually declared that Enright was a "rude person" and hung up. Enright then revealed that the interview had been fake. The Toronto comedian Ray Landry had been impersonating Carter's voice. The interview generated a number of angry calls from listeners who didn't find the joke amusing, but the next day the controversy reached even larger proportions when both the *Globe* and the *Mail* reported the interview as fact on their front pages. The editor of the *Globe* later explained that he hadn't realized the interview was a hoax because it was "a fairly strange issue and a strange person to choose as a spoof."

Whistling Carrots

In 2002 the British supermarket chain Tesco published an advertisement in the *Sun* newspaper announcing the successful development of a genetically modified "whistling carrot." The ad explained that the carrots had been specially engineered to grow with tapered airholes in their side. When fully cooked, these airholes caused the vegetable to whistle. Of course, there was no truth to this at all. Intriguingly, a month later a rival chain called Sainsbury's announced that it would soon be introducing purple carrots. Some immediately suspected that these, too, were a hoax. But they, by contrast, turned out to be quite real.

Death Hoaxes

Death hoaxes involve the false report of someone's demise. They're an old favorite of hoaxers, since the untimely departure of a well-known figure is always sure to gain publicity. But during the years 2000 and 2001 an unusually high number of these hoaxes occurred, perhaps reflecting the generally cynical mood of the period.

The Demise of Pop Stars

Between 2000 and 2002 a slew of pop stars were hastened prematurely to their graves. Rap star Eminem was eliminated by a car crash in December 2000. In May 2001 the BBC reported that Suzanne Shaw of the band Hear'Say had been found dead in her home. Also in May 2001 numerous radio stations reported the death by overdose of rock legend Lou Reed. In June 2001 a Los Angeles radio station shocked fans of Britney Spears and Justin Timberlake by informing them that the couple had died together in a car crash (like Eminem). It was a bad year for Britney Spears because in October she died again, once more in an automobile accident. In this second case a twenty-two-year-old hacker named Tim Fries managed to make it appear as if the report of her demise was part of CNN's Web site, thus adding far more credibility to the story. Of course, all of these celebrities are still very much alive.

Gabriel García Márquez's Final Farewell

In May 2000 the "farewell poem" of Nobel prize–winning author Gabriel García Márquez began to spread across the Internet. Supposedly he had penned the poem as he lay dying of cancer. The poem was highly sentimental and full of maudlin clichés that one would not expect from such a gifted writer. For instance, at one point the poet declared his desire to "live in love with love." Nevertheless, many who read it were deeply moved by what they took to be the author's dying message. The poem turned out to be the work of an obscure Mexican ventriloquist named Johnny Welch.

Safeway Says, "Shop Elsewhere!"

Stores don't usually advise their customers to shop elsewhere, but that's exactly what British Safeway seemed to do in an e-mail to hundreds of its customers on August 9, 2000. The e-mail, which came from Safeway's own e-mail server, stated that the store was planning a twenty-five-percent price increase. Customers who were unhappy about this plan were pointedly told to take their business elsewhere, such as to one of the rival supermarket chains, Tesco or Sainsbury. The e-mail was cheerily signed, "From the Safeway Team!"

Over a thousand customers telephoned Safeway to complain about the e-mail. The management of Safeway apologized profusely but explained that they had sent no such message. When investigators finally got to the bottom of the situation, they discovered that a hacker had somehow broken into Safeway's computer database and sent out the fake e-mail using the store's internal server, making it appear to its recipients to be a legitimate communication. Safeway immediately shut down its Web site to prevent any chance of a repeat hoax. It didn't feel confident enough to reopen the site until April of the following year.

Emulex: A Stock Market Hoax

On the morning of August 25, 2000, shareholders of Emulex Corporation were greeted by disturbing headlines that appeared on all the major wire services: "Emulex Announces Revised Earnings; SEC Launches Investigation into Accounting Practices. Paul Folino Steps Down As CEO." The company's stock price responded swiftly and violently to the news. It plunged from a morning high of $113.06 to a low of $43. Emulex shareholders were despondent.

Then more news hit the wires. Earnings weren't being revised. The CEO had no intention of leaving. The SEC was conducting no investigation of accounting irregularities. The entire nightmare scenario of corporate meltdown spelled out in the earlier press release was a hoax.

The bogus news release was swiftly tracked down to a relatively new wire service called Internet Wire. When confronted with this possible public relations disaster, Internet Wire immediately proclaimed its innocence. It explained that it had been the dupe of a sophisticated group of con artists. The criminals, posing as Emulex's PR firm, had sent a fake press release to the wire service's night staffers. The staffers, believing the announcement to be real, included it in with the other releases scheduled to go out at market open.

The following Thursday the FBI announced an arrest in the case. The "sophisticated" con artist turned out to be Mark Jakob, a twenty-three-year-old college student who had once been an Internet Wire employee. He had used his inside knowledge of the company to slip the release past its security checks. He reportedly made $250,000 from his scheme, though he had only one week to enjoy the money before the FBI caught up with him.

In the wake of the hoax pundits proclaimed that it revealed how vulnerable online trading of stocks was to such manipulation. They pointed out that a slew of similar, though lesser, frauds had occurred the previous year involving companies such as Pairgain Technologies and Bid.com. But curiously, Mark Jakob's crime resembled those cases less than it did one that had occurred a century and a half earlier—the Civil War Gold Hoax of 1864 (see Chapter Three). This earlier fraud also involved night staffers, a fake press release, and a media insider, demonstrating that although technologies may change, the basic techniques of hoaxers remain remarkably similar.

The Stone Age Discoveries of Shinichi Fujimura

By the age of fifty, Shinichi Fujimura had established himself as one of Japan's leading archaeologists. His skills were so legendary that it was said he had "divine hands," magically capable of finding ancient artifacts. He even became something of a popular hero in Japan because of the broad following that archaeology enjoys there.

During the 1990s Fujimura began excavating a prehistoric site near the town of Tsukidate in the Miyagi Prefecture, about 186 miles northeast of Tokyo. The town basked in the tourism that his site attracted. Local bartenders created a signature drink called "Early Man" that they sold to the tourists, and the politicians changed the town's official slogan to "The town with the same skies viewed by early man."

Then, on October 22, 2000, Fujimura and his team announced the discovery of a cluster of stone pillars that they believed to be over six hundred thousand years old, making them one of the oldest signs of human habitation in the world. The discovery immediately drew international attention. Unfortunately for Fujimura his moment of glory did not last long. On November 5 the *Mainichi Shimbun* newspaper published three pictures on its front page displaying Fujimura burying artifacts at the site. These were artifacts that he had later dug up and announced as major finds. The *Mainichi* newspaper took the photographs in secret, but did not publish them until it confirmed with Fujimura that he had indeed buried the artifacts himself.

At a press conference on November 5 Fujimura confessed that he had planted the Stone Age artifacts and had faked many other discoveries throughout his career. He kept his head bowed in shame as he said, "I was tempted by the devil. I don't know how I can apologize for what I did. . . . I wanted to be known as the person who excavated the oldest stoneware in Japan."

The revelations shocked Japan and angered Fujimura's colleagues. Inevitably people began asking how Fujimura could have gotten away with such grand deception for so long. Part of the reason lay in the inherent difficulty of dating stone implements. They can only be dated by the stratum in which they are found, meaning that it is almost impossible to differentiate between planted artifacts and real ones. Given how influential Fujimura's work had become, all agreed that it would be years before the misinformation he had placed into the archaeological record could be corrected. One of the first groups to be affected were academic publishers, who soon realized that their archaeology textbooks had become out of date overnight.

Hoax Web Sites

Given the vast amount of stuff that clutters the Internet, it's hard enough for a Web site to get noticed, let alone to make people believe that the claims it's offering up for public inspection are true. Despite this challenge all of these hoax sites, which were active between 2000 and 2002, managed to gain hundreds of thousands of visitors as well as believers. Given the constantly changing nature of the Internet it cannot be guaranteed that any of these sites are still active.

Spud Server: http://totl.net/Spud/

Getting a potato to power a clock is the stuff of high school chemistry. This site purported to take the concept a step further by using spuds to power a Web page server. Visitors to the site (which loaded agonizingly slowly) could marvel at their participation in such a technological feat. The site reached the peak of its popularity in March 2000 when both *USA Today* and the BBC, among others, ran stories about it. A few days later the media had to admit that it had been taken for a ride. The site was a joke created by the minds at the nonprofit net company Temple ov Thee Lemur. But Steve Harris, one of the hoaxers at Temple ov Thee Lemur, noted that while their site was a sham, the concept itself was technically feasible. He theorized that it might also be possible to build a beer-powered Web site.

Malepregnancy.com: http://www.malepregnancy.com/

Can men become pregnant? According to this site they can. It presented the case of Mr. Lee Mingwei, supposedly the first man to bear child. Visitors to the site could inspect a variety of evidence (news reports, pictures, video clips, Mr. Mingwei's EKG) in order to learn more about his pregnancy. All of the evidence was fake. The site first appeared online in 1999 but began to receive extensive media attention in 2000. The author of the site was a man named Virgil Wong, who claimed that it was intended to be a work of art. Others questioned whether art, if it represents itself as being real, can still be considered art. This same question is raised by the work of Joey Skaggs (see chapters Six and Seven). Wong claimed that his site inspired numerous men to contact him, seeking to be the next pregnant man.

Bonsai Kittens: http://www.bonsaikitten.com/

Bonsai describes the ancient Japanese art of growing miniature trees by rigorous pruning of their roots and branches. This site, which debuted in late 2000, claimed to apply that principle to kittens. The idea was to seal young kittens inside glass containers. As the kittens grew, their bones would supposedly conform to the shape of whatever container held them. At the end of the process a uniquely shaped "Bonsai Kitten" would be produced. "You no longer need be satisfied with a house pet having the same mundane shape as all other members of its species," the site declared. "With Bonsai Kitten a world of variation awaits you, limited only by your own imagination." The site also advertised that hand-grown Bonsai Kittens were for sale to the public. Almost immediately the site generated a huge amount of outrage and controversy. Furious animal lovers insisted that it be closed down, and thousands of people, believing the Bonsai Kitten Company to be real, lobbied the FBI to investigate it. The FBI did investigate but found no evidence of criminal wrongdoing. In fact, the site had been created as a prank by graduate students at MIT who represented themselves through the persona of "Dr. Michael Wong Chang" in interviews. Their intention had been to satirize "the human belief of nature as commodity." Although it has by now been thoroughly debunked as a hoax, the site still manages to generate controversy and calls for it to be shut down.

Manbeef.com: http://www.manbeef.com/

Expertly spoofing the specialty food sites that have proliferated on the Internet, this site claimed to sell human flesh for the "sophisticated human meat consumer." Visitors to the site could read the "recipe of the day" as they viewed pictures of attractively cut meat (species unknown). This site caused so much controversy (at one point it was receiving a half-million hits per day) that the U.S. Food and Drug Administration eventually felt compelled to investigate it. They found no evidence that human meat was actually being sold. In July 2001 a Los Angeles graphic designer who went under the alias "Joseph Christopherson" admitted to being its creator. He explained that his intention had been to outrage "sensitive" viewers. At this he definitely succeeded.

The Religion of the Jedi Knights

As the 2001 census geared up in Britain, an e-mail began to spread suggesting that if ten thousand people listed "Jedi Knight" as their religious affiliation on the census forms, the government would be forced to acknowledge it as an officially recognized faith. The British government dismissed the suggestion as nonsense. Nevertheless, as the census got under way the Office of National Statistics (ONS) found itself flooded with forms listing "Jedi Knight" under the category for religion. So many Jedi entries arrived that the ONS eventually gave the aberrant listing its own classification number, 896, to assist with the filing of the forms. While the British government still denies that it has officially recognized Jedi Knight as a religion, the receipt of a classification number represented a victory of a kind for the thousands of British Jedis. Since it is questionable whether those thousands actually do worship "The Force" of the Star Wars universe as their primary religion, the massive write-in campaign may qualify as one of the largest mass pranks in history.

The Day of No Joe

Students at prestigious Amherst College, like students all over the country, require large amounts of caffeine to fuel their late-night study habits. Therefore it was with horror that in May 2001, a week before final exams, they learned of the college's decision to ban coffee on campus. Signs were displayed at the cafeteria attributing the ban to "the alarming rise in caffeine use and the adverse side effects associated with this drug." Anticipating the withdrawal symptoms some students might face once denied access to their drug of choice, the college also established a "coffee detox center" in the infirmary.

The students were not pleased. The more vocal among them threatened to go straight to the college president with their complaints. The less vocal wearily trekked across campus to buy coffee in town, or purchased the black-market cups of joe that began selling for two dollars each.

Thankfully the students didn't have to wait long before the coffee started flowing again. The next day the event was revealed to be a hoax engineered by Andrew Epstein, a senior at the college. He had devised the elaborate deception with the help of the administration as a project for a "social sculpture" art class. His grade for the project is not known, but it surely was aided by the fact that teachers were exempted from his coffee ban.

Kaycee Nicole Swenson

Kaycee Nicole was a nineteen-year-old girl from Kansas dying of cancer. Or so believed the thousands of people who visited her Web site, on which she kept a diary of her fight against leukemia.

For over a year Kaycee Nicole added updates to her diary, letting people know about the ups and downs of her struggle with the disease, about her hope as the cancer went into remission, and about her fear as it reappeared. Kaycee's mother, Debbie, maintained a companion journal in which she discussed what it was like caring for a child with cancer. Many people grew extremely close to Kaycee. They communicated with her via e-mail, chatted with her in online chatrooms, and some even phoned her.

Then on May 15, 2001, Kaycee Nicole died of a brain aneurysm. Her online friends were distraught. They sought for ways to express their sorrow. They wanted to send gifts to her family. Some even wanted to attend her funeral. And that's when things began to get suspicious.

Kaycee's mother refused to provide anyone with information about where the funeral was being held or where to send gifts. This prompted a group of individuals who participated in the online community Metafilter, and who called themselves the

"ScoobyDoos," to find out what was going on. What they discovered was disturbing. Kaycee's death had not been recorded by any obituary they could locate. Nor could anyone remember ever having met Kaycee in person. They began to wonder if Kaycee actually existed.

Their fears were confirmed a few days later when Debbie Swenson, a forty-year-old woman from Kansas, confessed that she had invented Kaycee and written all the diary entries herself. The photos of Kaycee that appeared on the site were simply pictures of a neighbor, used without the neighbor's knowledge. Whenever anyone had thought that they were e-mailing Kaycee or instant-messaging with her, it was actually Debbie they were communicating with. Debbie did not reveal who had posed as Kaycee for the phone calls.

Debbie Swenson remained unrepentant and evasive in her confessions, claiming that Kaycee was real, in a way, because the character was a composite of a number of cancer victims whom Debbie had known, and that she had not realized that so many people were reading the diary. This hardly satisfied the thousands of people who felt their trust had been abused. The FBI even looked into the case, but determined that because Debbie Swenson had not gained money from the hoax, besides a few small gifts and the use of Web space donated by a sympathetic man in Hong Kong, she had not actually committed a prosecutable crime.

Kaycee's case was not the first of its kind (see Chapter Seven for the similar case of Janet Cooke). But while Kaycee's case was not unique, it did reveal how the rise of the Internet had removed many of the gatekeepers who previously guarded access to the public. Debbie Swenson, after all, wasn't a newspaper insider or a well-connected figure. She was simply a forty-year-old housewife who, from the comfort of her home, managed to fool thousands of people all over the world.

Snowball the Monster Cat

An image of an enormous cat (approximately the size of a large dog) being held in the arms of a bearded man began circulating around the Internet in early 2000. The picture immediately attracted attention because it didn't seem possible for a cat to be that large. But the chance that the cat was real couldn't be ruled out altogether. Like all the best tall tales the monster cat balanced delicately on the razor's edge of credibility.

At first the picture stood alone without explanation, but by the time it was featured on NBC's *The Tonight Show with Jay Leno* and ABC's *Good Morning America*, someone had written an explanatory narrative to accompany it. According to this narrative the image was of Snowball, a monster cat owned by Rodger Degagne of Ottawa, Canada. Mr. Degagne had supposedly adopted Snowball's mother (a normal-sized cat) after finding her abandoned near a Canadian nuclear lab. She later gave birth to Snowball, who proceeded to grow into the oversized, eighty-seven-pound cat that "Mr. Degagne" was shown holding.

Both Snowball's story and her picture were fake. In May 2001 Cordell Hauglie, a resident of Edmonds, Washington, came forward to admit that "Snowball" was actually his daughter's cat. The cat's real name was Jumper, and it weighed only twenty-one pounds. Hauglie had created the fake image by using widely available photo manipulation software and had then e-mailed the image to a few friends as a joke, never intending that it should pass beyond those friends. But a few months later the picture had spread worldwide. Hauglie only realized what had happened when the picture started appearing on TV shows, in newspapers, and in magazines. To his amazement he had unintentionally become an Internet celebrity simply by sharing a joke with a few friends.

The picture of Snowball recalled a far older American tradition of tall-tale photography. Lighthearted images of giant fish, whopper grasshoppers, and oversized farm animals of all varieties have been a staple of American culture ever since novelty

"Snowball, the Monster Cat" in the arms of Cordell Hauglie.
Copyright permission and photo courtesy of Cordell Hauglie.

picture postcards first became popular at the beginning of the
twentieth century (see Chapter Four). Back then photographers
had to painstakingly cut and paste images together to create the
trick effect. Nowadays, as Cordell Hauglie can attest, all it takes
is a click of the mouse.

Cordell Hauglie holds "Jumper," his daughter's twenty-one-pound cat who served as the model for "Snowball." Copyright permission and photo courtesy of Cordell Hauglie.

David Manning, Film Critic

No matter how bad the movies of Columbia Pictures were, there was always one reviewer who was willing to heap lavish praise on them. It was David Manning of the *Ridgefield Press*. For instance, while others reviewers were skewering *Hollow Man,* Manning declared that it was "one helluva scary ride! The summer's best special effects." The sophomoric comedy *The Animal* impressed him as "another winner," and he singled out Heath Ledger of *A Knight's Tale* as "this year's hottest new star." These comments all appeared prominently in print ads for these respective films.

David Manning's rave reviews might have gone forever unnoticed. After all, few people pay much attention to the hyperbolic comments that grace most movie ads. But during the course of investigating the journalistic subworld of movie junkets, *Newsweek* reporter John Horn uncovered the curious truth behind David Manning. The *Ridgefield Press,* a small weekly newspaper based in Connecticut, had never heard of the man. Nor was Manning known by any of the other reporters who frequented the junket circuit. In fact, Manning didn't exist at all. He was, instead, the fictional creation of a young marketing executive at Sony, the parent company of Columbia Pictures.

The executive, who has remained anonymous, created the Manning character around July 2000. He used the *Ridgefield Press* because he himself had grown up in Ridgefield. It is not clear whether others at Sony knew of the deception, or whether the executive acted alone.

John Horn exposed the reality behind David Manning in an article that appeared in early June 2001. He noted that the most curious aspect of the whole affair was why Sony should have felt the need to invent movie reviews in the first place. During movie junkets the studios pamper critics with all-expense-paid weekend getaways. In return for this star treatment many critics are happy to print whatever the studios want them to say about their movies. Perhaps Sony's real crime was taking a shortcut to the good reviews, thereby neglecting to pay the critics their due tribute.

Monkey Fishing with Slate.com

Jay Forman wrote an occasional "Vice" column for the online magazine Slate.com. It provided him with a mainstream outlet to detail some of the bizarre activities he had engaged in or witnessed over the years. For instance, one column probed the synergies between guns and liquor. Another discussed his short career in the pornography trade. But his column that appeared on June 7, 2001, was the most bizarre of all. It described his participation in the extreme sport of monkey fishing.

Monkey fishing, in Forman's usage of the term, was not a slang expression for some untraditional method of fishing for fish. Forman meant exactly what he said. He went fishing for monkeys.

The event in question supposedly occurred sometime in 1996 on the island of Lois Key in the Florida Keys. Lois Key was the home of a large population of rhesus monkeys used by a pharmaceutical company for experiments. Local fishermen, according to Forman, had developed the "sport" of rowing out to the island, attaching pieces of fruit to fishing rods, casting the fruit onto the shore, waiting for monkeys to pick up the fruit and impale their hands on the hook, and then yanking the primates off the island into the water. The fishermen would then cut the lines free, allowing the monkeys to swim back to shore.

The column was a colorful piece of reporting, full of vivid observations about the art of monkey fishing. Who would have guessed, for instance, that oranges are the fruit of choice for baiting monkeys? But almost as soon as the article was published it attracted criticism. *The Wall Street Journal* didn't believe a word of it, declaring, "Slate Gets Hoaxed." Michael Kinsley, Slate's editor, fired back, insisting that it stood behind the veracity of the story. But under the weight of continuing criticism Kinsley backed down. On June 25 he published an apology, acknowledging that key details in Forman's story were fictitious.

Was the article a complete fiction? No. Lois Key was inhabited by rhesus monkeys until 1999, when they were removed for environmental reasons. Kinsley assured his readers that once or twice a fisherman had rowed out to the island and thrown pieces of fruit attached to a line onto the shore. Fortunately for the monkeys, and unfortunately for Slate.com, the reaction of the monkeys to the fruit was somewhat underwhelming. A few of them had picked it up and then dropped it back down. This was the riveting reality behind the monkey-fishing scandal.

The Lovenstein Institute IQ Report

In July 2001 an e-mail began to circulate around the Internet claiming that the Lovenstein Institute, a think tank based in Scranton, Pennsylvania, had conducted research into the IQ of all the presidents of the past fifty years and concluded that George W. Bush ranked at the bottom, with an IQ of only 91. This news quickly gained attention from the international media. The *Guardian* (Manchester) broke the story on July 19, and on August 26 Garry Trudeau featured the report in his *Doonesbury* comic strip.

But both Trudeau and the *Guardian* had been taken in by a hoax. The e-mail had originated as a joke on a Web site called Linkydinky.com. In its original version the joke was obvious. For instance, Linkydinky.com cited the *Pennsylvania Court Observer* as its source for the news, while crediting the paper with a circulation of only five readers. Furthermore, Dr. Lovenstein was described as "living in a mobile home in Scranton, Pennsylvania." As the joke began to make its way through people's e-mail, these textual clues were removed, making it appear that the Lovenstein Institute was an actual research organization. Once they learned of their mistakes, both Trudeau and the *Guardian* published retractions.

Gorgeous Guy

Dan Baca, a twenty-nine-year-old network engineer, was going about his life, minding his own business, when suddenly people began staring at him. He noticed it first while he was standing at the bus stop in the morning. Crowds of people were gathering, looking at him, and whispering to each other. It happened a few days in a row. Finally he confronted them, and they told him that he was an Internet celebrity.

On May 11, 2001, his picture had been posted without his knowledge on a local Internet portal, craigslist.org, in the "Missed

Connections" forum. The picture's caption read, "Gorgeous Guy @ 4th and Market at the MUNI/Amtrak Bus Stop (Mon–Fri)." The poster of the message spoke sighingly of wanting to meet this "gorgeous guy" but as she didn't know his name, she was hoping he would see her message and contact her. This initial posting initiated a flood of follow-up messages. The Gorgeous Guy at the bus stop became the talk of San Francisco's online community. People theorized about who he was and speculated whether he was single, straight, or gay. Then people began going to the bus stop to see him in person.

Eventually David Cassel, a freelance journalist, caught wind of the Gorgeous Guy phenomenon and wrote about it in the *San Francisco Bay Guardian.* National media then picked up on the story, and soon Dan Baca found himself fielding calls from CNN and *The Tonight Show.* He had seemingly become a national celebrity just by standing at the bus stop looking gorgeous.

Cassel, meanwhile, did some more research and about a month later wrote a follow-up story revealing that the Gorgeous Guy phenomenon was all a hoax. No one knows who posted the original picture of Baca, but Cassel discovered that the majority of the initial follow-up messages that drew attention to the picture had been posted by Baca himself. He had created an array of online personalities to convey the sense that a crowd of people were talking about him. This strategy eventually succeeded in attracting the attention of a real crowd.

Baca's motivations are obscure. Perhaps he just craved attention, or perhaps he was hoping to segue his fame into a modeling or acting career. Either way, the hoax demonstrates how the Internet has allowed average people to access huge public audiences without going through the traditional gatekeepers of the print and broadcast media.

September 11, 2001

The events of September 11 stunned the world. During the weeks that followed, fear, panic, grief, and confusion reigned. This was a recipe for hoaxes and fear-driven rumors. The wild stories that circulated through e-mail included the following: that terrorists were going to strike again by blowing up malls on Halloween, that a large number of rented Ryder vans capable of being converted into truck bombs had gone missing, and that secret terrorist messages were coded into the Wingdings font of Microsoft Word. The hoaxes flourished because even at the best of times it can be difficult for people to differentiate between true and false claims. During periods of extreme emotion it becomes even more challenging. Just as for a person alone in a dark house at night, every stray noise is magnified into a threat. In addition, such periods act as an irresistible magnet for hoaxers motivated by the lowest desire—the longing to gain a sense of personal power by manipulating the fear of others. This appears to have been the root cause for the numerous anthrax and bomb-scare hoaxes that followed September 11. Listed below are some of the more benign hoaxes that spread during this period.

The Predictions of Nostradamus

Within a few days of September 11 an e-mail began to circulate claiming that the sixteenth-century astrologer Nostradamus had predicted the attacks on the World Trade Center. Two quatrains attributed to Nostradamus were offered as proof of this claim. They read: "In the City of God there will be a great thunder, / Two brothers torn apart by Chaos, / while the fortress endures, / the great leader will succumb, / The third big war will begin when the big city is burning." And "On the eleventh day of the nine month, / two metal birds will crash into two tall statues / in the new city, / and the world will end soon after." Nostradamus did not write these quatrains. The first was loosely derived from his writings, but the second was of completely modern invention. Nevertheless, numerous people were taken in by the claims, and interest in Nostradamus rose to an all-time high. His name quickly became the most popular search term on all the major Internet search engines. The evocation of prophecy during times of extreme national distress is ancient and understandable. It is a way for people to place momentous events within a larger framework of sacred meaning. In this case the meaning was supplied by the Christian belief in the movement of history toward an apocalyptic judgment day that will be anticipated by various catastrophes (see "Waiting for the Apocalypse," Chapter One). Nevertheless, since the quatrains in question were of demonstrably modern origin, their use in suggesting a link between the events of September 11 and ancient prophecy was deceptive.

NASA Satellite Photo

A widely circulated e-mail urged Americans to light a candle and stand outside of their homes at a specified time and date (which varied between e-mails). It was said that a NASA satellite would then photograph the entire nation illuminated by candlelight in order to demonstrate the solidarity of the American people in the face of terrorist aggression. The photo would supposedly appear on NASA's Web site the following day. Of course, NASA never planned to take such a photograph. After all, the candlelight would have been invisible from space. Nevertheless, at the specified time numerous people dutifully appeared outside holding their candles. As it turned out, they were joined by many more people who were holding candles simply to show their support to passing motorists and pedestrians, making this a harmless, but still misleading, hoax.

Touristguy

A photograph forwarded to millions of people through e-mail following September 11 showed a heavily clad tourist standing on the observation deck of the World Trade Center as a plane,

presumably one of the hijacked planes, approached from behind. An accompanying message explained that the photograph had been rescued from a camera found in the rubble of
the World Trade Center. Apparently the photo had been taken
just seconds before disaster struck. The image grabbed people's
attention and received coverage from both national and international media. Perhaps the source of the fascination with it
(besides its sensational subject matter) was that it counterposed
a scene of such innocence (a tourist posing for a holiday snapshot) with a scene of such horror (the hijacked plane approaching from behind). In this way it evoked the prevailing mood in
America immediately following the attacks, which was of having been wrenched from an age of innocence into a new nightmare reality. The picture also spoke to the surprise nature of
the attack (the tourist's back was turned, and he seemed un-
aware of the fate that was soon to engulf him). Of course, the
picture was completely fake. The man was wearing heavy clothing on what was a warm day. Also, the view behind him indicated that he was standing on the deck of the second tower
that was attacked. The first tower would therefore have been
burning fiercely while he happily posed for this snapshot.

The popularity of the "Touristguy" photo inspired the creation of parodies. One, for instance, replaced the plane in the
picture with an image of an enormous Stay Puft Marshmallow
Man approaching menacingly from behind (a reference to the
movie *Ghostbusters*). Other parodies placed the tourist at the site
of various disasters (the explosion of the *Hindenburg,* the crash
of the *Concorde,* the assassination of President Kennedy).

During November two men stepped forward to claim that
they were "Touristguy." The first was a Brazilian businessman,
who immediately began negotiating commercial endorsements
on the basis of his new identity. The second was an anonymous Hungarian man. The Hungarian man's case appeared to
be the better one, as he was able to supply what seemed to be
further pictures of himself posing on the WTC observation
deck. But given his anonymity it remained impossible to confirm his identity as "Touristguy" with any degree of certainty.

"Touristguy" poses as a hijacked plane approaches from behind.

"Touristguy" poses as the Stay Puft Marshmallow Man approaches from behind.

The Onion Dome Hoax

On June 3, 2002, the *Beijing Evening News* scooped its competitors with a shocking story from America—the U.S. Congress was threatening to leave Washington and relocate to a more hospitable host town, such as Memphis or Charlotte, if the city did not construct a new Capitol building that included a retractable dome. The article quoted House Speaker J. Dennis Hastert (R-Ill.) as saying, "Don't get us wrong. We actually love the dilapidated [old] building. But the cruel reality is, it's no longer suitable for use by a world-class legislature. Its contours are ugly, there's no room to maneuver, there aren't enough bathrooms, and let's not even talk about the parking."

The article struck Henry Chu, a reporter for the *Los Angeles Times,* as being slightly odd. After all, why would American papers not be covering such a dramatic political development? After a little fact-checking he discovered that they were. In fact, an American publication was the source of the news. But the publication was the *Onion,* a humor magazine whose stories are clearly identifiable as satire—at least to American readers.

Chu surmised that a reporter for the *Beijing Evening News* had simply translated the story from the *Onion* almost word for word, not realizing that it was a satire spoofing the relationship between sports teams and their host cities. The *Evening News* had then printed the tale as fact without indicating its source. Indeed, when Chu questioned the Chinese paper about the story, its international editor continued to stand staunchly behind the veracity of the coverage. "How can you prove it's not correct?" The editor intriguingly pointed out. "Is it incorrect just because you say it is?" The editor of the *Onion,* by contrast, happily admitted that the story contained not a word of truth. He commented, "Wow, even journalists now believe everything they read."

AFTERWORD

How to Avoid Being Hoaxed

There is a simple and foolproof strategy to avoid being hoaxed. Don't answer the phone. Don't look at newspapers. Don't turn on the TV. Don't listen to the radio. Don't check e-mail. Don't log onto the World Wide Web. Don't read books. And don't talk to anyone else.

If you're unwilling to take these steps, then the solution is a bit more complicated.

The most frequently offered suggestion is to use your common sense. This, ironically enough, is bad advice. False information possesses no inherent, identifying feature that common sense can reliably zero in on. In fact, the claims of a well-designed hoax will invariably appear possible within the context of current knowledge about the world. Fantastic, perhaps, but possible. By contrast, claims that most of us now regard as true often appeared ridiculous when first put forward. History shows that scientific theories such as the roundness of the earth, the heliocentric solar system, evolution, and plate tectonics all met stiff resistance from critics who insisted that they defied common sense.

Instead of examining evidence internal to a claim (i.e., how reasonable it sounds), it's far better to look at evidence external to the claim: where it came from, how it was produced, and why. This is the ultimate lesson of the Museum's Gullibility Test. The true claims sound just as far-fetched as the false ones. Without further contextual information about them, there is no reliable way to sort out the true ones from the fictitious ones.

The essence of a hoax lies in misdirection, in camouflaging the true origin of the information. Hoaxers will go to great lengths to disguise the source of whatever sham claim they are peddling, since their overly active imaginations are typically the actual source. They invent elaborate excuses to dissuade people from checking up on their stories. They try to create a false sense of urgency in order to rush people into making premature judgments. To resist these strategies, it helps to be able to recognize some of the more popular techniques of misdirection.

A classic ploy is the claim whose validity depends upon a unique, irreproducible source to which only the hoaxer has access. James Macpherson employed this technique in 1760 when he translated the Ossianic poems from an ancient manuscript that he alone possessed a copy of and which he would allow no one else to see (see Chapter Two). Generally speaking, the more sources can be used to validate information, the more trustworthy that information will be. If a claim is backed up by only one source, it should be more suspect. An important exception to this rule is when hoaxers create multiple identities or aliases, thus conjuring up a proliferation of phony sources. This is proving especially easy to accomplish on the Internet, as Dan Baca, aka Gorgeous Guy, proved in 2001 (see Chapter Nine).

Then there is the trick of alluding to supporting evidence that is conveniently inaccessible, and therefore impossible to check. In 1702 the Native of Formosa stumped his critics for years because it was hardly possible for them to travel to Taiwan to disprove his fantastic assertions (see Chapter Two). Embellishing a claim with the weight of phony authority is a perennial favorite. When an e-mail began circulating in 2001 claiming that George W. Bush had the lowest IQ of any president, most might have dismissed this as partisan politicking, except that the claim was backed up by the prestigious-sounding Lovenstein Institute (see Chapter Nine). Appropriating the name of an actual authority is also popular, though riskier since if that authority finds out about the misuse of its name it can bring the curtain down on the entire scheme. This happened to Clifford Irving in 1971 when he tried to peddle the phony autobiography of Howard Hughes (see Chapter Six).

The most devious strategy of all is when a hoaxer convinces a trusted authority of the truth of his or her claim. The hoax information is then disseminated as fact with the weight of real authority behind it. When this occurs, as it did in 1999 during the case of the Piltdown Chicken (see Chapter Nine), the public has little defense.

So how can you avoid being hoaxed? When presented with a new piece of information, ask yourself where it originally came from. What was its source? Is that source trustworthy? Does it have a reputation for honesty and reliability? If not, why not? Is the source previously unknown? If so, make a note of this. Consider the ways that hoaxers can hide information's true origin. Could any of these techniques be at work? What do other people have to say about the subject? It's always good to get a second, third, and fourth opinion before giving any new claim a stamp of approval (scientists call this process peer review). But finally, realize that with all the defenses in the world, it is still possible to fall prey to a skillful hoax. In fact, all of us are probably clinging to a few pieces of "hoax" information right now in the vain belief that they are true. This is an unavoidable fact of life in any age, but especially in the Age of (Mis)information.

THE GULLIBILITY TEST

(ANSWERS)

1) False

Thomas Crapper was a real person, who operated a plumbing business in nineteenth-century London, but he didn't invent the flush toilet. This is credited, instead, to Joseph Adamson, who took out the first patent for a flush toilet in 1853. A 1969 book by Wallace Reyburn, *Flushed with Pride: The Story of Thomas Crapper,* has helped to propagate the myth that Crapper was the inventor of the toilet. Reyburn's biography of Crapper is simply a fabrication.

2) False

The Eskimo language has two root words for snow: *qanik,* which means snow in the air, and *aput,* which means snow on the ground. Modifying nouns can be added to these root words to create more words, but root words in any language can be modified indefinitely by adding new endings. Think of *snow* in English (snowfall, snowdrift, snowshoe, etc.). The idea that Eskimo has more words for snow has been traced to a 1940 article by Benjamin Lee Worf in *Technology Review,* in which he said that the Eskimo language had seven different words for snow (he never said what those words were). The concept that Eskimo has a very large number of words for snow grew from there.

3) True

This is one of those stories that sound like a myth, but as far as historians can tell, it is actually true. A 1626 letter exists in which a Dutch merchant reports having heard that representatives of the West India Company "purchased the Island Manhattes from the Indians for the value of sixty guilders." Sixty guilders is approximately $700 in present-day currency. It sounds like the Europeans got a pretty good deal for such a valuable piece of property, but the real joke was on the Europeans. It turned out that the Native American tribe that sold Manhattan to the Dutch didn't live there, so by local custom they didn't have the right to offer the Europeans any kind of use of it. In other words, the Europeans were conned out of $700 by a tribe that just happened to be passing through the area.

4) True

The story of Squanto, the English-speaking Native American whom the Pilgrims met when they disembarked from the *Mayflower*, is one of the stranger tales American history has to offer. Squanto had been taken from his village by a British captain around 1605. He lived in England for nine years and was sold into slavery in Spain in 1614. He eventually made his way back to England, and from there back to Massachusetts in 1619. By that time he had crossed the Atlantic a total of six times, making him far better traveled than the Pilgrims who arrived soon thereafter. By the Pilgrims' own admission they would have had difficulty surviving their first years in Massachusetts without the help of Squanto.

5) True

The 1904 Olympic Games, held in St. Louis, Missouri, easily remain the most bizarre on record. They were only the third summer games ever held, since the modern Olympics began in 1896, and their organizers were uncertain which sports to include. They decided to set aside certain events to allow "primitive" tribes, such as Pygmies and Patagonians, to compete separately. The "primitives" were allowed to reach for Olympic glory in events such as mud fighting, greased-pole climbing, rock throwing, and spear throwing. The dates set aside for the "primitive" events were referred to as the "Anthropology Days." The 1904 summer games proved to be such a fiasco that the Olympic committee decided to rehold the games just two years later in Athens in order to get the festival back on a proper, more dignified footing.

6) False

There is a lake in Massachusetts that goes by that name. But the explanation of its meaning is incorrect. Larry Dale, editor of the *Webster Times*, made up the fanciful etymology for an article he wrote in 1921. He meant it as a joke, but people took his story seriously and continue to repeat it to this day. The long name actually means something like "the fishing place at the boundaries and neutral meeting grounds." The body of water in question is more commonly referred to as Lake Webster.

7) False

Very few people alive anywhere in the world in 1492 believed that the earth was flat. After all, you can see the curve of the earth simply by looking at the horizon. Washington Irving, in his 1828 biography of Columbus, first popularized the myth that most Europeans believed the earth to be flat back in 1492.

8) True

Archaeologists discovered a 3,800-year-old recipe for beer on a clay tablet in Sumeria. The recipe appeared as part of a hymn to the goddess Ninkasi. Beer seems to have played a major role in Sumerian culture. Those who have brewed the Sumerian recipe report that it produces a beer with a taste similar to hard apple cider but retaining the fragrance of dates. It should be no surprise that there was a goddess of beer. After all, the Greeks worshipped Bacchus, the god of wine.

9) True

Thomas Jefferson and John Adams, who were friends during life, did die within hours of each other on July 4, 1826. Jefferson was at his home in Virginia, and Adams was at his home in Massachusetts. Americans were fascinated by the coincidence and read great meaning into it. John Quincy Adams, who was President at the time as well as being son of John Adams, declared the twin deaths to be a "visible and palpable" sign of heavenly favor.

10) False

Legend has long connected Marco Polo with the introduction of ice cream to Europe, but no evidence supports this idea. Leaving aside entirely the question of whether Polo actually visited China, there is the fact that ice cream only began to be made in Europe during the seventeenth century. This was three hundred years after Polo died. Furthermore, there is nothing in Polo's *Description of the World* that even vaguely resembles a description of ice cream.

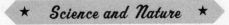

★ Science and Nature ★

11) True

Cockroaches do not have blood pressure as mammals do. Therefore, cutting off their heads would not cause them to die from bleeding. Nor do cockroaches need their heads to breathe. They only require their heads to eat. After about a month without their heads (though probably much sooner), they would die of starvation.

12) False

Sharks definitely do get cancer. However, they get it far less often than humans do. The idea that sharks are immune to cancer was popularized by the title of William Lane's 1992 book *Sharks Don't Get Cancer*. However, inside his book Lane admitted that sharks do get cancer. Although it is theorized that shark cartilage might inhibit the growth of tumor blood vessels, studies have shown that ingesting shark cartilage does not confer any anticancer benefits.

13) False

Monkey chains have long been rumored to exist, but no contemporary naturalist has ever seen one. The idea of monkey chains is a myth that was started by the early European explorers of South America.

14) True or False

This was a trick question (but also a freebie) because either answer is potentially correct. Physicists are still very undecided about whether or not the laws of physics change over time. Some current research in physics does seem to indicate that the laws of nature have subtly changed since the birth of the universe, but other physicists dispute these findings. The change, if there is one, may be due to the shifting elasticity of atomic bonds. For more about this topic, do a search on the Web for the work of John Webb, a researcher at the University of New South Wales.

15) True

Turtles exhibit what is known as "negligible senescence." In other words, unlike humans, they do not continue to biologically age once their bodies reach maturity. In theory they might be able to live forever, though in practice this would never happen. Injury, predation, or disease eventually kills them. They do not die of old age. In fact, turtles have been known to live beyond 150 years without exhibiting any signs of old age. Fish and amphibians also share this enviable characteristic.

16) False

Lemmings do not periodically commit suicide by hurling themselves off cliffs. The idea that they do is just a myth. Belief in this myth was strengthened by a 1958 Disney documentary, *White Wilderness,* in which the filmmakers herded some hapless lemmings off a cliff in order to show this supposedly natural behavior.

17) False

It was believed for many years that the residents of the Ecuadorian village of Vilacabamba lived to an unusually old age. This belief stemmed from a 1971 census that listed a high number of the village's 819 residents as being over the age of one hundred. But when anthropologists investigated this claim, they discovered that it was a hoax. Apparently, the Vilacabambans were lying about their age in order to attract more tourists to their village.

18) False

Nineteenth-century scientists dubbed this phenomenon keranography, and anecdotal accounts of it have long persisted. An actual example of it, however, has never been documented. Lightning can leave strange markings on those it strikes, but scientists do not believe that lightning possesses any photographic properties.

19) True

Researchers at the Harvard-Smithsonian Center for Astrophysics announced in January 2001 that they had used supercooled vapor to slow down the velocity of light waves to zero, thereby freezing the energy of the light in an atomic "spin wave." It may seem odd to think of light being frozen in place. After all, light moves faster than anything else in the universe, traveling at 186,282 miles per second. But that's only in a vacuum. Light does slow down when it hits a substance such as air, water, or glass. It was essentially a matter of finding the right material to slow down the light without destroying the delicate light photons altogether. The researchers said that they hoped to use their light-freezing technique to create superfast "quantum" computers.

20) True

The Earth is not perfectly round. It flattens out somewhat at the poles. Therefore, a person standing at the poles is exactly thirteen miles closer to the center of the Earth than he or she is when standing at the equator. The pull of gravity increases as you move closer to the center of a gravitational mass, making objects heavier. Conversely, when you move away from the center of a gravitational mass—such as when you fly into outer space—gravity weakens. In addition, the centrifugal spin effect at the equator slightly counteracts the pull of gravity. All of this translates into a difference of almost a pound between what a person would weigh at the equator versus at the poles.

If space were limitless, many more hoaxes could have been included in this tour of the Museum of Hoaxes. Since this was not the case, a number of worthwhile humbugs and hoodwinks unfortunately ended up on the cutting-room floor. But happily the Internet can now provide these homeless hoaxes a second chance at fame. All the Bridey Murphys, Count Balmoris, Nantucket Sea Serpents, and Minnesota Icemen of the world, this time turned away, will find a place to rest at the online Museum of Hoaxes (www.museumofhoaxes.com). Come by and visit it once you're done here. The Museum's curator can be reached at alex@museumofhoaxes.com. He is always happy to receive information about any hoaxes, both old and new.

★ *Suggestions for Further Reading* ★

General Reference Works

Arnau, Frank. *The Art of the Faker: 3,000 Years of Deception.* Boston: Little, Brown and Company, 1961.

Barnum, P. T. *The Humbugs of the World.* New York: G. W. Carleton, 1866.

Boorstin, Daniel J. *The Image: A Guide to Pseudo-Events in America.* New York: Vinatge Books, 1992.

Clough, Ben C. *The American Imagination at Work: Tall Tales and Folk Tales.* New York: Alfred A. Knopf, 1947.

Dance, Peter. *Animal Fakes and Frauds.* Berkshire, UK: Sampson Low, 1976.

Fedler, Fred. *Media Hoaxes.* Ames: Iowa State University Press, 1989.

Gardner, Martin. *Fads and Fallacies in the Name of Science.* New York: Dover Books, 1957.

Jones, Mark, with Paul Craddock and Nicolas Barker (eds.). *Fake? The Art of Deception.* Los Angeles: University of California Press, 1990.

Kerr, Philip (ed.). *The Penguin Book of Lies.* New York: Viking, 1990.

Lindskoog, Kathryn. *Fakes, Frauds, and Other Malarkey.* Grand Rapids: Zondervan Publishing House, 1993.

MacDougall, Curtis. *Hoaxes,* 2nd ed. New York: Dover Publications, 1958.

McBride, Robert M., and Niel Pritchie (eds.). *Great Hoaxes of All Time*. New York: Robert M. McBride Co., 1956.

Madison, Joyce. *Great Hoaxes, Swindels, Scandals, Cons, Stings, and Scams*. New York: Penguin Books, 1992.

Moss, Norman. *The Pleasures of Deception*. New York: Reader's Digest Press, 1977.

Mound, Andrew. *Heroic Hoaxes*. London: MacDonald & Co., 1983.

Newnham, Richard. *The Guinness Book of Fakes, Frauds, and Forgeries*. Middlesex: Guinness Publishing, 1991.

Randi, James. *An Encyclopedia of Claims, Frauds, and Hoaxes of the Occult and Supernatural*. New York: St. Martin's Press, 1995.

Rieth, Adolf. *Archaeological Fakes,* trans. Diana Imber. London: Barrie & Jenkins, 1970.

Roberts, David. *Great Exploration Hoaxes*. New York: Modern Library, 2001.

Saunders, Richard. *The World's Greatest Hoaxes*. Chicago: Playboy Press, 1980.

Sifakis, Carl. *Hoaxes and Scams*. New York: Facts on File, 1993.

———, (ed.). *The Big Book of Hoaxes*. New York: Paradox Press, 1996.

Silverberg, Robert. *Scientists & Scoundrels: A Book of Hoaxes*. New York: Thomas Y. Crowell Company, 1965.

Spencer, John and Anne. *The Encyclopedia of the World's Greatest Unsolved Mysteries*. Fort Lee, NJ: Barricade Books, 1999.

Stein, Gordon. *Encyclopedia of Hoaxes*. Detroit: Gale Research Inc., 1993.

Steinberg, Neil. *If at All Possible, Involve a Cow: The Book of College Pranks*. New York: St. Martin's Press, 1992.

Time-Life Books (eds.). *Hoaxes and Deceptions*. New York: Time-Life Books, 1991.

Wade, Carlson. *Great Hoaxes and Famous Imposters*. Middle Village, NY: Jonathan David Publishers, 1976.

Williams, Stephen. *Fantastic Archaeology: The Wild Side of North American Prehistory*. Philadelphia: University of Pennsylvania Press, 1991.

Yapp, Nick. *Hoaxers and Their Victims*. London: Robson Books, 1992.

Chapter One
Before 1700: Female Popes and Vegetable Lambs

Darvill, Timothy, Katherine Barker, Barbara Bender, and Ronald Hutton. *The Cerne Giant: An Antiquity on Trial*. Oxford: Oxbow Books, 1999.

Findlen, Paula. "Jokes of Nature and Jokes of Knowledge: The Playfulness of Scientific Discourse in Early Modern Europe." *Renaissance Quarterly* 43 (1990): 292–331.

———*Possessing Nature: Museums, Collecting, and Scientific Culture in Early Modern Italy*. Berkeley: University of California Press, 1994.

Geary, Patrick J. *Furta Sacra: Thefts of Relics in the Central Middle Ages*. Princeton: Princeton University Press, c.1978.

Grafton, Anthony. *Forgers and Critics: Creativity and Duplicity in Western Scholarship*. Princeton: Princeton University Press, 1990.

Hankins, James "Forging Links with the Past." *Journal of the History of Ideas* 52 (July–September, 1991): 509–518.

Johnson, Donald S. *Phantom Islands of the Atlantic: The Legends of Seven Lands That Never Were*. New York: Walker and Company, 1994.

Kieckhefer, Richard. *Magic in the Middle Ages*. Cambridge: Cambridge University Press, 1989.

Mencken, Johann Burkhard. *The Charlatanry of the Learned*, reprint of 1715 edition, trans. Francis Litz, with notes by H. L. Mencken. New York: Alfred A. Knopf, 1937.

McCuaig, William. *Carlo Sigonio: The Changing World of the Late Renaissance*. Princeton: Princeton University Press, 1989.

Phillips, J. R. S. *The Medieval Expansion of Europe*. Oxford: Oxford University Press, 1988.

Tout, T. F. *Mediaeval Forgers and Forgeries*. Manchester, UK: Longmans, Green & Company, 1920.

Wood, Clement. *The Woman Who Was Pope: A Biography of Pope Joan, 853–855 A.D*. New York: Willaim Faro, 1931.

Wood, Frances. *Did Marco Polo Go to China?* New York: Westview Press, 1995.

Chapter Two
The Eighteenth Century: Rabbit Babies and Lying Stones

Adams, Percy G. *Travelers and Travel Liars, 1660–1800*, 2nd ed. New York: Dover Publications, 1980.

Beringer Johann. *The Lying Stones of Dr. Beringer: being his Lithographiae Wirceburgensis*, trans. and annotated Melvin E. Jahn and Daniel J. Woolf. Berkeley: University of California Press, 1963.

Hall, Max. *Benjamin Franklin and Polly Baker. The History of a Literary Deception*. Chapel Hill: University of North Carolina Press, 1963.

Haywood, Ian. *The Making of History: A Study of the Literay Forgeries of James Macpherson and Thomas Chatterton in Relation to Eighteenth-Century Ideas of History and Fiction*. Rutherford, NJ: Fairleigh Dickinson University Press, 1986.

Mayhew, George P. "Swift's Bickerstaff Hoax as an April Fool Joke." *Modern Philology* 61 (May 1964).

Pickover, Clifford A. *The Girl Who Gave Birth to Rabbits: A True Medical Mystery*. Amherst, NY: Prometheus Books, 2000.

Stafford, Barbara Maria. *Artful Science: Enlightenment Entertainment and the Eclipse of Visual Education*. Cambridge, MA: The MIT Press, 1994.

Standage, Tom. *The Turk: The Life and Times of the Famous Eighteenth-Century Chess-Playing Machine*. New York: Walker & Company, 2002.

Swiderski, Richard M. *The False Formosan: George Psalmanazar and the Eighteenth-Century Experiment of Identity*. San Francisco: Mellen Research University Press, 1991.

Chapter Three
1800–1868: Lunar Bison and Solar Armor

Adams, Bluford. *E Pluribus Barnum: The Great Showman and the Making of U.S. Popular Culture*. Minneapolis: University of Minnesota Press, 1997.

Cook, James W. *The Arts of Deception: Playing with Fraud in the Age of Barnum*. Cambridge, MA: Harvard University Press, 2001.

Coulter, E. Merton. "The Great Georgia Railway Disaster Hoax on the London *Times*." *Georgia Historical Quarterly* 56 (1972): 25–50.

Crawford, Martin. "The Great Georgia Railway Disaster Revisited." *Georgia Historical Quarterly* 58 (1974): 331–339.

Gutch, J. M. *Caraboo: A Narrative of a Singular Imposition Practiced Upon the Benevolence of a Lady Residing in the Vicinity of Bristol*. London: Baldwin, Cradock and Joy, 1817.

Harris, Neil. *Humbug: The Art of P. T. Barnum*. Chicago: University of Chicago Press, 1973.

Locke, Richard Adams. *The Moon Hoax, or, A Discovery That the Moon Has a Vast Population of Human Beings,* reprint of 1859 edition, ed. Ormond Seavey. Boston: Gregg Press, 1975.

Mott, Frank Luther. "Facetious News Writing, 1833–1883." *The Mississippi Valley Historical Review* 29 (June 1942): 35–54.

Ord-Hume, Arthur W. J. G. *Perpetual Motion: The History of an Obsession*. New York: St. Martin's Press, 1977.

Reiss, Benjamin. *The Showman and the Slave: Race, Death, and Memory in Barnum's America*. Cambridge, MA: Harvard University Press, 2001.

Rose, Joel. *New York Sawed in Half*. New York: Bloomsbury, 2001.

Saxon, A. H. *P. T. Barnum: The Legend and the Man*. New York: Columbia University Press, 1989.

Wells, John. *Princess Caraboo: Her True Story*. London: Pan Books, 1994.

Wonham, Henry B., *Mark Twain and the Art of the Tall Tale*. New York: Oxford University Press, 1993.

Chapter Four
1869–1913: Stone Giants and Antlered Rabbits

Boyer, Richard O. "The Nature Man." *The New Yorker* (June 18, 1938): 21–25.

Breeden, James O. "'The Case of the Miraculous Bullet' Revisited" *Military Affairs* 45 (1981): 23–26.

Cohn, Norman R. C. *Warrant for Genocide: The Myth of the Jewish World Conspiracy and the Protocols of the Elders of Zion*. New York: Harper & Row, 1967.

Rubin, Cynthia Elyce, and Morgan Williams. *Larger Than Life: The American Tall-Tale Postcard, 1905–1915*. New York: Abbeville Press, 1990.

Seitz, Don. *The James Gordon Bennetts*. Indianapolis: Bobbs Merrill, 1928.

Spencer, Frank. *Piltdown: A Scientific Forgery*. Oxford: Oxford University Press, 1990.

Stansky, Peter. *On or About December 1910: Early Bloomsbury and its Intimate World*. Cambridge, MA: Harvard University Press, 1996.

Stephen, Adrian. *The "Dreadnought" Hoax*, reprint of 1936 ed. London: The Hogarth Press, 1983.

Walsh, John Evangelist. *Unravelling Piltdown: The Science Fraud of the Century and Its Solution*. New York: Random House, 1996.

Welsch, Roger L. *Tall-Tale Postcards: A Pictoral History*. New Brunswick, NJ: A. S. Barnes and Company, 1976: 78–84.

Woodruff, Douglass. *The Tichborne Claimant*. New York: Farrar, Straus & Cudahy, 1957.

Chapter Five
1914–1949: New Jersey Martians and Van Gogh's Ear

Anonymous. *Death in the Air: The War Diary and Photographs of a Flying Corps Pilot*. London: William Heinemann, Ltd., 1933.

Cooper, Joe. *The Case of the Cottingley Fairies*. London: Robert Hale, 1990.

Heyward, Michael. *The Ern Malley Affair*. London: Faber and Faber, 1993.

Holmsten, Brian, and Alex Lubertozzi, eds. *The Complete War of the Worlds: Mars' Invasion of Earth from H. G. Wells to Orson Welles*. Naperville, IL: Sourcebooks, Inc., 2001.

Johnson, James, and Floyd Miller. *The Man Who Sold the Eiffel Tower*. London: W. H. Allen, 1962.

Smith, William Jay. *The Spectra Hoax,* reprint of 1961 edition. Ashland, OR: Story Line Press, 2000.

Traprock, Walter E. *The Cruise of the Kawa: Wanderings in the South Seas*. New York: G. P. Putnam's Sons, 1921.

Chapter Six
1950–1976: Naked Animals and Swiss Spaghetti Trees

Abel, Alan. *The Great American Hoax*. New York: Trident Press, 1966.

————*The Confessions of a Hoaxer*. New York: Macmillan Company, 1970.

Chorvinsky, Mark. "The Makeup Man and the Monster: John Chambers and the Patterson Bigfoot Suit." *Strange Magazine* 17 (Summer 1996).

Culf, Andrew. "The Day They Harvested a Typical Italian Spaghetti Crop." *The Guardian* (November 8, 1993): 4.

Irving, Clifford, and Richard Suskind. *'Project Octavo': The Story of the Howard Hughes Hoax*. London: Allison and Busby, 1977.

Meiklejohn, M. F. "Notes on the Hoodwink (*Dissimulatrix spuria*)," *Bird Notes* 24 (1950): 89–92.

Nance, John. *The Gentle Tasaday: A Stone Age People in the Philippine Rain Forest*. New York: Harcourt Brace Jovanovich, 1975.

Packard, Vance. *The Hidden Persuaders*. New York: Pocket Books, 1962.

Palmer, Allen W. "Primitives Among Us." *Science Communication* (March 1, 2000): 223–243.

Reeve, Andru. *Turn Me On, Dead Man: The Complete Story of the Paul McCartney Death Hoax*. Harbor Springs, MI: Popular Culture Ink, 1994.

Stümpke, Harald. *The Snouters: Form and Life of the Rhinogrades,* trans. Leigh Chadwick. Garden City, NY: Natural History Press, 1967.

Chapter Seven
1977–1989: Australian Icebergs and Cockroach Pills

Calonius, L. Erik. "Stiff Upper Lips Get a Bit More Relaxed on the First of April." *The Wall Street Journal* (March 30, 1984): 1,17.

Frazier, Kendrick, and James Randi. "Prediction After the Fact: Lessons of the Tamara Rand Hoax." *Skeptical Inquirer* (Fall 1981): 4–7.

McFadden, Robert D., ed. *Outrage: The Story Behind the Tawana Brawley Hoax.* New York: Bantam Doubleday Dell, 1990.

Plimpton, George. "The Curious Case of Sidd Finch." *Sports Illustrated* (April 1, 1985): 59.

Rorvik, David. *In His Image: The Cloning of a Man.* New York: Lippincott, 1978.

Taibbi, Mike, and Anna Sims Phillips. *Unholy Alliances: Working the Tawana Brawley Story.* New York: Harcourt Brace, 1989.

Chapter Eight
The 1990s: Crop Circles and Cross-Dressing Ken

Lingua Franca (eds.). *The Sokal Hoax: The Sham that Shook the Academy.* Lincoln: University of Nebraska Press, 2000.

Marin, Rick. "Grunge: A Success Story." *New York Times* (November 15, 1992): 9:1.

Sherrill, Martha. "Forget Gwyneth, Forget Mira. Here's Hollywood's Next Dream Girl: The Allegra Coleman Nobody Knows." *Esquire* (November, 1996): 70–77.

Thomas, Andy. *Vital Signs: A Complete Guide to the Crop Circle Mystery and Why It Is Not a Hoax.* Seaford, Sussex: S. B. Publications, 1998.

Thomas, David E. "'Pi' April Fools' Joke Gets Out of Hand—And Goes Around the World." *Skeptical Inquirer* (September/ October 1998).

Chapter Nine
After 2000: Bonsai Kittens and Monster Cats

Cassel, David. "'Gorgeous Guy' is San Francisco's new cyberlebrity." *San Francisco Bay Guardian* (May 30, 2001).

Forman, Jay. "Monkey fishing: Cruel and unusual? Or good sporting fun?" *Slate* (June 8, 2001).

Horn, John. "The Reviewer Who Wasn't There; Sony resorts to some questionable marketing practices to promote new movies." *Newsweek* (June 2, 2001).

Simons, Lewis M. "Report to Members: Archaeoraptor Fossil Trail." *National Geographic* (October 2000): 128–132.

Sloan, Christopher P. "Feathers for T. rex?" *National Geographic* (November 1999): 98–107.

Advertising: Hoaxes of P. T. Barnum (64); Feejee Mermaid (66); Free Grand Buffalo Hunt (68); Harry Reichenbach (120); Jim Moran (121); Subliminal Advertising (137); I, Libertine (143); BMW Crop Circle (185); Sibuxiang Beast (198); David Manning, Film Critic (225).

Animals/Zoology: Duckbilled Platypus (49); Feejee Mermaid (66); Free Grand Buffalo Hunt (68); Paulding County Hyena (74); Tall-Tale Creatures (81); Jackalope (81); Fur-Bearing Trout (83); Ice Worms of the Klondike (83); Central Park Zoo Escape (87); Winsted Wild Man (88); Magic Turtle (109); Sea Serpents (122); Surgeon's Photo (122); *Mauretania* Sights a Sea Serpent (123); Great Monkey Hoax (134); Unusual Animals (145); Bare-Fronted Hoodwink (145); Snouters (146); Bigfoot (146); Society for Indecency to Naked Animals (147); Bonsai Kittens (218); Snowball the Monster Cat (223); Monkey Fishing with Slate.com (226).

Anthropology: Patagonian Giants (42); Stone-Age Tasaday (154).

April Fools' Day: Origin of April Fools' Day (25); Predictions of Isaac Bickerstaff (33); April Fools' Day Hoaxes (40, 68, 90, 129, 148, 162, 189, 210); Sleeveless Errands (40); Street Pranks (41); Train to Drogheda (68); Great Cave Sell (69); Edison Invents Food

Machine (90); Monster of Deadman's Hole (91); Wisconsin State Capitol Collapses (129); World To End On April 1 (130); New Zealand Wasp Swarm (130); Swiss Spaghetti Harvest (138); Around the World for 210 Guineas (148); Spiggot Metric Boycott (149); Eruption of Mount Edgecumbe (149); Planetary Alignment Decreases Gravity (150); San Serriffe (162); Sydney Iceberg (163); Operation Parallax (164); Eruption of Mount Milton (165); British Weather Machine (165); Interfering Brassieres (166); Sidd Finch (166); *Tass* Expands Into American Market (171); Kremvax (171); Soviet Missile Lands on Air Force Base (172); UFO Lands Near London (174); Nixon for President (189); China Ends One-Child Policy for PhDs (190); Drunk Driving on the Internet (190); Taco Liberty Bell (191); Life Discovered on Jupiter (193); Left-handed Whoppers (194); Alabama Changes the Value of Pi (194); Webnode (195); Guinness Mean Time (204); Y2K Solved (205); Y2K CD Bug (205); Fifteenth Annual New York City April Fools' Day Parade (210); FatSox (211); IPO for F/rite Air (211); Interview with President Carter (212); Whistling Carrots (212).

Archaeology/Paleontology: Cerne Abbas Giant (26); Lying Stones of Dr. Beringer (34); Giants in the Earth (78); Cardiff Giant (79); Piltdown Man (98); Piltdown Chicken (208); Stone Age Discoveries of Shinichi Fujimura (216).

Art: Renaissance Forgeries (22); Art Hoaxes and Forgeries (111); Disumbrationist School of Art (112); Alceo Dossena (113); Hans Van Meegeren (113); Hugh Troy (120).

Astronomy/Extraterrestrial Life: Great Moon Hoax (60); Great Monkey Hoax (134); Planetary Alignment Decreases Gravity (150); Aliens and Abductions (173); Alternative Three (173); UFO Lands Near London (174); Crop Circles (183); Operation Blackbird (184); Doug and Dave (184); BMW Crop Circle (185); Life Discovered on Jupiter (193).

Biology: *Lusus Naturae* and Museum of Hoaxes (23); Cloning of a Man (158); Malepregnancy.com (218).

Business/Financial: Great Stock Exchange Hoax of 1814 (55); Sawing the Island Off (58); Civil War Gold Hoax (71); Keely Motor

Company (84); Cassie Chadwick (85); Con Men and Pranksters (117); Charles Ponzi (118); Count Victor Lustig (119); Financial Hoaxes (179); Dayton Hudson (180); Savings and Loan Branch Opens on the Moon (180); IPO for F/rite Air (211); Emulex: A Stock Market Hoax (215).

Death: Predictions of Isaac Bickerstaff (33); Death of Titan Leeds (38); Empire City Massacre (75); Strange Death of Adolf Hitler (132); Paul Is Dead (152); Death of Alan Abel (160); Death Hoaxes (213); Demise of Pop Stars (213); Gabriel García Márquez's Final Farewell (214).

Exploration/Travel: Medieval Travel Lies (15); Letter of Prester John (15); Marco Polo's Description of the World (16); Travels of Sir John Mandeville (18); Great Balloon Hoax (63); First to the Pole (95); Alone in the Wilderness (100); Cruise of the Kawa (116); Around the World for 210 Guineas (148); San Serriffe (162).

Hate Crimes: Protocols of the Elders of Zion (94); Tawana Brawley Case (178); September 11, 2001 (230).

Historical: Renaissance Forgeries (22); Donation of Constantine (9); History of Crowland (10); Tale of a Tub (111).

Imposters: Pope Joan: The Female Pope (11); Native of Formosa (31); Princess Caraboo (56); Joice Heth (65); Imposters and Con Artists (84); Tichborne Claimant (84); Cassie Chadwick (85); Last German Prisoner of War (106); Stanley Clifford Weyman (118); Allegra Coleman (201); Kaycee Nicole Swenson (221).

Internet: Kremvax (171); Drunk Driving on the Internet (190); Life Discovered on Jupiter (193); Webnode (195); Microsoft Buys Catholic Church (197); World Wide Web Hoaxes (202); Ourfirsttime.com (202); Ron's Angels (203); eBay Auctions (203); Y2K Hoaxes (204); Safeway Says "Shop Elsewhere" (214); Hoax Web sites (217); Spud Server (217); Malepregnancy.com (218); Bonsai Kittens (218); Manbeef.com (219); Kaycee Nicole Swenson (221); Snowball the Monster Cat (223); Lovenstein Institute IQ Report (228); Gorgeous Guy (228); Predictions of Nostradamus (230); NASA Satellite Photo (231); Touristguy (231).

Inventions/Free-Energy: Great Chess Automaton (48); Charles Redheffer's Perpetual Motion Machine (54); Keely Motor Company (85); Edison Invents Food Machine (90).

Literary/Linguistic: Renaissance Forgeries (22); Hoaxes of Jonathan Swift (32); Eighteenth-Century Literary Hoaxes (44); James Macpherson and the Ossianic Controversy (45); Thomas Chatterton and the Rowley Poems (46); William Henry Ireland's Shakespeare Forgeries (46); Hoaxes of Edgar Allan Poe (62); Vrain Lucas (72); Literary Hoaxes (114); Spectric Poetry (114); Ern Malley (115); I, Libertine (143); Autobiography of Howard Hughes (153); Hitler Diaries (175); Grungegate (196); Garbriel García Márquez's Final Farewell (214).

Medical/Health: Mary Toft and the Rabbit Babies (41); Facts in the Case of M. Valdemar (63); Case of the Miraculous Bullet (86); Dr. Gregor's Cockroach Pills (169); Fat Squad (170); FatSox (211).

Military/Propaganda: Captain of Köpenick (96); *Dreadnought* Hoax (97); World War I Hoaxes (106); World War I Armistice Signed (106); Veterans of Future Wars (107); Hugh Troy (120); Hitler Hoaxes (131); Hitler's Silly Dance (132).

Movies: Harry Reichenbach (120); Hitler's Silly Dance (132); Subliminal Advertising (137); Allegra Coleman (201); David Manning, Film Critic (225).

Music: Milli Vanilli (188); Grungegate (196).

Newspapers: Silence Dogood (37); Supplement to the Boston Independent Chronicle (39); Great Moon Hoax (60); Great Balloon Hoax (63); Great Cave Sell (69); Railways and Revolvers in Georgia (70); Locals: The Hoaxes of Mark Twain, Dan De Quille, and Artemus Ward (73); Paulding County Hyena (74); Empire City Massacre (75); Solar Armor (75); Travelling Stones of Pahranagat Valley (76); Journalism Hoaxes (86); Central Park Zoo Escape (87); Winsted Wild Man (88); Great Wall of China Hoax (89); William Randolph Hearst and the Spanish-American War (89); Edison Invents Food Machine (90); Monster of Deadman's Hole (91); *Mauretania* Sights a Sea Serpent (123); Wisconsin State Capitol Collapses (129); Around the World for 210 Guineas (148); San Serriffe (162); British Weather Machine (165); Interfering Brassieres (166); Jimmy's World (167); Tass Expands Into American Market (171); China Ends One-Child Policy for PhDs (190); Y2K Solved (205); FatSox (211); Onion Dome Hoax (234).

Photography: Photographic Fakes (91); Sympsychography (93); Silent City (92); Tall-Tale Postcards (102); Cottingley Fairies (108); Surgeon's Photo (122); Wisconsin State Capitol Collapses (129); Baby Adolf (131); Snowball the Monster Cat (224); NASA Satellite Photo (231); Touristguy (231).

Physics/Chemistry: Von Kempelen and His Discovery (64); Solar Armor (75); Sympsychography (93); Alabama Changes the Value of Pi (194); Sokal Hoax (200).

Political: *Supplement to the Boston Independent Chronicle* (39); Roorbacks (70); Hugo N. Frye (125); Milton Mule (125); Wisconsin State Capitol Collapses (129); Dick Tuck (142); Report from Iron Mountain (150); Cold War Hoaxes (170); Tass Expands into American Market (171); Kremvax (171); California High School Announces War with Soviet Union (172); Nixon for President (189); Russia Sells Lenin's Body (195); Interview with President Carter (212); Lovenstein Institute IQ Report (228); Onion Dome Hoax (234).

Pranks: Pranks and Truth Spells (21); Street Pranks (41); Berners Street Hoax (52); Hugh Troy (120); Alan Abel (141, 159); Ultimate Lie (209); Cross-dressing Ken (186); Day of No Joe (220).

Radio: Radio Panics (126); BBC Radio Panic (127); War of the Worlds (128); New Zealand Wasp Swarm (130); I, Libertine (143); Planetary Alignment Decreases Gravity (150); Operation Parallax (164); Nixon for President (189); Call to Queen Elizabeth (199); Y2K CD Bug (205); Interview with President Carter (212).

Social Commentary: Hoaxes of Jonathan Swift (32); Hoaxes of Benjamin Franklin (37); Polly Baker (38); Jesters and Tricksters (140); Joey Skaggs (142, 169); Omar the Beggar's School for Panhandling (160); Dr. Gregor's Cockroach Pills (169); Fat Squad

(170); FAINT (177); Fifteenth Annual New York City April Fools' Day Parade (210).

Religion/Prophecy: Donation of Constantine (9); Pope Joan: The Female Pope (11); Medieval Relic Trade: True Crosses and Fake Shrouds (12); Shroud of Turin (14); Waiting for the Apocalypse (20); Protocols of the Elders of Zion (94); Microsoft Buys the Catholic Church (197); Religion of the Jedi Knights (220); Predictions of Nostradamus (230).

Sports: Rosie Ruiz Wins the Boston Marathon (161); Sidd Finch (166); Monkey Fishing with Slate.com (226).

Television: Television Hoaxes (137); Twenty-One (137); Swiss Spaghetti Harvest (138); Spiggot Metric Boycott (149); Eruption of Mount Milton (165); Alternative Three (173); Talk Show Hoaxes (176); FAINT (177); Fake Guest Scandal (177); Sibuxiang Beast (198).

Alabama Changes Value of Pi, 194

Alan Abel, 141, 159

Alceo Dossena, 113

Aliens and Abductions, 173

Allegra Coleman, 201

Alone in the Wilderness, 100

Alternative Three, 173

April Fools' Day Hoaxes, 25, 40, 68, 90, 129, 148, 162, 189, 210

Around the World for 210 Guineas, 148

Art Hoaxes and Forgeries, 111

Autobiography of Howard Hughes, 153

Baby Adolf, 131

Bare-Fronted Hoodwink, 145

BBC Radio Panic, 127

Berners Street Hoax, 52

Bigfoot, 146

BMW Crop Circle, 185

Bonsai Kittens, 218

British Weather Machine, 165

California High School Announces War with Soviet Union, 172

Call to Queen Elizabeth, 199

Captain of Köpenick, 96

Cardiff Giant, 79

Case of the Miraculous Bullet, 86

Cassie Chadwick, 85

Central Park Zoo Escape, 87

Cerne Abbas Giant, 26

Charles Ponzi, 118

Charles Redheffer's Perpetual Motion Machine, 54

China Ends One-Child Policy for PhDs, 190

Civil War Gold Hoax, 71

Cloning of a Man, 158

Cold War Hoaxes, 170

Con Men and Pranksters, 117

Cottingley Fairies, 108

Count Victor Lustig, 119

Crop Circles, 183

Cross-dressing Ken, 186

Cruise of the Kawa, 116

David Manning, Film Critic, 225

Day of No Joe, 220

Dayton Hudson, 180

Death Hoaxes, 213

Death of Alan Abel, 160

Death of Titan Leeds, 38
Demise of Pop Stars, 213
Dick Tuck, 142
Disumbrationist School of Art, 112
Donation of Constantine, 9
Doug and Dave, 184
Dr. Gregor's Cockroach Pills, 169
Dreadnought Hoax, 97
Drunk Driving on the Internet, 190
Duckbilled Platypus, 49

eBay Auctions, 203
Edison Invents Food Machine, 90
Eighteenth-Century Literary
    Hoaxes, 44
Empire City Massacre, 75
Emulex: A Stock Market Hoax, 215
Ern Malley, 115
Eruption of Mount Edgecumbe,
    149
Eruption of Mount Milton, 165

Facts in the Case of M. Valdemar,
    63
FAINT, 177
Fake Guest Scandal, 177
Fat Squad, 170
FatSox, 211
Feejee Mermaid, 66
Fifteenth Annual New York City
    April Fools' Day Parade, 210
Financial Hoaxes, 179
First to the Pole, 95
Forgeries of the Medieval Church, 8
Free Grand Buffalo Hunt, 68
Fur-bearing Trout, 83

Gabriel García Márquez's Final
    Farewell, 214
Giants in the Earth, 78
Gorgeous Guy, 228
Great Balloon Hoax, 63
Great Cave Sell, 69
Great Chess Automaton, 48
Great Monkey Hoax, 134

Great Moon Hoax, 60
Great Stock Exchange Hoax of
    1814, 55
Great Wall of China Hoax, 89
Grungegate, 196
Guinness Mean Time, 204

Hans van Meegeren, 113
Harry Reichenbach, 120
History of Crowland, 10
Hitler Diaries, 175
Hitler Hoaxes, 131
Hitler's Silly Dance, 132
Hoax Web sites, 217
Hoaxes of Benjamin Franklin, 37
Hoaxes of Edgar Allan Poe, 62
Hoaxes of Jonathan Swift, 32
Hoaxes of P. T. Barnum, 64
Hugh Troy, 120
Hugo N. Frye, 125

I, Libertine, 143
Ice Worms of the Klondike, 83
Imposters and Con Artists, 84
Interfering Brassieres, 166
Interview with President Carter,
    212
IPO for F/rite Air, 211

Jackalope, 81
James Macpherson and the
    Ossianic Controversy, 45
Jesters and Tricksters, 140
Jim Moran, 121
Jimmy's World, 167
Joey Skaggs 142, 169
Joice Heth, 65
Journalism Hoaxes, 86

Kaycee Nicole Swenson, 221
Keely Motor Company, 85
Kremvax, 171

Last German Prisoner of War, 106
Left-handed Whoppers, 194

Letter of Prester John, 15
Life Discovered on Jupiter, 193
Literary Hoaxes, 114
Locals: The Hoaxes of Mark Twain, Dan De Quille, and Artemus Ward, 73
Lovenstein Institute IQ Report, 228
Lusus Naturae and Museum of Hoaxes, 23
Lying Stones of Dr. Beringer, 34

Magic Turtle, 109
Malepregnancy.com, 218
Manbeef.com, 219
Marco Polo's Description of the World, 16
Mary Toft and the Rabbit Babies, 41
Mauretania Sights a Sea Serpent, 123
Medieval Relic Trade: True Crosses and Fake Shrouds, 12
Medieval Travel Lies, 15
Microsoft Buys the Catholic Church, 197
Milli Vanilli, 188
Milton Mule, 125
Monkey Fishing with Slate.com, 226
Monster of Deadman's Hole, 91

NASA Satellite Photo, 231
Native of Formosa, 31
New Zealand Wasp Swarm, 130
Nixon for President, 189

Omar the Beggar's School for Panhandling, 160
Onion Dome Hoax, 234
Operation Blackbird, 184
Operation Parallax, 164
Origin of April Fools' Day, 25
Ourfirsttime.com, 202

Patagonian Giants, 42
Paul Is Dead, 152

Paulding County Hyena, 74
Photographic Fakes, 91
Piltdown Chicken, 208
Piltdown Man, 98
Planetary Alignment Decreases Gravity, 150
Polly Baker, 38
Pope Joan: The Female Pope, 11
Pranks and Truth Spells, 21
Predictions of Isaac Bickerstaff, 33
Predictions of Nostradamus, 230
Princess Caraboo, 56
Protocols of the Elders of Zion, 94

Radio Panics, 126
Railways and Revolvers in Georgia, 70
Religion of the Jedi Knights, 220
Renaissance Forgeries, 22
Report from Iron Mountain, 150
Ron's Angels, 203
Roorbacks, 70
Rosie Ruiz Wins the Boston Marathon, 161
Russia Sells Lenin's Body, 195

Safeway Says "Shop Elsewhere!", 214
San Serriffe, 162
Savings and Loan Branch Opens on the Moon, 180
Sawing the Island Off, 58
Sea Serpents, 122
September 11, 2001, 230
Shroud of Turin, 14
Sibuxiang Beast, 198
Sidd Finch, 166
Silence Dogood, 37
Silent City, 92
Sleeveless Errands, 40
Snouters, 146
Snowball the Monster Cat, 223
Society for Indecency to Naked Animals, 147
Sokal Hoax, 200

Solar Armor, 75
Soviet Missile Lands on Air Force
    Base, 172
Spectric Poetry, 114
Spiggot Metric Boycott, 149
Spud Server, 217
Stanley Clifford Weyman, 118
Stone Age Discoveries of Shinichi
    Fujimura, 216
Stone Age Tasaday, 154
Strange Death of Adolf Hitler, 132
Street Pranks, 41
Subliminal Advertising, 137
Supplement to the Boston
    Independent Chronicle, 39
Surgeon's Photo, 122
Swiss Spaghetti Harvest, 138
Sydney Iceberg, 163
Sympsychography, 93

Taco Liberty Bell, 191
Tale of a Tub, 111
Talk-Show Hoaxes, 176
Tall-Tale Creatures, 81
Tall-Tale Postcards, 102
Tass Expands Into American
    Market, 171
Tawana Brawley Case, 178
Television Hoaxes, 137
Thomas Chatterton and the Rowley
    Poems, 46
Tichborne Claimant, 84
Touristguy, 231
Train to Drogheda, 68

Traveling Stones of Pahranagat
    Valley, 76
Travels of Sir John Mandeville,
    18
Twenty-One, 137

UFO Lands Near London, 174
Ultimate Lie, 209
Unusual Animals, 145

Veterans of Future Wars, 107
Von Kempelen and his Discovery,
    64
Vrain Lucas, 72

Waiting for the Apocalypse, 20
War of the Worlds, 128
Webnode, 195
Whistling Carrots, 212
William Henry Ireland's
    Shakespeare Forgeries, 46
William Randolph Hearst and the
    Spanish-American War, 89
Winsted Wild Man, 88
Wisconsin State Capitol Collapses,
    129
World to End on April 1, 130
World War I Hoaxes, 106
World War I Armistice Signed, 106
World Wide Web Hoaxes, 202

Y2K CD Bug, 205
Y2K Hoaxes, 204
Y2K Solved, 205

★ *Acknowledgments* ★

Five years ago I was doing research in the Library of Congress when I first came across the work of Curtis MacDougall and Gordon Stein. During guilty breaks in my work I read their tales of bizarre hoaxes from years gone by. Gradually those guilty breaks grew longer until I had developed a full-fledged obsession with the history of hoaxes. Without the initial inspiration and sheer fun of their scholarship, this book would never have existed.

I am indebted to the many people who have found my Web site in the years since it began and sent me their comments, questions, and encouragement. Please keep sending those e-mails!

My thanks to my editor, Mitch Hoffman, who saw the potential for a book in the Web site and gently shepherded it through the writing process. My thanks also to Stephanie Bowe and all the others at Dutton for their help.

Finally, without the support of my family and friends I would have been lost: my parents, Janet and Klaus Boese, who have always been my number one fans; Kirsten, Ben, and Astrid (and now Pippa) for their constant encouragement; Boo, who sat with me throughout the entire process; Ted Lyons, for all the mind-clearing coffee breaks; the many others who provided help along the way; but most of all Beverley and Charlie, for their love and for keeping my feet firmly on the ground.